Sing Me Home

Judith Cuffe

POOLBEG

Published 2020
by Poolbeg Press Ltd
123 Grange Hill, Baldoyle
Dublin 13, Ireland
E-mail: poolbeg@poolbeg.com
www.poolbeg.com

A catalogue record for this book is available from the British Library.

ISBN 978-1-78199-352-1

Typeset by Poolbeg Press Ltd

www.poolbeg.com

ABOUT THE AUTHOR

Judith Cuffe lives in County Wicklow, Ireland with her husband, three children and faithful writing companion, Wilbur, the dog. A book lover and a fan of the written word, she finally got round to following her dream and writing that book. *Sing Me Home* is the second novel in the Evolve trilogy, following on from the first, *When Destiny Sings*. She is currently working on the third. When she isn't writing, she can be found in the gym, running, following the latest fashions or ferrying the children around as Mum's Taxi. To find out more about Judith, follow her on Facebook (Judy in The Middle) and Instagram (@judy_middle), or on her website www.judyinthemiddle.com.

For Martha-Lily – my brave one

Work hard, love freely, cry openly, enjoy your own
company, laugh – laugh until you pee your pants
(you are the reason I pee mine!) and sing, loud.
Enjoy the peaks, tolerate the troughs.
I'll be there for them all.

This is life – live it.

"Everything will be okay in the end.
If it's not okay, it's not the end."
John Lennon.

PROLOGUE

It had become such a part of her life again – so familiar and yet somehow, each time she set eyes on it, it was as though she were seeing it for the first time. It was difficult to comprehend how she could feel so intrinsically linked to it yet repelled by it, in almost equal measures. Like others before her, she, too, had developed a morbid fascination with this place, this structure, this house, and try as she might, she couldn't seem to break away.

The immaculate gravel drive – not a weed allowed to rise between the stones – wound its way towards those three granite steps, leading to the imposing red-panelled door. The half-moon window above it, the white pillars either side. Directly opposite the pillars, in perfect symmetry, two enormous grey stone pedestal pots sat each side of the steps, built into the low wall, containing identical topiary trees – so perfectly coiffed that they couldn't be anything but artificial. But they were real – pruned to within an inch of their lives, snipped and trimmed into an unnatural shape, defined by what they ought to be. She knew how they must feel, having spent half of her life trying to be what other people expected of her. When she closed her eyes, she could visualise what lay beyond the bright red door, leading into the large hallway – a vase of fresh flowers perched on the large round table in the middle, the winding staircase, the chandelier glistening above it all. Perfection.

Deception.

How could she have been so naïve?

It seemed a lifetime ago now, when she'd hoped, believed, that having all the answers, finding the truth, would set her free. Snip her loose. Allow her to spread her wings and uncover the kind of life she desired. It hadn't. Instead, she'd willingly stumbled back into an ornate web, throwing herself at it – catapulting herself right at the centre, to the most vulnerable part. Perhaps she was being superstitious, but she couldn't help thinking the house had something to do with it all, that it had somehow beckoned to her, lulled her home.

No matter what happened after today, it would always be a part of her, that was for sure – the big house on the hill. It was, after all, where her story had begun. Her past wound its way through the wisteria growing either side of the columns flanking the front door, up the stone walls, past the sash windows to the eaves.

How could something so beautiful be linked with such pain, suffering, lies? And there was no doubt it was beautiful – now, more than ever. Months and months of restoration, improvements, expansion – and yet to her, it still seemed unchanged, as if the original structure was all she could see.

"Houses have souls," her mother used to say. "And this one is black."

Perhaps Mam was right, but she didn't want to believe it. Even on a sunny day, some rooms still appeared dark and cold, like the sunlight would attempt but not quite manage to penetrate the glass. She'd read an article about it once – how some properties are filled with negative energy, a sombre vibe, a foreboding sense. Years ago, she'd have laughed it off – the part of her brain that adored numbers and deciphering problems in search of a logical solution – poking fun at such nonsense.

That was before.

Once she uncovered the real history of the house – her own mother's tragic story – she was convinced that the truth would liberate her, maybe even set the house free, if you believed in that kind of thing. Allow a new phase to commence, a better story. But impossible as it might seem, it was as if the history of the house had filtered its way up through the foundations, wrapping itself around the beams, running along the skirtings, leaking into the plasterboard, settling into the bricks and mortar, becoming the very fabric of the building. Perhaps whoever lived there afterwards would always be tarnished by its past. She didn't want to believe that, still imagining that it somehow held the key to her future.

She remembered the first morning she'd arrived here in an official capacity, excited by the opportunity that awaited her. Standing at the gateposts and looking up at the house, exactly as she was now, she'd noticed a single magpie perched on the decorative ridge tiles on the roof, staring down at her. She'd stared back, defiantly, sure that a lonely bird couldn't destroy her recent fortune. She'd saluted it like her mother had taught her, to ward off danger. Waited for it to fly away, as it usually did, once you acknowledged its presence. It didn't move.

"There are signs everywhere, little one. You have to look for them," her mother would say.

She hadn't thought much of that magpie at the time. Had it been trying to tell her something? Issue her with a warning to stay away?

Of course, she hadn't ever anticipated being so involved with the house again, nor with the people living there. Before then, she used to walk past it sometimes, stop to stare up at it woodenly, unconsciously drawn towards it, trying to imagine her mother and the life she'd had there – an unbelievable experience of pain and cruelty. She'd wanted to hate it, despise it as her mother had done. But it was just a house, wasn't it? A house with a past, energy that transferred from owner to owner. She was certain of that now.

She didn't want to be part of the mess *they* had created. Walk away, she told herself, knowing she wouldn't. She'd miss it too much – the bits that made her instantly connected to her mother, like being in her mother's childhood bedroom, where she felt enveloped in warmth. She'd spent a lot of time there over the past few months, looking out over the gardens, supervising the construction work, trying to see it as it had once been, through her mother's eyes. She'd sat in that window seat, looking out at what lay below, trying to imagine how her mother must have felt as she'd peered out of the same window all those years ago.

Perhaps it would take a miracle to break the negative cycle of the house. It would undoubtedly take more than laying salt on the floor, or rubbing sage on the walls. Even though it wasn't hers, she'd fallen in love with it and as strange as it seemed, it had somehow become her destiny, her mission to set it right, free it.

Yes, maybe it would take a miracle, or at least the truth, or perhaps something more. She suspected that the draw to the house was the something more – something she knew she should give up on, something she told herself she'd walked away from but deep down knew she hadn't. All she did know was that she'd never settle until she tried.

Ann Maguire wondered how many times in one lifetime you could come full circle before it was time to stand still for a while, be content in your present. She ran her hand over the name on the gate before taking a deep breath and walking, once again, towards Knockmore House.

CHAPTER ONE

Sounds drifted towards her, rousing her from an already broken sleep. Ann didn't bother fighting against the noise, covering her head with the pillow or pulling the duvet over her head. Instead, she lay back, allowing the rhythm of the day, the symphony of everyday life, to wash over her. She could hear doors slamming, little metal gates creaking open and closed, engines starting, frantic voices.

"Hurry up."

"Have you got your lunch?"

"Where's your bag?"

"I told you to brush your teeth. Go!"

It was as if they all waited there until the exact moment – three, two, one – before swinging their front doors open and commencing the day in unison, marching to the beat of the same drum.

"Morning."

"Lovely day."

"Looks like rain."

"How's your Mam? Tell her I was asking for her, won't you?" they called to each other before stepping into their cars or trekking up the road laden with bags, pushing buggies, children trailing behind. It lasted only five minutes, maybe ten, if you counted the last stragglers who habitually managed to miss the communal exodus. They could be heard several minutes later making the final dash towards the exit onto the main road.

Ann listened as Tracy Doyle, her neighbour, rushed from room to room beside her, slamming doors, calling the kids – four of them, *all* boys – ushering them out of the house. Tracy dropped her keys on the front step, picking them up with a muffled curse. Then the driver's door banged shut and the car crunched into gear, ready to join the string of vehicles that would impatiently queue up, awaiting their turn to swing right towards the national school to deposit their precious cargo.

Then they'd make their way to work, or towards one of the local coffee shops, or even the local gym that had recently opened – did you ever think you'd see the day? The teenagers would all be meeting at the top of the road, inching towards the secondary school to watch the seconds tick by until four o'clock, where freedom awaited on the green – the girls watching the boys, the boys playing football, pretending not to look back.

Ann allowed her body to relax back into the pillows, determined to enjoy the additional twenty minutes of morning silence she was always rewarded with before tuning in to the return journey – a brief respite from the constant whirr of her thoughts. It had been this way for the last six months since she'd uttered the words that erupted from a place of rage, a reaction to twenty-six weeks of frustration and doubt. Once Ann had made the decision, she hoped it would all end – the wondering, the detachment – so at last she could cross the threshold into a new phase. Anything had to be better than where she'd been: jobless, living out of a suitcase, a broken marriage tucked into her already straining emotional baggage.

"You can't be serious?" Sophie attempted to make her see reason.

"I am. I'm done here, feeling as if I'm public enemy number one. No one will hire me. I'm imposing on you. I can't do it any more."

"But all alone, there, in Hicksville? You said it yourself. There's nothing there. No opportunities. You don't know anyone."

"Well, then I'll have to make opportunities."

"Please don't do this, Ann. Please don't let him drive you away. Don't go back to being alone. You can stay here with me – forever, if you want."

"It's done, Sophie. Besides, some journeys you have to take alone," she'd told her concerned best friend in a fist-pumping surge of power.

It *was* what she needed to do. Ann had read a quote that week, written at the top of the page in her diary – one of those that you only pay attention to when you're desperate for guidance. She hadn't been able to remember the exact words to repeat it back to Sophie, but it had resonated with her – something about not being able to fix the past but being able to control a new beginning. It was time.

Nothing would change her mind. No lectures from Sophie about her tendency to make snap decisions, no amount of pleading, telling her to hold tight, that it was a passing phase that would soon cease.

"Soph, my parents weren't that much older than me when they died. I can't keep putting off life. I made a promise I wouldn't settle. I have to try. Anyway, it's the only choice that makes sense right now. You know that."

"If it doesn't work out . . ."

"I know." Ann cut across her, not wanting to be told

again that she could always return to Dublin *when* it didn't work out.

"I think you're really brave."

The word stung. Ann didn't feel brave, nor remotely worthy of the label. What had she ever done to warrant it? Brave because she'd survived her parents' death? Brave because she'd chosen not to forgive her cheating husband? Brave because she was still standing after life had catapulted every iota of waste it could muster and continuously sling at her? Ann hadn't made a decision to be brave – it had been imposed upon her.

The whole way there on the bus, her three suitcases beneath her, her entire twenty-nine years packed into them, she tried to give herself a pep talk. To harness the stubbornness she'd inherited from her father, to convince herself she was doing the right thing. The adrenaline pumped in her veins, surging with the disappointments life had presented.

"Don't look back. Always forwards," she repeated as the taxi drove from the bus station towards her new beginning. "This *is* the right thing."

She'd still believed it all the way there, even when she turned the key in the lock and the door shut behind her with a thud.

The emptiness echoed while she clenched her muscles and tightened her jaw, waiting for the familiarity to hit with force. She braced herself for the memories to pierce her flesh. To tear open the wounds that hadn't yet healed and rupture her heart open further. Instead, a stench of soured milk engulfed her, turning her stomach, then dank air, coupled with an obscured vision of the past.

Nothing was the same.

Ann flung the door open, gasping for fresh air to counteract the musty reek.

"Hi."

Ann looked up to see a woman standing there, watching Ann suspiciously, arms crossed, tight dark curls sticking out in every direction, eyes darting.

"I'm Ann. Your new neighbour." Ann reached her hand across the little metal fence that separated them.

"Tracy Doyle." Her thin hand travelled over the barrier like a claw to take Ann's hand reluctantly – more a light touch than a handshake. "The girls are gone? They never said." Tracy regarded Ann. "They used to babysit the odd time for me. That's a shame. I have the four, you see – all boys. Gifts from heaven or karma from my youth." Tracy forced a nervous laugh. "Don't suppose you babysit? Are you renting with a few others?"

"Oh. Eh. No."

"Are you a nurse?"

"No."

"Teacher?"

"Nope."

"What are you, then?"

"I'm an accountant. Well, I was. I'm not working at the moment."

Tracy raised her eyebrows. "What are you doing here, then?"

"It's my house."

"I didn't realise the house had sold." Tracy wrinkled her nose. "So, where's the hubby and kids?"

Ann didn't get a chance to correct her.

"The houses are all right. Old," Tracy continued, pulling her cardigan around her, pinching it closed with her claw, taking a breath through her teeth. "Bit on top of each other, but there's plenty of other families around here. It's all families. No one in their right mind would live here unless they had to.

"There's plenty of activities out there . . ." She gestured her head towards the green area opposite the house. "I'd have loved one of those new apartments near the hotel, but apartments and families don't mix. Bedrooms are a bit pokey, too, don't you think? We have the two sets of bunks, but we manage. How many do you have?"

"Bunks?" Ann asked, confused, and Tracy rolled her eyes.

"Kids?"

"None. It's just me. I . . . I'm . . . It's just me."

"Oh." Tracy's nose turned up again, unable to hide the disappointment.

Ann could almost hear the common thread that had the potential to spark a friendship snap.

"Well, I don't suppose you're old enough."

"I'm twenty-nine."

"Right. Not that much younger than me. I turned thirty last year. Well," Tracy whispered out of the corner of her mouth, "I was caught out the first time, but it all worked out. I always wanted my family out of the way nice and early. Still, you've plenty of time left, but don't go leaving it too late. Your eggs have a sell-by date and it doesn't get any easier. The last one nearly broke me. Did I say I had the four?"

"You did."

"I can't remember what it's like to be footloose and fancy-free. Lonely, I'd say." Tracy's curls moved as she shook her head. "Anyway, I hope we don't disturb you, Ann, the accountant. Imagine? You all alone in a house that we have to fit six in. All that space, alone. I wouldn't know what to be doing with myself. Will you get lodgers? A lot of weirdos out there. I like to know who's living next door. You understand?"

"It'll just be me. Alone." Ann emphasised the word.

"Right, so." Tracy nodded and went to walk away before turning and quickly looking Ann up and down curiously.

Ann might have missed the glare, but Tracy's eyes had rested for a moment too long on Ann's velvet ballet shoes before travelling back up the length of her body to her eyes.

"We should do drinks," Tracy said at last. "I can introduce you around. First Thursday of the month, we all go out. Well, all the other mothers, but us girls should stick together. No? Not that it would matter to you, but the children's allowance comes in on the first Tuesday. Sure, what else is the allowance for but for us mams to kick the heels up a bit?

"Well, apart from Una Dealy. She's one of those who hasn't spent a penny of it since the day hers were born. Saving it all in her post office account for university, she says. Miserable! There's nothing wrong with a good trade, I always say. Una only has the two kids, so I get double what she does – not a bad old income. The only decent thing the government does is reward the mothers. Then again, here I am raising the future," Tracy tutted.

"Absolutely. Well-deserved. Thanks, Tracy. It would be nice to get to know a few people."

"Una comes along anyway." Tracy continued her rant. "Always has the cheap wine with her. Still, I'm not one to judge. And it's nothing fancy, now – just a bite to eat in the Italian. They let us bring our own booze. Might not be what you're used to. Still, we have a good time and you never know, someone might have a half-decent brother tucked away who we can introduce you to . . ." Tracy paused for a moment. "If you hurry, you could be pregnant by Christmas," she snorted and then exhaled loudly.

"Well, the drinks part I can do, but not the half-decent brother, or the Christmas pregnancy. Not sure I'm ready for that so soon after . . . after moving," Ann corrected.

"I'll knock in on you the next time we're going."

Tracy's eyes had narrowed at Ann's slight delay. Ann could almost picture an invisible radar sprouting from Tracy's curls and beginning to rotate, primed to detect her new neighbour's real story.

"See you, *Ann*."

Tracy said her name as if it were an accusation and then disappeared inside, leaving Ann staring, confused, at her front door, unsure if she'd just encountered an act of kindness or a glimpse of trouble. Ann waited for the door to close, then uncharacteristically stuck two fingers up at Tracy Doyle's front door and mouthed, "Fuck off," before picking up her bags.

It hadn't been the start Ann expected – sour milk and what appeared to be an intensely bitter neighbour. What did Tracy want? For Ann to offer to take a couple of her kids, so as not to seem greedy taking up *all* that room for herself?

Ann could sense that she'd have difficulty keeping Tracy's curiosity at bay, but she was still determined to embrace her new life. Who knew? Maybe Tracy would turn out to be a valuable lifeline. After all, Ann didn't know anyone here and beggars can't be choosers – but for now, she wasn't ready to be placed under the spotlight of village life, becoming the new slice of gossip on the block.

Damn it. She should have had her story straight before

she'd arrived, with an explanation as to why she was turning up out of nowhere to live in a place that most young people longed to flee–often spending years planning their earliest possible escape route. Of course, Ann hadn't expected that the first person she'd encounter would be the local internal intelligence, and just moments after her arrival.

Ann could feel the anger start to bubble out of nowhere as it so often did lately. Sophie had called her out on it before she left.

"You're so bloody fiery. It's not like you to fly off the handle so easily. I mean, I like it, if it's just a temporary thing, but can you go back to being calm soon, please? I'm not sure our friendship would survive two sarcastic narks."

Ann had noticed it, too. Her usual outward serenity replaced with a short fuse, reason replaced with tempestuousness – determination and sheer hatred driving her to prove everyone and everything wrong.

A year ago, when everything had started to fall apart, Ann refused to be conquered. But wasn't that always how it was when you had a life-changing revelation? The truth of the past, and the discovery that she'd married a cheat, had gifted her temporary invincibility. Nothing else could possibly happen . . .

Those first six months, living with Sophie, trying to find her feet, had been nothing short of hell on earth, but then Dom, her ex, was never going to make things easy. No, he'd made it impossible, practically erasing her from her life in Dublin, putting up as many blockades as he could to prevent her from moving forwards.

"Show me a marriage breakdown that doesn't turn nasty and I'll show you a pig that can fly. I've seen it a hundred times, Ann. It *never* goes smoothly," Aunt Lucie, her father's sister who lived in Australia, had said when Ann told her just how bad things were. "But there's always a way."

Deep down, Ann had known it, too. She just never expected she'd need to use her trump card so soon. There was only one place left for her to go where she could take back control and begin to emerge from the limbo-like state . . .

Knockmore – to the tiny terraced house she'd left behind in the Estates, the same one her aunt had kept for her all those years, in case she needed it.

Home.

CHAPTER TWO

Ann threw back the covers, hearing her first cue of the day: Tracy's voice drifting up through the window. She swung her long legs from the bed, placing them on the floor, and scrunched her toes against the fibres of the carpet, relishing the softness beneath her feet. There were some things worth being alone for – everything was almost how she liked it. She crept towards the window, where she could see Tracy below, dressed in her hybrid pyjama stroke leisurewear, her dark curls thrown into a topknot, chatting to another mother, who was gradually attempting to edge away.

"Ah, sure, it'll be the holidays soon. Christ, I don't know what to be doing with them all. But then I have the four. Oh! yeah. You were wise. You only had the two. Are you heading off yourself, Una? No, sure, we couldn't be affording to go away with the four. But look, they're all healthy, isn't that the main thing?"

Every day was the same – Tracy holding court at the front gate, her voice booming with identical dialogue, forcing Ann out of bed, preventing her from drifting backwards into disturbed sleep and spiralling thoughts. It was curiosity that first started Ann's pattern of peering out of the window, studying the morning interactions of the Estates, spectating, watching those who'd safely delivered their children to school.

Ann watched them day after day, robotically wheeling a buggy back home again – a blabbering toddler strapped into it, a piece of soggy toast clasped in a chubby hand. She could identify those who'd thrown on a pair of tracksuit bottoms and a Puffa jacket over their nightie, hoping no one would clock their state of undress – dark sunglasses to hide their tired eyes. From her altitudinous viewpoint, Ann would watch them reach around self-consciously to ensure their nightwear remained safely inserted into the back of their trousers when Tracy summoned them to the gate.

At first, Ann was sure Tracy had been standing in her driveway, having a full-on conversation with herself. She'd been relieved to spy another woman there, leaning against the gatepost, talking back, her inaudible lips moving. Not like Tracy – long arms flying everywhere as she spoke, so loud that Ann often wondered if Tracy was permanently hooked up to a roving mic, complete with amplifier. Still, she supposed as the head of a busy household, there was only one way to be heard.

Over the months, Ann had become what Aunt Lucie would describe as a "curtain-twitcher" – hiding behind the blinds, watching people go about their lives instead of living her own. In one way, it felt as if she'd left behind a form of limbo in Dublin, to plunge straight into what she described to Sophie as purgatory – suspended here, atoning.

"Don't be ridiculous," Sophie told her down the phone when Ann first mentioned it shortly after her return to Knockmore. "You're better off without Dom. He was a cheat, a liar."

"Do you think I'm being punished?"

"For what? You're not the first woman to ditch a prick. No. The only person punishing you is yourself. You have to stop this. I feel like you're . . . what's the word?

Unravelling. Make it fast, won't you? Unravel and then pull yourself together.

"It's not like you. You're the one who crumbles then faces a problem and finds a solution. Remember? You're the one who doesn't go down without a fight. Have you gone out with that neighbour yet? The one who asked you for drinks," Sophie encouraged.

"That's this week."

"Well, try to enjoy yourself. Be young!"

Of course, Ann hadn't unravelled straightaway. It was a gradual process, like watching a piece of string, tied in a bow, levitating and then ever so slowly coming undone. But, bit by bit, the fight in her started to diminish.

Ann had almost ignored the harsh knock on the door that came a week after meeting Tracy while she sat at the kitchen table aimlessly staring at the wall. The sharp rapping had broken her thoughts. Glancing at the front door, Ann waited for whoever it was to give up and withdraw until she noticed the letterbox begin to ease open.

"Ann. Are you in there? Ann?" came the tuneful voice through the gap.

Terrified that Tracy might stick a telescope through the opening to observe her, Ann unwillingly made her way into the hall to open the door.

"Morning." Tracy was flushed and out of breath. "Oh, sorry, were you asleep?" Tracy took in Ann's dressing gown and tried to crane her neck over Ann's shoulder for a glimpse beyond the hall door.

"No. I was just getting into the shower," Ann lied and stepped outside, closing the door behind her.

"Well, for you. I've been up for hours. I'm just back from my run." Tracy wiped the sweat from her brow and waited for an invitation inside. When Ann didn't offer, she continued, "It's Wednesday," nodding encouragingly. "Tomorrow's Thursday."

Ann stared at her blankly.

"First Thursday of the month," Tracy explained. "Girls night, remember?"

"Oh. Yes, right."

"I've told all the girls you're coming. They're dying to meet you. What are you going to wear? We like to get dressed up, but you know, one or two insist on jeans, so anything goes. Except for dressing gowns," Tracy grimaced. "Pick you up at seven? We like to escape before bedtime. Gives us a bit of extra time and a night off trying to battle the kids into bed."

"I'm not sure . . . I . . ."

"Great. See you then."

Tracy was gone before Ann could object.

Ann could feel her stomach instantly clench with nerves, or perhaps it was excitement – she wasn't sure. Either way, she couldn't spend the rest of her life wallowing and staring into space. Maybe a night out was just what the doctor ordered.

It started well enough, with Tracy knocking on the door at 7 p.m. sharp, an enormous grin plastered on her face. Tracy looked like a different person, dressed to the nines in a sparkly top and leather pencil skirt, a far cry from her usual attire, her hair straightened to within an inch of its life. It must have taken the entire day to uncoil each dark corkscrew curl carefully and iron it so that her hair now hung in a sheet down her back.

"You look fab, Tracy. I almost didn't recognise you."

"And you're dressed, I see! And you went for the jeans – not to worry. As I said, there's always a few who don't bother, either." Tracy patted Ann's arm.

Ann had thoroughly agonised over what to wear, deciding it was best to stick with jeans and a nice top, unsure as to how dressy Tracy had meant. She could see now that she should probably have made more of an effort. Grabbing her coat, and a bottle of wine off the table in the hall, Ann closed the door and Tracy linked her arm as they set off up the Estates towards the little Italian over the post office.

"Now, don't go telling everyone all about yourself without telling me first," Tracy laughed as they went. "And don't mind Una. Like I said, she's fierce nosy. Wouldn't tell you anything in exchange, mind. She's closed, that one. I'll make sure you're sitting next to me."

"There's nothing to tell, honestly."

Tracy looked unconvinced. "I'll get to the bottom of you, Ann," she giggled, her face flushed with excitement. "Sure, we've years to get to know each other."

Ann wondered if Tracy had already dipped into her stash of "bring your own booze", which was clinking enthusiastically in her shopping bag as they went.

No sooner were they inside the restaurant than Ann found herself seated at the very end of a long table of twelve women, at least six people away from Tracy and tucked tightly beside the infamous Una.

As suspected, after downing just one glass of tepid white wine, Tracy was already well on her way, her volume developing with each second, her eyes flashing up and down the length of the table. The other women were a mish-mash of mothers who ranged from their late thirties all the way down to one who looked young enough to be in school still.

"Twenty-two," Una mouthed when she noticed Ann glance surprisingly at the slight blonde girl. "Had her first when she was seventeen. Unmarried. There's some around here who make a living out of having babies," Una whispered with disdain. "I work. Nothing for nothing."

Tracy was right about one thing: Una was a bore – drab clothes, flat hair and downturned mouth, thankfully more interested in the economics of the evening than quizzing Ann.

"How are we going to split the bill? Should we share starters? I think it'll be cheaper to get the platters for everyone," Una called up the table apprehensively before turning to Ann. "Last time, I ended up chipping in for two bottles of red. I drink white."

Actually, Una seemed just as disappointed to be sitting beside the new girl instead of in the thick of things near Tracy, where she could keep an eye on what the others were ordering, as Ann was to be sitting next to thrifty Una, every accountant's dream.

"Clink, clink."

Ann watched as Tracy banged her fork against her glass, as some of the liquid slopped over the side and as Tracy licked the glass.

"Waste not, want not."

The other women giggled.

"Now, I just want to introduce you all to Ann, all the way from Dublin, no less, and I'm privileged to have her as my new neighbour."

Ann smiled and waved up the table.

"This is . . ."

Tracy went through all the women as each name drifted hopelessly over Ann's head. Most of them smiled as Tracy issued their name – a few raised their glasses.

"Nice to meet you all." Ann raised her glass in return.

"As a little welcome and to cut past all the boring small talk, let's get straight to the nitty-gritty." Tracy was grinning like the cat that got the cream. "I've tried to find out Ann's story, but she's as cagey as Una!" Tracy exploded with laughter and Una shot Ann a quizzical look. "So, what is it, Ann, what brings you away from the Big Smoke – and here, of all places?" Tracy erupted with laughter.

Ann could feel her face burning as all twelve heads turned towards her expectantly.

"Honestly, no story. I just fancied a change from Dublin. All a bit hectic up there. Thought I'd try out the easier life."

"Ah, come on. There must be a reason why a Dublin girl would come all the way here. Haven't you everything up there that we don't? All the American shops and loads of men . . ."

"Not that many men, believe me." Ann tried to keep it light. "And sure, isn't Knockmore as good a place as any? Dublin is far too expensive." Ann was ready with the story she'd invented earlier about soaring house prices and the cost of living in the capital.

"Slumming it with the country-folk, more like," Tracy threw out, her joke falling flat and many of the women shifting in their seats.

"Did you have a big break-up, Ann? Was there some hotshot who let you down?" Tracy persisted.

"Sort of . . ." Ann was still playing her cards close, much to Tracy's obvious frustration.

"Anyone have a fella for Ann? She's single again and ready to mingle. Isn't that right, Ann?"

Ann nodded weakly and pretended to root in her bag for something.

"Lock up your husbands," Tracy squealed.

There was an uncomfortable pause before the woman next to Tracy smiled briefly at Ann and moved the conversation on.

"Talking of single, and wishing I was," the woman started. "I took the young lad out last week with his scooter. He loves going up Church Hill and then scooting back down. Well, Jesus, Mary and Joseph, he nearly got milled over by a guy driving out of the gate of the big house."

"Which one?" someone asked.

"The big one! Knockmore House," the woman continued as Ann's ears perked up from the end of the table. "Driving a big tank of a car, he was. Range Rover, or at least one of those huge ones. I nearly lost my life. 'Be careful,' I said to him. To be fair, he hopped out of the big tank and asked were we all right. Fierce apologetic, he was. Then he rooted in his pocket and threw the young lad a few euros to buy some sweets.

"Gorgeous, so he was – not the usual Knockmore fare. Wouldn't have minded a root in his pocket myself."

The other women erupted with laughter.

"Mark, he said his name was. Mark my words, I thought, I think we'll scoot past again."

"Be careful! You know what they say – the bigger the car, the smaller the gear-stick," another chimed in, to peals of laughter.

The mention of Mark's name took Ann by surprise, sending an unexpected fluttery feeling through her insides.

Ann had walked past Knockmore House a few times since her return, finding herself strangely drawn to it. Had she been hoping to see Mark again? she wondered, thinking about the man she'd encountered there almost a year ago, when she'd first made the journey back to Knockmore to delve into the past after twelve years away. Ann often wondered about him and whether or not he'd told his parents about the day she'd called there with her aunt Lucie, to discover the letter in the tree, revealing the truth of her mother's childhood. He'd promised he wouldn't.

He'd been so easy to talk to, so open that Ann had ended up telling him the whole story that weekend. How she'd been sent away at seventeen, her mother, Felicity, trying to protect her from the clutches of the grandmother she'd never even met.

"It's your story to tell," he'd assured her at the time.

Mind you, she'd also promised to call him, maybe meet up for a drink. He'd been so kind to her that day and she'd be lying if she said she hadn't been attracted to him, but Ann hadn't worked up the courage to lift the phone, imagining him answering and saying, "*Who?*"

Ann struggled her way through the main course. Lately, her appetite had disappeared, almost as much as her desire for life. After her initial outburst, Tracy was now practically ignoring Ann, who was miserably failing at making polite conversation with the other women whose names were still eluding her. Feeling entirely out of her depth as the conversation edged towards teachers in the school, which mother was an interfering know-it-all and who was now running the parent committee into the ground, Ann excused herself early.

"Thanks, everyone." She set her share of the bill on the

table. "I've got an early start tomorrow. I'm going to shoot off. I had a great time."

"It's only eight thirty. Did you even have a drink? You've had the same glass of wine in your hand all night," Tracy slurred, waving her wine glass around.

"Next time. Enjoy."

Ann slunk out of the door self-consciously, understanding full well there probably wouldn't be a next time. While the conversations had been different from those she'd suffered with Dom's friends' wives back in Dublin, the theme was all too familiar – women taking down other women – and tonight, Ann wasn't interested.

"Drip."

Ann heard Tracy's voice as she headed down the stairs.

It stung and not for the first time, Ann began to feel like she'd made a mistake coming back here, but one she wasn't quite ready to admit.

When she reached the bottom of the stairs, instead of turning right towards home, Ann swung left, heading up town, past the shops and towards the hill. Looking around the sleepy village, Ann couldn't help but feel she was somehow in a foreign place and not the town where she'd grown up. So much had changed.

As she reached the brow of the hill, Ann paused at the gate of Knockmore House and peered up the driveway at the imposing structure. Her eyes caught a sudden glimpse of movement in the illuminated bay window. A figure walked past and then reversed slowly to look back out. Ann watched the slight frame in the shining glass and before she could stop herself, she automatically raised her hand in acknowledgement. The figure edged back from the glass and Ann walked away, berating herself for waving at a total stranger.

Sauntering away, Ann realised she might have to look a little further afield to find a like-minded tribe. Tonight hadn't been what she'd expected and evidently, Tracy wasn't going to be her saving grace, but at least she'd given it a go. Wasn't that what was important?

Ann glanced back at the gates of the house once more, shaking her head. Perhaps she'd been hoping someone, or at least a big tank of a car, would emerge through them to knock her off her feet.

Ann knew one thing for sure: she wasn't going to find what she was looking for among Tracy and her crew, and she certainly wasn't going to find what she was looking for inside those granite gates. Fascinated as she was by Knockmore House, it had already gifted her the key to her past, but Ann was sure the door to her future lay elsewhere.

CHAPTER THREE

Olive

Olive Dempsey walked past the window of the study, stopped and took a few steps back. Olive had noticed her before, during the day, peering up the driveway into the house, but this was the first time she'd seen her in the evening. There was very little Olive missed nowadays as she perused the activity outside the gates of the house from her study window. The familiarity of the scene sent a shiver up her spine. The girl was standing there motionless, staring at the house, then she looked straight at the window, directly at Olive, and lifted her hand.

Olive stepped back immediately, putting her hands in the pockets of her cream wool trousers, and narrowed her eyes. Should she be concerned? Perhaps she'd mention it to her husband, Eugene, later. Although she knew he'd have the same answer he always did.

"Sure, who'd be looking at us, Olive? You're paranoid." Before adding, "There's no need any more. No need for those thoughts."

Perhaps she was paranoid, but not without good reason. Olive hadn't always been what her husband called paranoid and she labelled cautious. Perhaps it was old age getting the better of her. Mind you, you could hardly call sixty-three old age, especially nowadays.

"Life begins at forty," her friends back in Wicklow

used to say. "You're only as young as you feel. Or the man you feel!"

A decade later, they'd assured one another, once again, that life, in fact, began at fifty. And then ten years later, sixty was the decade to start afresh. Olive wondered if this would go on through each decade until one day, life ceased. Her second phase had begun at sixty, here in Knockmore. But not the chapter she'd expected, far removed from her previous existence in Wicklow, when life was simple, comfortable. Not perfect – but then, nothing ever was. They'd been good days back in Wicklow – early on, anyway. Her happiest times, perhaps, living on the narrow country lane, their little house at the very end, all the neighbours helping each other when the kids were small.

Back then, Olive adored her three-bedroom bungalow, with its fine-sized garden, watching the trees they'd planted mature with each passing year. Eugene had built the house himself, his strong arms ploughing into the earth, Olive looking on as he'd constructed their future, stone by stone, brick by brick.

"He's not exactly refined. A bit country," her father told her when he'd first met Eugene. "But then one shouldn't aim too high, Olive. Those who aim too high often miss."

Had she settled? No. She wouldn't have put it like that. At first, she felt secure that Eugene had aimed higher with her, achieved more from their union than she had, and that perhaps he loved her that bit more.

"That's the secret to a happy life, Olive," her mother had advised. "Keep them keen."

But with each passing day, Olive fell more and more in love with Eugene until the balance slowly shifted and she felt as though she'd won the lotto, with her fine, big builder husband and their house with all the mod cons.

After the wedding, Eugene had stood at the front door of their new home grinning before scooping Olive up to carry her over the threshold.

"You're as light as a feather."

"Don't drop me, Eugene," she whispered into his chest, stretching her legs out like a doll, relishing the feel of his strong arms around her.

"I'll never drop you, my little olive tree."

"And I'll never let go. Never," she promised.

"No peeking," he whispered, covering her eyes with his hand. "Now, look . . ." He dropped his hand, pointing towards the dishwasher he'd plumbed in as a wedding present.

"Eugene! That's far too extravagant. What would I be doing with that? No one has a dishwasher. They'll be thinking I'm too lazy to wash-up."

"No. They'll be thinking Olive Dempsey has it all. No wife of mine will be scrubbing dishes all day. Look out there," he'd smiled with pride, pointing out at the vast washing line running the length of the house, ready for her to hang their clothes out to dry. "I told you, Olive, we're going to have some life."

"Some life," she'd repeated.

Eugene Dempsey was as smart and ambitious as he was strong.

"Eugene working late again? You see, when you come from nothing, one is often on a mission to prove oneself," her bank manager father had warned. "I see it all the time. Let's hope it stays fine for him. All a bit flashy, isn't it?"

Olive listened as her father's admiration had morphed to jealousy.

"We've everything we need, Eugene, rest now," Olive would say when he returned home from work, to wolf his dinner and head straight back out to do another nixer.

"It's the cash jobs that'll make us, Olive, just wait and see."

He'd worked hard, gradually developing his business, from the man building extensions, fitting those gaudy conservatories, to buying land. Thwarted by Wicklow's stringent planning rules, it wasn't long before Eugene spread his wings towards Dublin, building housing estates and apartment blocks while Olive stayed in Wicklow. So different from how it all began, she found herself experiencing the weight of being alone with the kids, looking after Mark and Jessica, day in, day out.

"Do it, Daddy," the children would squeal when Eugene arrived home.

His clothes were covered in cement, his hair a shade lighter from the layer of dust resting there, ready to escape like a snowdrift as soon as they asked him to shake his head. The children would run at him and he'd throw his arms around them, lifting them into the air, while Olive waited for her turn to bury her face in his chest, inhaling the scent of masculinity and hard work.

As his work attire evolved from dusty trousers and old black shoes – at one time reserved for best – to suits and ties, so, too, did his working hours. ED Construction sometimes took him away for months on end. Then when he returned home late on a Friday evening, the children would dash to greet him, ready to play the game. Alternatively, he'd keep them at arm's length, at a safe distance from his expensive pinstripe suit.

When Olive greeted him, smiling sheepishly at how handsome he looked, he'd bend to kiss her brusquely, the smell of cement replaced by a musky aftershave and once or twice, with a hint of something floral. There were constant presents for her and the kids. Trinkets. Toys. Jewellery. All delivered to ease the discomfort of his absence. On more than a few occasions, over the years, Eugene had tried to encourage a move to Dublin, tempting Olive with some four-storey house in the city, complete with vast rooms to clean and a postage stamp for a garden.

"But I'm happy here, Eugene. This is our life."

That was her first mistake.

So they'd remained in the bungalow, watching it age over the years – as they were. What was it her father used to say? "Cobblers' children have no shoes." Eugene never wanted to put the work into their own house when he was home, preferring to sit in the same chair he'd sat in for the last twenty years, resting for another strenuous week ahead.

The children grew up as children do. Mark: handsome, steady, kind. Jessica: flighty, wild, rarely home. Olive looked forward to spending time with Eugene again, just the two of them, their time – the reward for all the years left waiting.

Then Olive started to see *her* lurking around outside. Of course, she'd had an inclination – in hindsight, perhaps she'd always known – but it was the overheard conversation that drove the final nail into the coffin, making it impossible to ignore the indiscretions any longer.

"She hasn't a clue, absolutely none. God love her, living here, with the house falling down around her ears, and him swanning around up there in Dublin, with a girlfriend and a young son. Old enough to be the boy's grandfather. All this time! It's hard to imagine.

"Frank said the girlfriend is pushing him now for the

divorce. She wants the boy to grow up with his father around. Eugene told him all about it, with a few drinks on board."

Olive had arrived late to girls' night at Rosemary's house, letting herself in the back door as she always did, pausing to wipe her feet on the mat.

"Poor Olive. Ordinary Olive, Frank calls her."

Olive hadn't waited to hear the rest before reversing out of the door, running home and stumbling in the driveway, to land on all fours. *Ordinary Olive.* It stung more than her scraped knees.

Later, she'd stared at herself in the mirror, lightly touching her neglected hair, tugging at the sagging skin of her now lined face, finally able to see herself as they did: pale, old, grey, drab, ordinary. Poor little Olive. Teeny-weeny, capable Ordinary Olive, with her elfin face and delicate hands, her clothes old and worn, always making do.

"Small packages can be deadly, Olive, remember that," her mother, who was even smaller than Olive, used to say. "There's more bite in a Jack Russell than a Rottweiler."

Olive's inner Rottweiler was unleashed almost overnight, confronting Eugene without delay, to watch him squirm as he revealed the shattering truth of his mistress and son.

"Don't say his name. I don't want to hear it. Don't tell me anything about them." Olive had covered her eyes.

There would be no divorce – no separation.

Olive was a shareholder in ED Construction and could make his life a misery if she so chose. Eugene was smart, but she was, too. Unless he wanted to be left with nothing, he'd have to hold tight, as tight as she'd once promised she would.

She knew what he'd choose.

"Walk away," Olive told *her* when she saw her appear again a few days later, teetering up and down outside the house in a pair of high heels, a spray-on dress under an expensive coat and huge sunglasses trimmed with gold. It was the sunglasses that irked Olive the most, the twisty, ornate arms looping garishly into a golden spiral.

"At least have the decency to look at me," Olive spat and then regretted it, as *she* removed the glasses and stared back, doe-eyed, at Olive. "I know everything. If you don't leave, you'll never see a penny – and you won't have him, either. I'll never let him go. Never!" Olive warned the bleached blonde girl.

She couldn't have been much older than Jessica. So, this is what he wanted – everything Olive wasn't. *She* had tried to object, but Olive clocked the euro signs flashing beneath her curtain-like lashes.

"The child will be looked after, if that's what you're worried about. It's not his fault his father's a philanderer."

She still couldn't accept it – that her children shared a father with a stranger, an unknown boy who perhaps had Mark's eyes, or Jessica's smile, or that Olive had shared her husband with a rival who was nothing more than a girl.

"I'm not a monster, but if you ever darken my door again, or go near my husband, so help me God, you'll be sorry. If you want your son to have any sort of decent life, then leave. And believe me, he'll do better without a father like that in his life. He'll learn that in time. And you! A woman who preys on married men . . . disgraceful!" Olive could almost hear her mother cheering for her in her ear, her father telling her he'd seen it coming.

Afterwards, she'd stayed put in the house in Wicklow, keeping her head down, avoiding the neighbours, intent on keeping Eugene on a tight leash while he sulked like a child.

"Why, Eugene, why?" Olive had asked over and over.

"We had everything! Why?"

"Because you didn't want any of it, Olive," he'd finally told her. "I wanted to give you everything, but you didn't want it. You didn't want any of it."

At first, Olive had tried to hide it all from Mark and Jessica, but there was tension in the house – you could cut it with a knife. It was Eugene who'd eventually told them the truth, attempting to absolve himself. Olive would never forgive him for that.

"How could you!" Jessica screamed at her. "How could you let him make a fool of us all? It's your fault. All your fault."

Her fault? It wasn't until that moment that Olive let herself fall to pieces. All she'd done for them over the years and it was her fault. Her fault for trying to ground them all, give them a simple life. It was how Olive was reared: sensible, demure, careful.

"I have a brother!" Mark repeated incessantly, looking disappointed in her. In her!

Then one phone call had altered it all, suddenly making her husband's indiscretions seem irrelevant. Olive had pulled herself back together in an instant. Her family needed her. Jessica needed her. Soon after that, Eugene got sick. What do they say? When it rains, it pours. The world had been pouring on top of Olive for years now.

While Eugene was recovering, Olive began to delve. It was only then that she realised just how successful her husband was and how much they were actually worth. It was then Olive knew it was time to reinvent, somewhere new.

Olive looked out again. The girl was gone. She caught a glimpse of herself in the reflection of the glass – no longer *Ordinary Olive*. Perhaps it was her imagination playing tricks on her, but she'd keep an eye out, just in case. She'd learned that the hard way, never to take her eye off the ball again. Olive had the house now to focus on and plans to make it even more spectacular. She'd be careful to maintain the external grandeur. They'd already worked on the front of the property, but at the back and internally, Olive was sure she could improve it further. Wasn't internal improvement what was always needed? First, she'd tackled the exterior – of herself and the house – and now it was time to delve deeper still.

From the outside, the house was almost ideal – turn of the century, all original features, sash windows, granite steps leading to the front door, sweeping drive. It was everything that she could have had in Dublin years ago, if she'd wanted it, except for the enormous gardens. They'd never have secured such land there. No, for a fraction of the price, and peace of mind that they were tucked away safely, she was still secure in her decision to abscond to Knockmore.

Back in Wicklow, Olive Dempsey had taken care of the past and was now certain that the pillar-box red panelled door of Knockmore house was the entrance to her future.

CHAPTER FOUR

"Alarm bells," Aunt Lucie told her during her weekly call from Australia after Ann divulged the story of Tracy and the abysmal introduction to her Knockmore peers. "When I first arrived in Australia, I ended up making friends with this nurse at the hospital. Nurse-in-Your-Face, they called her. She used to wear flesh-coloured fish-net tights with her uniform! Can you imagine? Anyway, it made sense after I found out she was always fishing for information – and not in an engaging way, but to gather ammunition to use against you.

"She wanted to know everything about everyone. It was her way to take you down eventually, in an effort to make herself feel better. Always the drunk one on the nights out, stuffing her boobs in the doctors' faces. Oh, and the best bit – she used to try to get all the other girls in trouble by diddling the roster. Mad yoke.

"Well, Nurse-in-Your-Face saw me coming. Turns out she'd already burned her bridges with everyone else and was only too keen to take the poor new little Irish eejit under her wing. I figured her out soon enough," Lucie laughed. "Sounds like this Tracy one might be cut from the same cloth. Could you give her a wide berth, Ann?"

"I suppose I thought because we're the same age, we should get on."

"Sure, what's age got to do with it? Why on earth would

you be hanging around with school mothers when you don't need to? I'm telling you, that's the best bit of advice Mam ever gave me. Don't get involved.

"I only wish I'd listened earlier. What a minefield! A bunch of women with nothing in common except the fact they've had children. Who'll do anything to make sure little Jimmy or Mary doesn't get left out in the playground, or get given the shite part in the Christmas play, or not get invited to a party . . . I've seen street fighters softer than some of them," Lucie laughed. "You'll find a few like-minded people in time. Cull the crazies!"

Ann had found a few like-minded friends over time, far from where she'd expected and ever so slightly outside her self-imposed age bracket. Denise from the coffee shop and Ian from the hardware store had graciously taken Ann under their wing, in a non-airway blocking, slackened headlock grip sort of way. And bit by bit, Ann had managed to distance herself from Tracy: Neighbour-in-Your-Face.

"Did you not have a nice time?" Tracy had asked her the day after the evening out at the Italian.

"I did. Everything's all so new still. It always takes me a while to get settled and I have my hands full here trying to get the house in order. It was left in a bit of a state, but thanks for including me."

"Suppose. Coffee, later? There's still so much I want to ask you."

"Ah, I can't today, Tracy. I've someone coming to look at the bathroom."

"Sure, my fella can look at the bathroom for you. He's a plumber. I'll come in and take a few pictures and send them to him."

"Thanks, but I've already called a guy Ian recommended. I wouldn't want to let him down."

"Not Liam? He'll charge you through the nose. Honestly, let me—"

"If it's okay, Tracy, I'd prefer to keep it separate from neighbours. You know, in case anything goes wrong, then—"

Tracy held up her hands. "Say no more. Not really how Knockmore works – bit hard to separate business from pleasure when we all live on top of each other. Anyway, no offence taken. Dublin will do as Dublin will do."

"Great, thanks for understanding." Ann started to back away, unconvinced that no offence had been taken, when Tracy stuck her head back round the door.

"I'll call in later to check on you . . ."

Unfortunately, keeping her distance from Tracy often entailed Ann spending more time than necessary at home. Tracy was everywhere, and Ann was wary of plunging herself into a friendship that in time may see her pinned to a chair and hooked up to a lie detector machine. It wasn't that she disliked Tracy, they were just too different. And if they weren't neighbours, they'd never gravitate towards each other in the real world.

"Neighbours should smile at you over the fence and not climb over it," Denise warned her over coffee one morning.

"Or ask you to babysit!" Ann giggled.

Ann supposed in one way she should be grateful to Tracy. As the months went by and Ann attempted but failed to find her place, it was the din from next door that would somehow anchor Ann and prevent her from floating away. Her boisterous next-door neighbour became excellent company, albeit one-sided. Ann could tell most days what

Tracy was up to next door as she lay in bed listening, or strolling from room to room, trying to fill the days. Ann wasn't sure exactly when she'd started using her neighbour's routine to prompt one of her own, shadowing Tracy on the other side of the wall, but it had helped.

Each day, Tracy would return home from the school run to replace her hybrid leisurewear with full leisurewear and go for a jog. Ann would watch Tracy sprinting up the road, looking as though she were running away, never to return.

While she was gone, Ann would shower and dress. On a good day, the route took thirty minutes, on a bad day, up to thirty-five. While Tracy showered and dried her hair with her extraordinarily powerful hairdryer, Ann would make her bed, collect her washing and clean the bathroom.

They'd proceed downstairs, together, separated by the wall, where Tracy would switch on morning television and possibly eat breakfast. Ann couldn't be sure of this, but she took the silence as a suggestion that Tracy was chewing.

After probable sustenance, Tracy would make several lengthy phone calls, first to her sister, then her mam. From what Ann could gather, Tracy's sister was a little more well-to-do than Tracy, judging by the number of times Tracy asked, "How much did that set you back?" and the fact that Tracy could often be heard saying, "Well for some."

The mother must have been hard of hearing, as Tracy's voice would increase by several decibels during their chat. Ann knew everything about *Mam*, from her love of cake to her irritable bowel and how many times each day it moved, which Tracy would repeat loudly several times.

"Four, Mam? In the space of an hour? That is excessive. Well, jot it down and we'll tell the doctor next week."

Ann would then force herself to leave the house for a

while, drop in on Denise or Ian before returning for the afternoon schedule: four screaming boys and a frantic mother. At times, Tracy shouted so loud that once or twice, Ann had almost gone to tidy her own room.

Certain that she couldn't be heard over the racket of next door, Ann would play music in the evenings. Songs she remembered from her childhood – ones that helped to fill the emptiness of the house and her heart with sound. Sitting in the kitchen, sipping wine, forcing herself to relish the solitude, the upbeat music of her youth helped to smother the pangs of uncertainty.

"Me ma says will you turn down the music? The baby can't get to sleep."

"Oh, gosh, sure. Sorry," Ann told the gangly young boy with the spiky red hair and freckles staring at her from the doorstep.

"She said, 'Tell *yer one* to turn down that shite,'" he grinned, wrinkling his nose.

"Is that right?" Ann couldn't help smiling.

"Yeah, she says you're a pain in the hole. I think you look nice," he blushed, surmising that this wasn't a term of endearment.

Ann put her hands on her hips and grimaced. "Thanks. I think. So, which one are you?"

"The oldest one. I get all the jobs," he called before jumping the metal fence separating the two houses.

Ann turned down the music, only to be met immediately with the sounds seeping through the walls once more: the TV on full blast, children screaming at each other, Tracy screaming back.

Oddly, Ann became dependant on the sounds that penetrated the paper-thin walls, finding comfort in being part of the comings and goings of the Doyles behind the safety of her barrier. It wasn't that she was trying to be elusive or standoffish – she just wasn't ready to immerse yet. For the moment, it was all she could manage to restore her little house to how it once was and observe other people going about living from behind her window. In time, she hoped it might somehow give her the prompts she needed to get on with her own.

"Do you know who popped into my mind the other day," Aunt Lucie had said yesterday. "That Mark, from Knockmore House. Did you ever call him? He seemed like a genuine guy."

Ann had moaned. "Lucie, please. I'm not ready to meet anyone."

"It doesn't have to be like that. Why not reach out as a friend? It would be nice for you to reconnect. Make a few plans."

CHAPTER FIVE

Mark

He hadn't planned to come this weekend. Mark rarely planned on visiting, but somehow, he managed to end up here. It wasn't the drive that bothered him – if he left late enough, he could manage to avoid the weekend traffic. Mark gazed in front of him as the leaves above threw moving shadows on the tarmac of the tree-lined country road along the final stretch. It wasn't Knockmore that troubled him, either. Knockmore wasn't a bad old town – not that different from where he grew up. Small but not too small. Big enough so you could remain anonymous, or right at the heart of things if you were that way inclined. Mark knew how he was inclined, always preferring to stay on the outskirts, not get too involved, hold back a little.

"You'll never meet someone if you don't throw yourself out there. You're like your father," his mother would say, not meaning it as a compliment. "A closed book. Guarded."

Mark didn't know about that. He was relatively open with the right people, not seeing the point in trying to break through to the very soul of every person he encountered, content with his few close friends, his job, his golf. It wasn't that he had no interest in meeting someone, but he was busy, all the time, especially since his father's forced retirement from the company.

"I wish I could give you a hand, son, but she has me

practically locked up down here," Eugene would complain. "All marching to the beat of her drum. Even you."

"Can you blame her?"

"No. I suppose not."

"Welcome to Fort Knox." Eugene was sitting on the steps at the front door, his walking stick beside him, his left side noticeably stooped. He looked old, frailer than Mark remembered, dressed in rust-coloured corduroy trousers and a beige checked shirt with a khaki cardigan.

"Don't you mean Knockmore?"

"No, I think Fort Knox suits it better, don't you? Or Knoxmore, there's a new one for you."

"Hi, Dad." Marked hugged him. "It's good to see you. It's been a while. New clothes? All you need now is a rifle and a peaked hat. At last, a look that suits the old moustache!"

Eugene rolled his eyes. "Yes, I think she calls this look 'country pile', or something like that. I do what I'm told nowadays. Apparently, the moustache is now approved, since it goes well with the house and all the tweed."

Mark laughed as his father twirled one corner of the familiar moustache, once deemed common by his mother and now accepted as distinguished.

"It's good to see you too, son. You're the only one who talks to me in this sprawling metropolis. How have you cleverly succeeded in avoiding this place for . . . what is it . . . a month, now? What brings you here this weekend?" Eugene reached for Mark's hand to help him up.

Mark glanced up at the house, wondering what his mother had on the agenda for the weekend. It must be something huge, judging by her panicked phone call earlier that day.

"I need you to come down for the weekend. I want to discuss something with you. It's vital."

"Can't it wait, Mum? I've been busy all week. I was hoping to relax this weekend."

"Is there something you're not telling me, Mark? Are you seeing someone?"

He could picture her standing at the end of the stairs, below where the staircase looped up to the split-level balcony, holding the house phone away from her face so it didn't disturb her hair.

"No, Mum. Nothing like that. I haven't time to see anyone. You know that."

Why did he need to explain himself? He was a grown man, for Christ's sake.

"Mum," he said now, looking up.

The door swung open dramatically, to reveal Olive, dressed head to toe in cream, mincing down the steps, coiffed to within an inch of her life. Her once salt-and-pepper hair was now platinum blonde and her top lip was curling up, unable to close over her suddenly perfect white teeth.

"You look well, Mother."

He bent to kiss her cheek, coughing as he inhaled her overpoweringly pungent perfume – another change. She used to smell of lemons. He remembered it, cuddling into her on the brown corduroy sofa with the wooden arms, where she'd read him story after story to get him to try to stay awake to say goodnight to Dad. Nine times out of ten, Dad never made it home before Mark's eyes fluttered closed. Nine times out of ten, he didn't come back at all.

"Thank you, darling," she purred, doing a little turn. "This old thing? It's winter white – all the rage for summer, apparently. Can you imagine? I said to the girl, in my day it was just plain white. She couldn't believe I was over sixty. I see you didn't dress for dinner," Olive grimaced, taking in the cargo shorts and T-shirt he'd thrown on for the drive.

Mark smiled woodenly, pondering how exhausting she must find it never to allow the veil to slip from her face. It had happened almost overnight, his little mum morphing from someone who was more like Mrs Doubtfire into Krystle Carrington from *Dynasty*.

"So, what's the big panic?" he asked, taking his bag out of the boot and locking the car.

"No panic, darling. I just wanted to see my little soldier and maybe discuss a few plans with you."

"What plans?" Mark looked from Olive to Eugene.

Eugene shrugged his shoulders. "Damned if I know. No one tells me anything."

"I've decided to do a job on the house. You remember, we had the plans drawn up, but in the end, we decided against it," Olive began. "I know we did a little band-aid job a while back, but there are a few bits I still want to do. We already have planning permission and we've got a few months before it runs out."

"Really? I can't imagine what else there is to do to the house." Mark walked through the front door and dropped his bag on the parquet floors.

Olive picked it up immediately, tucking it neatly under the stairs.

The house had already been redecorated thoroughly – like his mother, he supposed. It was completely different to how it was when they first bought it but still maintained the charm of an old house, now with some modern additions. The house had got updated sash windows and a new roof – his mother had got porcelain veneers and new breasts.

"I want to knock through some walls and make the living area bigger at the back. Have the kitchen and the living room in one. Oh, and I saw this wonderfully modern kitchen that I adore . . . Also, a glass wall separating the second living room. I need light. Air! All these pokey little rooms irk me," Olive announced, gesturing towards the dining room.

"There'll be no hiding now."

Olive whipped round to look at her husband. "Shut up, Eugene. We have the money. Besides, developing properties is what we do. Develop this," she quipped, followed by her irritating quirk of adjusting her hair without touching it, as if brushing away a cobweb.

"It's a waste of money," Mark attempted, glancing around again at the house that was already too big for them. He was fascinated how someone who used to remove the uneaten mashed potato from their plates as children to save for the next day could now be so flippant with money.

Olive flicked her hair from her face forcefully this time, causing a few strands to anchor to her lip gloss. Lip gloss! On his mother . . .

"I'm not asking for your opinion, Mark. I'm asking you to coordinate it."

"I barely have time to coordinate taking a shower at the moment, let alone a job like this. Kate from accounts just told me she's going to be taking her maternity leave early, so I'm up to my eyes trying to manage wages and everything else." Mark threw his hands in the air.

"Then find someone who can," Olive smiled sweetly, pursing her lips further, still trying to remove the hairs from her patent lips. "Why must men make a mountain out of a molehill?" She threw her hands up, mimicking Mark's theatrics. "Besides . . . other news. We're heading to Spain for a few months soon. I've taken a house in Marbella. Jessica needs a break." Olive looked at the ground, trying not to meet his gaze. "As do your father and I. The warmer weather will do us all good. So it'll give you time to get the project going. Perfect timing."

Mark was about to question why his sister, Jessica, who lay in bed all day, could possibly need a break, but decided against it. The thought of a few months' respite from them all was far too tantalising.

Mark could see his dad watching Mum from the corner of his eye. Was this who his father had wanted all along? Could his mother have held his father's attention if she'd always been this way, looking as if she were going to an eighties fancy dress party, living the life of a lottery winner? He wondered what she – the other woman, the mistress, his bit on the side, his bit of fluff, or whatever the latest term Mum was employing – was like. Mark thought about it a lot, wondering what had been so great that it had kept his father away all those years. Mark also knew that somewhere out there, he had a little brother. He must be what? Fourteen, now? Mark didn't even know his name. It was as if he didn't exist. He almost felt an affinity with the poor kid.

"I know how you feel, kiddo," he'd say if they ever met. "He was the same with us."

It made Mark feel slightly better to know *they* were being well looked after. Mark noticed the generous sum exit the system each month, destined for the unnamed bank account. Not even Kate, the accountant, dare question where it was bound.

His mother had arranged it all. His mother, who'd never changed a light bulb, hung a picture or paid a bill in her life but who was perfectly capable of orchestrating a sophisticated production when she had to.

"So in here, I'd like to knock down this wall, tear out the . . ."

Mark tuned out. Already, his mother's voice was grating on his nerves. In a way, he supposed he should admire how she'd clung to her sinking marriage, making the problems vanish. In another, it infuriated him. He almost despised her for it, but not as much as his sister, Jessica, did. Jessica blamed her for everything, but then she'd always been a daddy's girl, constantly vying for his attention. Perhaps that's why she'd taken the whole thing so badly. When Jessica was young, she was just short of backflipping into the room and doing a triple somersault to get Dad to notice her. Now, she hated him, too.

Mark didn't exactly hate his father. He didn't admire his actions, but he was human, flawed, and he'd admitted his mistakes – he'd just forgotten to deal with them.

He wondered if Dad hadn't fallen ill, would things have been different. Would his father have done the right thing? Then again, what was the right thing? If he'd left their mother, Mark would have hated him for it, but perhaps that would have been better than this charade. Strangely, through it all, it was Mark's relationship with his mother that had broken down, but then again, that's what happens when you keep secrets – dangerous ones.

Mark followed Olive out to the garden.

"Wait until I show you the plans of the orangery." She was elated. "And that blasted shady oak will have to go."

Mark glanced towards the tree, remembering the day

he'd been a party to the past secrets of Knockmore House. He wondered what had happened to Ann Maguire and what her aunt's name was . . . Lucie, wasn't it? Ann had promised to call him. Perhaps if she had, he'd have told her that her family weren't the only ones to harbour secrets.

Yes. That was the reason Mark avoided coming here. His family – mostly his mother and his sister. His father didn't know the half of it. The parts Mark knew, he wished he didn't. Mark had been in the wrong place at the wrong time. Being around them, knowing what he knew, was like torture, but he wasn't sure he ever wanted to know the entire truth of what he'd overheard between his sister and his mother that night.

Mark looked back at the house from where they now stood beside the oak tree. Funny, he thought, how no amount of restoration could restore some things. And then he whispered her name.

"Ann Maguire."

CHAPTER SIX

"Ann Maguire, calling Ann Maguire. Come in, Ann, over. Okay, now I know you're avoiding me. You can't be *that* busy. Call me later. I have news – two-week countdown is on. Over and out."

Ann listened to Sophie's voice message, unable to stop smiling. In two weeks, Sophie would be arriving for the weekend, for Ann's thirtieth birthday – just the two of them, like old times. The house was still a bombsite and her plan to return it to some form of homely familiarity had stalled, her initial enthusiasm for restoring both it and, in turn, herself beginning to ebb. Ann was growing weary of stepping over empty paint tins and boxes from Ikea filled with furniture yet to be assembled. At least there was no one to fight with – she had only herself to blame for a poor paint choice, or for putting the leg of a chair on backwards.

Pulling back the curtains in her bedroom, Ann paused for a moment before lifting her hand to Tracy, who was returning from the school run. The movement above caught Tracy's eye, who glanced up briefly, her expression altering slightly – not enough. She didn't wave back. With the deadline of Sophie's arrival spurring her into action, she didn't have time to shadow Tracy today through the wall. Instead, she padded into the bathroom to run the shower.

It was the one thing she'd changed straightaway, immediately employing the local handyman, Liam, to rip out the murky-coloured bath and replace it with the most significant shower they could fit in the tiny bathroom. The intense guilt she felt at removing her grandmother's prized bathroom suite, the height of fashion in the 1980s, took her by surprise.

"It's not green. It's avocado." Grandma Tess defended her fruity choice.

"That's not avocado, that's snot, isn't it, Felicity?" her father, Sammy, echoed.

"It's more sage." Mam being diplomatic.

After Liam had dismantled it, the avocado porcelain had remained dejected for weeks in the yellow skip, passers-by choosing to ignore her precious family memory in favour of selecting a broken picture frame, or a chair with three legs, from the rubbish pile outside. Peering out at the sad mass of green had almost made Ann rush out, once or twice, to retrieve it, to drag it back inside, scared that by removing all traces of the past, she'd also be erasing it.

"This will be lovely, Ann. It's fierce mod-ren. Are you sure you don't want a bath?" Liam had tried to convince her in his thick Irish accent. "Don't all you young wans like to sip wi-en in de bath, reading those rags about the Karflu-shians and the likes? I think it's a mistake you'll be regrettin'."

"I'm sure, Liam. I prefer my wine on dry ground and the Kardashians aren't my thing."

"But you may want de babbies one day. They love de bath, so they do."

"I'm not sure that's on the cards for me, Liam, not any more," she smiled sadly as he'd coughed to hide his embarrassment and shuffled away.

While Liam had worked on the bathroom, Ann took the opportunity of the skip to have a clear-out. It took days to rid the house of the threadbare sofas and wobbling kitchen chairs, and discard the boxes of rubbish left behind by the four nurses who'd rented the terraced house for the past few years.

"It'll take months to get rid of them, at least six," the estate agent had told her the day after she'd decided to flee Dublin.

"I don't have six months. I need them gone now."

"Not going to happen. I can find you a place nearby to rent. There's a lovely—"

"Offer them their deposit and two months' rent, if they leave by Friday. Final offer," she'd snapped, remembering Dom's habit of using money to get what he wanted.

In hindsight, she could have offered just the deposit. The house was wrecked. Ann had scrubbed every surface until her hands were raw.

"Leave it twenty-four hours to dry before you go gettin' in, making a mess of my fine work," Liam had winked, applying the last sealant around the shower door. "And good luck with your new . . . eh . . . place." He'd looked over his shoulder at the empty, dismal space.

It was only then, when the door had shut behind him, that the initial euphoria had snapped and Ann crashed to earth, allowing the tears to spill. And only then that she could picture it all as it had once been.

There they were – their ghosts lurking behind every door, hanging in the atmosphere of each room, haunting her heart. She ran her hand over the pencil marks on the wall behind the kitchen door, jumping her hand higher with each year to mark her growth. Ann stood against it, placing the flat of her hand on her head, moving it slowly towards the wall and stepping away.

Her hand rested on the final line, just where she'd left it: Ann – 17 years old. The same. She hadn't grown in height since she first left, nor did it seem that she'd advanced at all. The dent on the living room wall was still visible where her dad would fling the door open dramatically to let them know he was home, leaving a hollow reminder in the plasterboard. "Hi, Dad," she whispered.

Tiny remnants of Blu-Tack remained on the kitchen wall, where her mam would proudly display her pictures, her certificates, her achievements. "Hi, Mam." The patterned carpet: the same one she used as an obstacle course as a child, jumping over and around the brown-and-maroon diamond-shaped pattern. The tenants had painted over the wallpaper, but when Ann scratched at it with her nail, she could still see the embossed floral design she used to pick at unconsciously while watching TV.

"Hi, Tess."

"Stop that, Annie. You're ruining my beautiful wallpaper." Tess's words rang in her ears.

"Grab your coat, kiddo. Come for a stroll with your old dad." The door flung open.

"Goodnight, Annie. I love you." Her mother blew a kiss.

Over and over, it played in her mind as she floated through the house, touching the walls, running her hand up the bannister, pressing her head against the doors – remembering. She needn't have worried about banishing the avocado bathroom suite. Nothing would ever force their memories from this place they'd never left – Ann just hadn't been able to see it until then.

"Am I looking at it through rose-tinted glasses?" she

asked her aunt Lucie over the phone, trying to explain what it was like to be back in their childhood home.

"No, pet. It was a rose-tinted life. Are you sure about this? Are you sure Knockmore is the place for you? It's your house. Your mam wanted you to have it and I know it was me who planted the seed in your head, but maybe you'd be better off in Dublin, with your friends, where there's a bit of a buzz."

"I knew it wouldn't be easy being back. I just didn't imagine how hard it would be."

"It *will* pass, Ann. You just have to ride the storm."

Ann knew she was right. It just didn't make it, or the thought of reinventing herself once more, any easier. She lay awake night after night, wondering did she have the strength, fretting that she'd fall asleep and never wake up, her body left to decompose for weeks before anyone noticed. Would the house be broken into at night with her here, alone? At least Tracy would probably hear that. Would she come to her rescue? Well, perhaps if Ann offered to babysit once or twice . . .

Sometimes Ann wished she could rewind it all, stay ensconced in her sheltered life in Dublin. In one way, she wished she'd never discovered her husband, Dom, and Sabrina together. Or found her aunt Lucie again. Or uncovered that darn letter explaining how *that woman*, Margot Montgomery, had stolen her mother as a baby. Would Ann have been able to continue her life if she never knew the secrets of the past? Perhaps she could forget.

"We've all been placed here to find our way, Annie. Some paths are easier than others, but you'll never be happy until you uncover what path is for you. Your mam was the bravest person I knew. Now, you must be brave, too," her great-aunt Florrie told her when it all first happened, when Ann had gone to visit her to relay what she'd unearthed in the letter she'd found buried in the tree at Knockmore House.

"I'm not brave. Everything was a lie. We're not even family any more – not even related," Ann sobbed.

"Maybe not by blood, but you know as well as I do that family comes from the heart. Maybe the one thing my sister Margot did without even knowing it was link us all together. There was a reason for that, of that I am sure," Florrie soothed, rubbing Ann's back as she once had for Felicity.

"I just want to know how it will all end."

"Well then, my love, you must go back to the start and work your way forwards from there."

Ann stood in her bedroom now, running her hands over the designer clothes in her wardrobe, left behind from her life in Dublin, which now seemed as though it'd never happened. She should have tossed them all in that stupid skip, or hurled them over the fence at Tracy for girls' night. Ann's eyes rested on three identical baseball hats hanging in a row: grey, yellow, black. It was the yellow one that irritated her the most – bright sunshiny yellow, trapped in between the other two murky colours. She grabbed it and pulled it on, hoping that the colour might inject her brain, then made her way downstairs to the kitchen.

Tracy was on the phone already, earlier than usual. Today, Ann didn't want to listen. What had once helped to occupy her mind and banish her thoughts suddenly seemed ridiculous. She flicked open the bank app on her phone and watched the Quick Balance icon spin, closing her eyes for a moment before opening them to look at the daunting amount on the screen. Time and money were running out.

Back then, it had seemed a fortune – an amount deposited into her account to get rid of her, fast – but the money wasn't going to last forever, no matter how much she employed her thrifty accountancy tendencies. Doing the house up had depleted the fund faster than expected. She needed a job.

One thing she knew for sure was she didn't want Dom's money – she never had. Perhaps six months in a self-appointed cocoon was enough and it was finally time to emerge – to stop using the house as an excuse, to finish it once and for all and then dip her toe into life again.

"I agree, Tracy – four in an hour is excessive."

Ann was tired listening to other people's problems, especially the bowel motions of her neighbour's mother.

Ann stood up and grabbed her bag as the thought entered her mind.

Surely there were worse things in life than to be in a small town as a separated, single, practically impoverished daughter of a stolen baby. Weren't there?

CHAPTER SEVEN

Ann made her way onto the main street towards the aptly named Tea and Sympathy local funeral home-cum-coffee shop. That was one thing that was still the same – how almost every person or nearly every business in Knockmore had a double function. The local garda moonlighted as a DJ, the electrician ran a very successful cake decorating business on the side, her builder friend, Liam, was the bouncy castle man, not to mention the lady who did the make-up at the funeral home, who also did face painting at children's parties. That one almost made Ann spit out her coffee as she listened to Denise, proud proprietor of Tea and Sympathy, bringing her up to date on the comings and goings of downtown Knockmore.

"A soya cappuccino when you're ready, please."

Ann had happened on the coffee shop soon after arriving in Knockmore, to be met with a shocked expression that was comparable with having walked in stark naked asking for a donation to purchase a pair of knickers.

"A whaty-what what-a-ccino, now?" Denise had burst out laughing, folding her arms.

The other customers stared, waiting for a reaction from the immaculately dressed blonde, who looked as though she'd just ridden into the wrong town.

Ann quietly repeated her order, wanting the ground to swallow her.

"Ah! It's only a regular coffee, a pot of tea, scones and muffins at the front here, or a full Irish breakfast you'll get at this time," Denise told her. "None of that fancy-pants stuff."

"Don't forget the sympathy," someone shouted from one of the pine tables near the back.

Accompanied with, "Go on you, boyo," from another punter.

"That's my husband's department. You won't get sympathy from me," Denise grinned back at them.

"Just any old coffee, please, and a scone." Ann sat at the counter, feeling the heat from several pairs of eyes boring into her cashmere sweater.

"There you are now, love." Denise placed a cup of what transpired to be the most bitter coffee Ann had ever tasted in front of her. "Get that into you. Don't suppose you'll be wanting milk. Cow's milk, that is," Denise added, raising an eyebrow.

Ann shook her head and drank the entire cup of acidic liquid, terrified to insult by leaving even a drop behind.

When the place quietened down, Denise rested her ample bosom on the counter in front of Ann.

"Are you just passing through?"

"No. I've already passed through. I'm returning home. I grew up here."

Denise stood back from the counter, crossing her arms and tilting her head to the side. She blew a stray bit of brown hair from her face where it had escaped from beneath her hairnet.

"What's your name?" Her eyes narrowed.

"It's Ann."

"Ann what?" She squinted further.

"Ann Maguire."

"Jesus, Mary and holy Saint Joseph. It can't be. Not Sammy's wee girl?"

Denise looked even more taken aback than she had done after the convoluted coffee request.

"The very one," Ann smiled, her heart surging at the mention of her father's name.

"Well I never! That's only gas. G-A-S. Jesus, you're your mam's girl. I knew you looked familiar." Denise shook her head in disbelief. "Would you look?" She pulled up her sleeve, hoisting it over her forearm. "I've feckin' goose bumps."

Ann giggled, suddenly feeling as if her pony had happened into the right place, after all.

"Christ, Sammy was a fine-looking man, and I mean *fine*. Do you mind me saying? By Jaysus, I'd get the sweats every time he talked to me. Ride. R-I-D-E." Denise spelled it. "I used to be up watching him play in Lennon's with the girls. Bashing each other out of the way, so we were, just to get to the front, hoping he might give us one of those sexy little winks." Denise's blue eyes twinkled at the memory. "You won't believe it now, but I was there the night he met your mam. Not a word of a lie."

This time, it was Ann's turn for goose bumps, her entire body breaking into a shiver.

"Really?"

"Oh, hell yeah. A group of us went to see Sammy and the band, but mostly Sammy." Denise shook her head again. "After that night, it was game over for us all and I got stuck with yer man instead. Isn't that right, Steve?" she laughed, gesturing towards the back office, where Steve popped his head out and waved. "The local undertaker. Not exactly every young girl's dream."

"I *can* hear you," he called.

Denise lowered her voice to a whisper. "Of course, the girls slagged the shite out of me for years for going out with the undertaker's son, asking did he have a constant stiffy. Stiffy Steve, they used to call him. A shower of wagons, they were. Used to say if I stood still long enough, he'd embalm me.

"Anyway, it made sense that Steve took over from his father. And as I always say, the business will never die, only the customers. And sure, we haven't done too badly. So I suppose it all worked out in the end," Denise chuckled.

Ann couldn't help smiling as she listened.

"We all thought Felicity was a stuck-up yoke at first. Never seen outside. And, of course, she was a leftie. We didn't mix with the Protestants back then. It was different in those days. But then after you came along . . . well, wasn't that the gossip doing the rounds for a while. The reverend's daughter, up the duff!

"Then her parents legged it and yer mam was left behind. The Maguires took her in like that . . ." She clicked her finger. "Felicity's mother was a weapon, my own mam used to say. Whatever happened to them? They were no loss to Knockmore."

Ann looked down, not knowing where the conversation was going and unprepared for such honesty.

"I'm not entirely sure. I never met them."

"Anyway, after a while, people stopped talking when they saw how in love that pair were. It was like a real-life love story and your mam . . . well, she was one of the good ones. Not a bit of snobbery in her. Proud as punch of her little family. We all loved her. Loved them." Denise stopped for a moment, softening and placing her hand on Ann's. "It was a tragedy them passing so young. A tragedy. Welcome home, Ann Maguire."

Ann didn't mean for the tears to well so fast as Denise gave Ann a glimpse of the sympathy part of the operation and poured her another bittersweet coffee.

"So, what brings you back after all this time?"

"I needed a fresh start." Ann lowered her voice. "I'm separated. It didn't work out with *him*, my husband, in Dublin." She looked down as she spoke. It was only the second time she'd divulged that piece of information since her return. "But it hasn't exactly been the start I expected. I don't know . . . it's so different. Maybe I haven't tried hard enough. Seems being separated is still a little taboo around these parts."

Ann forced a smile and told Denise about her encounter with her childhood friend's mother. Craving familiarity, Ann had called round at Ciara's mam's house. Mrs Sullivan nearly fell over when she saw Ann standing there.

"Ciara's just had her third baby – a little girl. Up to her eyes, she is. She lives a few miles out the road now. We wondered whatever happened to you, Ann. Ciara was devastated at the time, you leaving like that. No goodbye. You've lost your accent, too. Dublin, was it?"

"Have I?" Had she? "Yeah, Dublin. I should have called. I was with relatives," Ann told her, sticking to her original story. Lately, she seemed to have so many versions of the truth. It would have been so refreshing to let it all spill out. "It was . . . complicated." Ann didn't know how to explain.

"Life's complicated," Mrs Sullivan had answered before telling her she'd get Ciara to call. "Did you marry, Ann, any kids yourself?"

"No. No kids. I was married. Recently separated."

"Oh." The rounded sound lasted longer than it should have before Mrs Sullivan muttered, "That won't go down well."

Ciara hadn't called. But what did Ann expect?

"There's nowt so queer as folk. They'll get over it. You grew up here, you know what it's like. But you listen to me, if anyone gives you any shite, mention Sammy Maguire's name or send them here to me, all right? Most people are great, by and large, but there are the odd small-minded ones who like to gossip and are full of suspicion. Don't let it get to you. Keep your head down for a while and sooner or later, you'll settle back in. Knockmore is your home as much as theirs. Remember that."

"Usual, Ann?" Denise asked now as Ann pushed open the door of the shop.

"I'll take it to go, please, Denise. Still more painting to do, would you believe."

"Coming right up. Would you like me to send the young lad round to give you a hand? The great big lazy lump has finished college now and is hanging around me like a bad smell."

"Nah. Thanks, though. I've got it all under control."

Ann took the polystyrene cup that could burn the skin from your hand in seconds and placed some euros on the counter. That was another positive about living in Knockmore – it was cheaper, with far less fuss. Ann's taste buds had even adjusted to the insanely bitter coffee, in the same way she'd once forced herself to drink one of Dom's really expensive bottles of red wine.

"I'm looking forward to your birthday night out, Ann. I'm dying for a good bop," Denise added.

"Are you sure you want to come? Don't feel you have to. My friend Sophie told me to invite *all* of my friends. I think she'll be shocked when it's just Ian and us."

Ann was embarrassed, hoping her thirtieth birthday celebration wouldn't be like tumbleweed, complete with rent-a-crowd.

"Stop that now. We wouldn't miss it for the world. And we *are* your friends, as you are ours. Remember, you only need one or two good ones. The rest can feck off. In a small town like this, keep your circle tighter than your knickers. Let nothing unnecessary wriggle in there."

"Now that I can live by."

Ann continued up the road towards the hardware store, where Ian, the second of her two friends in Knockmore, would be waiting with her order. She wasn't sure what made her glance towards the charity shop. Perhaps it was the mannequin dressed from head to toe in every shade of yellow imaginable, with a giant straw picture hat balanced precariously on its head, or the sign beside it, written on a blackboard: Create Your Own Sunshine. She reached up to touch her yellow baseball hat and stared beyond it at the guitar that sat unloved at the back of the window display.

"Sing with me, Annie. Here, let me show you. Life is a song, now sing it, child." She could hear her father's words.

There was a pep in her step as she returned home later that morning, two pots of paint in one hand and a guitar in the other. It was years since she'd played, since Dad had held her fingers around the chords, showing her how. Would she still be able? Hopefully, it would come back to her, like riding a bike or returning to life.

Sooner or later, it would all come back.

CHAPTER EIGHT

"So, Jack and I walked into the pub and there they were, Dom and Sabrina, packed up each other's arses, thick as thieves," Sophie told her on the phone later that evening.

Ann had just finished the first coat of paint on the two bedrooms and the living room and was about to start the second, when the phone rang. Ann slumped down on the living room floor, half listening to the story about her ex-husband and his girlfriend, and half looking for any patches she'd missed on the wall. The rest of the furniture would be arriving in the next few days and the carpets replaced with a pale grey – no more patterns, plain and simple, just how she liked it.

"Ann? Are you even listening?" Sophie asked when Ann didn't respond.

"Sorry, yes. Go on."

"I gave them some look. Daggers. Jack had to drag me away," Sophie continued. "The head on Sabrina. The auburn hair is gone. Now, she's all peroxide extensions and double-layer spray tan, like a cheap version of you! Pathetic. I wonder if he calls her Sabrina, or if he's come up with some stupid name for her. Maybe he calls her Ann – wouldn't surprise me. Weirdo. Anyway, beat on the street is they're moving in together, looking for a place to rent. I drove by your house today and the For Sale sign is still up. Any news?"

Ann sighed. She knew Sophie meant well, but every time she told her another snippet of news from Dublin about Dom and that tramp, Sabrina, her stomach lurched. Regardless of the discovery that Sabrina was Dom's little bit on the side during her short-lived marriage, Ann hadn't expected them to last.

"Not yet. Apparently, no one's offered anywhere near the asking price. Dom's dealing with it and credit where credit's due, amassing money *is* his thing. Besides, it's an odd house, Soph. Not exactly a family home and too big for a young couple." Ann had never warmed to the large, shiny house on Pembroke Street in Dublin that reminded her of a hospital rather than a starter home. "You know what? They're welcome to each other. If I never see him again, it'll be too soon."

There had been minimum contact since their last encounter, when Dom accused Ann of being a gold digger and only marrying him for his money. The cheek of him. It had never been about that, his wealth always making her slightly uneasy as if he had the lion's share of say in their life because he had *all* the money.

"Yeah, forget 'em," Sophie replied. "I'm sorry I brought it up. They're not worth the oxygen. What a crowd of arseholes. I told you that circle were all too cool for school." She was referring to his friends.

At one time, Ann had mistaken them for her own, but some circles were hard to break. She supposed it was why she was still so wary of making new friends. It had hurt, finding herself dropped like a hot potato as soon as she left Dom. There had been no phone calls from her former pals to check she was coping. Instead, they'd hastily removed her from the WhatsApp groups (praise the Lord) and blocked her on social media. His family hadn't been much better, aside from his father, who'd been accepting of her decision, albeit not thrilled about it.

Ann soon realised you're never really part of someone else's family and had been foolish to think she was a Fitzgerald in anything but name. No. She'd always be a Maguire – infidelity and turning a blind eye simply wasn't how she'd been reared.

"You're so unreasonable, Ann."

"Dom's devastated. He wants you back."

"Where is your sense of forgiveness? How could you be so cold?"

In the end, they all had Dom's back, no matter how badly he'd screwed up. Of course they did! Her parents would have been the same. In their absence, Lucie in Australia and Sophie had stepped in as her cheerleaders.

"You can do this," Lucie told her. "Stand on your own feet. Start again. Find a job."

Unsurprisingly, Ann had been unable to obtain any references from Fitzgerald Stock Brokers, where she'd once forged a successful career before packing it all in for Dom and her joke of a marriage. Dom kept his promise.

"I'll make sure you never work in Dublin again. You'd better crawl back under your rock. You're finished around here."

Any job Ann applied for in similar companies would be met with a polite letter of refusal. The Fitzgeralds were a force to be reckoned with, and Dublin was too small to dirty your bib and expect to be forgiven.

"What am I going to do? I'm holding you back, Sophie. I know you want to move in with Jack. I'm just a thorn in everyone's side."

Of course, Sophie had met the fantastic Jack within weeks of Ann's life falling apart, so that while Ann's marriage was disintegrating, Sophie's new romance was going from strength to strength.

"You can stay here as long as it takes. Don't give up now, Ann. When you're at the point where you can take no more, that's when everything will turn around," Sophie pleaded as she'd watched Ann slip into despair.

Ann supposed she had Dom to thank for finally turning that despair to anger and her fury into action.

"I need the car back," he'd told her while standing in the underground car park of Sophie's apartment one evening, his shoulders pumped, trying to appear taller than he was.

"What the hell are you doing here?"

"You won't answer my calls." He sounded childish. "I need the car."

"You're having a laugh! Where's your car? You wouldn't be seen dead driving a Mini."

Dom said nothing and the penny dropped.

"Ah! I see. It's for her!" Ann spat.

"It's in my name. It's mine."

Ann stared through him, all of a sudden engulfed with rage and finally summoning the bravery she'd wished for so many times.

"Tell Sabrina she can have it. Take it, you shit. Take the car. Take your rings back, too." Ann removed the diamond rings she was still wearing for fear of misplacing them and threw them at him. "Take it all, you poisoned dwarf." She walked towards him, towering over him as he scrambled about on the ground, pawing for the rings in the dark. "I don't need you and I don't need your stupid family or your arsehole friends, you sad excuse for a man," she shouted, shocking both him and herself with her venom. "I want a divorce as soon as possible. You'll be hearing from my solicitor and if you come near me one more time, you little hobbit," she said, pressing a finger into his chest, "I'll get a restraining order. I'll make it up if I have to, but I can destroy you, too." Ann pushed him.

"You wouldn't dare," he sniggered, stumbling backwards.

"Oh yes I would. Isn't that exactly what gold-digging country muckers with thick accents do? And what was it you said – inbred? Screw you, Dom, because I wouldn't screw you if you were the last rich prick on earth," she'd finished, turning on her heel.

It had worked. The next day she'd received an email from his father, Bernard, apologising on behalf of Dominic and telling her an amount of twenty-five thousand euros would be in her account by morning to help get her started.

Would she like the car back?

No.

Where she was going, she didn't need a car.

"So, how's Knockmore?" Sophie asked now.

"It's great."

"I know you're lying. You didn't have to do this. You are always, and I mean always, welcome with me."

"I know," Ann smiled. "But I did have to come here, Soph. It's my home. I can't explain it. Even though I haven't a clue what I'm doing, clearly," she laughed.

"But am I right in saying there isn't a man for miles? What about that Mark?"

Ann exhaled. That name again. Was someone trying to tell her something?

"No. I haven't seen Mark again. Besides, you know as

well as I do, things like that don't happen to people like me."

"Eh, that sounds defeatist. Why don't you give him a call?"

"You sound like Lucie. Nah. That's a fairytale ending and I'm more of a tragedy kind of girl."

"Wouldn't you like to meet someone again?"

"Of course I would. Maybe. Ah, I don't know, Sophie. I'm better on my own."

"You're impossible. And fairy tales do happen. Real love *is* out there. I mean, if I can find it, you can."

After she hung up, Ann stretched her legs in front of her and lay back on the floor, her blonde hair splayed out around her, splashes of paint covering her face, and stared up at the ceiling. Maybe there still was a piece of her that believed in love – a fragment of faith left from earlier days.

Ann sat up suddenly, remembering the guitar she'd bought earlier that day. Fetching it from the hall, she sat back down in the living room, crossing her legs and cradling it like Dad had taught her. Plucking at the strings, Ann turned the tuning pegs. With the fingers of her left hand, she began to form keys. With her right thumb, Ann started to strum, letting the sound ring through the room until she could feel something that resembled home. Engulfed by the moment, she began to sing a fragmented tune.

"Just promise you're not running away again, Ann?" Sophie had asked earlier.

Ann focused on a tiny patch on the wall in front of her that she'd missed, one little spot that was slightly different, paler against the rest of the wall, as the thought struck. Maybe she was running towards something.

CHAPTER NINE

Denise popped up from behind the counter, from where she was sweeping up a bag of spilled coffee.

"You'd better get a move on." Denise's hairnet was down over one eye and her floral apron twisted from the exertion. "Won't your friend be here soon?"

Ann looked at her watch, feeling a tingle of excitement. Today was the day Sophie was arriving.

"Plenty of time yet. I'm going to go for a quick run before I head home and get everything ready."

"You and this running! Aren't you only a slip of a thing already! You'll damage your knees, not to mention your face."

Ann giggled. "My face?"

"Oh, yeah. If you saw the broken veins on some of the faces passing through here . . ." Denise gestured towards the door that separated her office from that of the funeral home. "Well, you wouldn't be out running in the Irish weather. Better to stay indoors and eat cake," Denise chuckled and then unexpectedly hugged Ann. "I love having you working here, Ann. It's great to see you finally turn things around. I had a bet with Ian you'd hotfoot it out of Knockmore as fast as you arrived. I'm glad I was wrong.

"And don't mind me about the running. I'm only jealous. At least it has you eating again. Here . . ." She handed her a brown paper bag filled with scones and muffins. "For the morning. Or stick them in the freezer, or throw them at moving cars for all I care. Imagine, a day old and no use to anyone."

"And people starving on the streets," Ann finished for her.

"I'm telling you, Ann, even beggars would turn their noses up. The world's gone mad. In my day, the bread was eaten until it was so hard it could kill a seagull from a height."

Ann laughed. Being with Denise was like a tonic. Denise was still young enough to love a laugh and old enough not to care about anyone else's opinion, giving Ann the snippet of guidance she needed.

It had been two weeks since Ann's epiphany – well, her latest one, at least. Just fourteen days since she'd allowed a seed of hope to flourish. She wasn't sure exactly what suddenly stopped her from feeling as if she were being dragged underwater by a current she couldn't control. A concoction of everything, she supposed.

Romantically, Ann liked to imagine the moment her fragmented thoughts started to mesh together, coincided with the first time she'd picked up the guitar. At that moment, she'd felt only the best parts of her past. Life kept chugging forwards, but it slowly began to dawn on Ann that she'd never be who she once was. Only, who she could become was better. Maybe, just maybe, everything that had happened up to now was how it was meant to and that what she'd been dealt wasn't another abysmal hand but a second chance.

The next day, her renewed energy had forced her to finish painting the rooms of her house – her previous excuse for standing still for so long. With each coat, Ann imagined she was painting a new future, covering the hurt and the pain, preparing a blank canvas.

As soon as she'd finished, she grabbed her bag and slammed the door behind her. She'd no idea why she hadn't thought of it before now. It was so glaringly obvious.

"Denise, I need a job." Ann had stood at the door of Tea and Sympathy as if preparing to go into battle.

"A job? Is that a question or a statement?" Denise asked.

"It's both."

"Do I have a choice?" Denise crossed her arms in her usual stance.

"There's always a choice. Isn't that what you keep telling me? Always a solution. Always an option. You said it yourself. Baby steps. Get yourself into a routine," Ann grinned smugly while Denise pursed her lips.

"It's here, or I'll have to ask Ian for a job in the hardware store, and I'm not sure I can listen to him talking about blue-greys, pink-greys, green-greys, grey-greys all day." Ann grimaced, referencing the time she'd asked for a pale grey paint and received a full lecture on all the various greys on the spectrum.

"Ah, that fella's more fifty bales of hay than fifty shades of grey and you know he's totally colour blind." Denise ignored Ann's question, disappearing behind the counter to empty the dishwasher.

Ann waited for her to reappear and resume the arm-crossing.

"Do you have any experience in the catering industry?" Denise raised her eyebrows in an attempt to deter her.

"Well, I did waitress in Dublin before I became an accountant and I do make a mean soya cappuccino." Ann raised her eyebrows.

"Nah. Feck off." Denise disappeared again. "You're overqualified and overqualified people know it all. You'll be trying to get me to get a coffee machine, and I don't like anything that spits and fires more than I do," she called from beneath the counter.

Ann walked over and leaned against it.

"Jesus!" Denise shrieked, emerging once more to see Ann in front of her. "You frightened the shite out of me."

"Well?"

"Now I mean this, love. I'm mad about you, but this is *not* where you should be working. You need to get yourself a proper job, back doing books and the likes, working with numbers, you know that. You'd be wasted here."

Ann looked at the ground. "I know, Denise. But right now, all I need is a bit of money to get by and some headspace to figure out the rest. I'm idle. My brain isn't working. Just a few shifts. I'll take minimum wage and you know I'll work hard."

"No. No way." Denise shook her head. "You're not sympathetic enough," she said, picking up a mug and ignoring the pleading eyes.

"Denise," Ann called after her. "Denise!"

Denise turned to regard her. Ann's blonde hair was thrown into a bun on top of her head, her paint-streaked clothes hanging from her tiny frame like a child dressed in her mother's clothes. Christ! she *was* only a child, Denise thought to herself, watching her standing there, all forlorn. It was hard not to fall in love with Ann Maguire. She had the sweetness of her mother, mixed with a little of the Sammy Maguire edge. But by God, she was lost – more than lost, she was positively vanishing.

It was months now since she'd first started calling in on Denise for a bit of company and the poor thing seemed to be getting worse than better. It twisted Denise's stomach to think of all Ann had been through, losing her parents and then discovering she was married to a total gobshite. Then again, we all find that out eventually.

But not after a year! Most fellas have the decency to wait until the first baby's born before you realise that their mother was responsible for creating another eejit to walk the face of the earth. It sounded, to Denise, like Ann had had a lucky escape from Dom, but Christ! the girl still couldn't see it. Then again, you never can see what's staring straight at you, waving at you, standing on a pedestal, winking, practically jumping up your nose.

"What?" Denise looked at Ann again and then narrowed her eyes.

Something was different. Some small glint of colour visible on the girl's cheeks, the once flat eyes glistening back with defiance.

Ann stood up straight, her hands by her side as if citing from the Irish Constitution.

"My father was Sammy Maguire, loved and revered in this town. If anyone gives me any trouble, I'm to mention his name, you said so yourself."

"Don't you dare, Ann! Don't you dare play the Sammy Maguire card! You know I can't resist." Denise put her hands on her hips. "Arghhh, Ann." Denise put her hand up to stop Ann from replying. "If I were to give you a job, and it would be only temporary, I need to see proof that you're looking for something more suitable to match your qualifications, or Sammy will be haunting me. Lord knows I could do with a few days off over the summer. But come September, I want you out of my hair." Denise put her hand down and thrust it at Ann.

"Deal," Ann said, shaking Denise's hand. "Except for Saturday week. That's my thirtieth."

"Go on, but it'd better be a good night. I have the dress out and ironed on the spare bed in anticipation of a night in Lennon's."

Ann had been so excited that she'd run back down the hill to the Estates. There was something so liberating about the sensation of feeling her feet move automatically, without having to think.

That evening, she'd dusted off her old trainers and rooted in the back of the wardrobe for a pair of leggings and a vest top. If Tracy could do it, so could she. Ann used to walk every day, the relaxed pace complementing the hectic lifestyle of Dublin. Here in Knockmore, her life had slowed to a stop, so it seemed natural to up the tempo of her activity to match.

Now, with her new-found love of running and her job, Ann wasn't sure how she'd managed without either. For months she'd felt sluggish and weak, but when she ran, it made her feel capable, strong – and starving. So hungry that her appetite returned, her curves slowly re-emerging, her muscles gaining strength. It was a slice of the day when it was just her, being herself, with nothing to focus on except finishing.

Working with Denise, Ann had the company she'd been missing and bit by bit, she was starting to feel part of Knockmore again. Some remembered her, many didn't, but day by day, she was beginning to feel accepted. Swapping her designer clothes for jeans and T-shirts did little to hide her looks, nor stop the customers from asking her out. Some things never changed – although nowadays, her suitors were in their seventies, minus a full set of teeth.

"You know, I might have severe cataracts, but I'm not blind," Gerry, who took seven sachets of sugar, said one morning as she delivered his pot of tea and six sausages to the table. His bottom jaw jutted out and his cheeks reached his eyes with his broad smile. "My Vera was a handsome woman. You remind me of her, Blondie. She could deliver a calf at the same time as boiling the ham and cabbage for lunch. Capable, she was. Sturdy. A fine woman. God rest her," he barely paused. "Will you go for a shandy with me sometime? We'd be the talk of the town. Vera would be turning in her grave. Feck all she could do about it. I always wanted a young one on my arm."

"Now, Gerry, I told you. I've sworn off men, but I'll share a cup of tea with you. Easy on those sugars. They'll rot your teeth," Ann said affectionately, her Knockmore accent growing thicker by the day.

"Blondie, you know as well as meself that a newborn has more teeth than I do," he said, reaching for the little silver pot stuffed high with sugar.

"The dirty old fecker," Denise giggled as Ann walked past, trying to keep a straight face. "I'd say it's more a hand shandy he's after," Denise whispered out of the side of her mouth. "And Vera. Handsome! She'd a beard thicker than his. She looked better laid out in the coffin with the make-up on than I'd ever seen her when she was alive. Steve nearly had to get the strimmer out for her chin."

Ann had barely made it round the counter before the pair exploded with laughter.

"I'll see you tomorrow, Denise," Ann called from the door of the coffee shop now before running out of the door and up the town.

Ann waved as she passed Ian, who was out watering the plants.

"See you tomorrow," she shouted over the music of her headphones.

Ian made a sort of running motion, like a dad dancing at a wedding.

Ann's eyes glinted as she approached the big hill, ready to take it on and using her arms to power her way to the top. When she reached the brow, she stopped to catch her breath, bending over and placing her hands on her legs before looking up the driveway of Knockmore House.

"They keep themselves to themselves," Denise told her on the one occasion when Ann had plucked up the courage to ask. "I heard he was a developer or something. Always something funny about that house, but I suppose you know that." Denise watched Ann quietly for a reaction, but Ann changed the subject.

Ann switched the music on her phone to the eighties playlist, knowing the songs would get her home, where she'd soon be laughing with Sophie. Filling her lungs, she glanced once more up the beguiling driveway of Knockmore House – today, the past didn't seem so important. Then she took off down the hill, back to the Estates.

CHAPTER TEN

Olive

There she was again, that same girl. Olive pushed back one of the wooden shutters and stood behind it, observing the road through the crack. The girl was bent over with her hands resting on her legs. She looked like she was out for a run. Innocent enough, Olive supposed, but still, there was something about it that wasn't quite right.

Perhaps she'd mention it to Mark instead of Eugene. He was coming again this weekend to discuss further the plans for the house. He'd sounded irritated on the phone earlier. Of course, he had a lot on his plate, but the house renovation was top of Olive's agenda. She wouldn't rest until everything was how she wanted.

Olive watched as the girl righted herself and took off back down the hill.

Sitting back into her armchair, she allowed her head to sink into the soft cushion behind her. She closed her eyes, pressing her tongue against the roof of her mouth, breathing in slowly. She held her breath for a moment before releasing it through her mouth in little puffs, just like Dr Wilson, her therapist, had demonstrated. She did it twice more before opening her eyes.

Why did she bother? It did nothing to eliminate the feeling of panic residing in the pit of her stomach, always waiting to rear its ugly head when she least expected.

Keeping busy was the only thing that helped, but then it was hard to act busy when you weren't. Not like when the kids were small.

Back then, she was always rushed off her feet, with barely a minute to breathe, let alone sit in a chair and think about breathing. There was always a shoelace that needed tying, dinner to be cooked, homework to do, dropping them here, there and everywhere, washing, ironing, baking. But then the balance had shifted, suddenly and unexpectedly – their needs less physical, more psychological. Olive hadn't excelled in that arena. Perhaps she'd always suffered from the blanket term her mother used to describe as "nerves".

"Those who talk about their nerves are weak, Olive. Get up, get dressed, get on with your day. Don't succumb. It's indulgent."

Back then, Olive was anything but self-indulgent, always placing the needs of her family above her own, the "nerves" only rising to the surface when the children no longer needed her – and her husband no longer wanted her. She wondered sometimes if she'd ever really felt at ease with herself. It was impossible to decipher what she felt any more, or how she used to feel. The move from Wicklow had helped – for a time, anyway. Being here in Knockmore eased the everyday struggle, the dread of not knowing what lay around the next corner.

"You'll have to come and visit, stay the weekend," she'd announced to the neighbours at their leaving party.

Over her dead body.

It had been Eugene's idea to host a soirée to bid their Wicklow friends farewell.

"We had good times here, Olive, they were good

people," he told her, unconcerned that he'd made her the laughing stock.

She'd put on a brave face the entire evening, ignoring the glances, the whispers. *They all knew.* Every last one of them had known what her husband had been up to for years. She could never forgive them.

"I'll be sorry to see you go." Rosemary had grabbed Olive's arm as Olive swept past, unable to believe she'd had the gall to come. It was the first time they'd spoken since their last confrontation, the day after Olive overheard her gossiping.

"You never came last night. I tried calling, but there was no answer." Rosemary had popped her head through the back door.

Olive sat for a moment at the kitchen table, staring ahead before turning to glare at the woman she'd once considered her best friend.

"But I did come, Rosemary. I let myself in the back door, but something came over me. I felt too *ordinary*. Too *Ordinary Olive* to be with the likes of you, *Rotund Rosemary*," she shouted.

"Oh, God," was all Rosemary could manage, the colour slipping from her face. "Olive, I . . . I . . . I wasn't sure . . . I didn't . . . I'm sorry. I didn't know what to do."

"All this time. All these years . . ." Olive stood up and walked past her, opening the door.

"What will you do?" Rosemary asked.

"Oh, I know perfectly well what I'm going to do and it's no longer your concern. Get out, Rosemary. Run home. The exercise will do you good."

There was a part of Olive that had been sad to leave Wicklow, to wave goodbye to the happy memories, until she reminded herself it had all been a lie. Mark and Jessica were the only truths she had left, in one way. In another, she'd lost them, too.

Olive looked out of the bay window again and up the driveway towards the gate of Knockmore House. It was a beautiful house. She'd transformed it, and herself along with it, but there was always room for improvement. Now, when she looked in the mirror, she barely recognised herself. She'd never had time to consider her looks much before – until she let the sales assistants in those big department stores loose on the emergency credit card, to unlock a large commission and a body to envy. As she twisted and turned in the array of outfits they produced – the likes of which she'd never have been brave enough to wear before – Olive was happy she'd resisted eating her way through those foggy years of young motherhood.

Once Olive got to grips with spending money on herself, she realised she was quite good at being extravagant. Relished the tingle of excitement when she left the shop with bags bigger than herself and the sales assistants pandering to her.

"Do you think you might use your excessive spending to mask deeper feelings? Like putting a Band-aid over your emotions," Dr Wilson had asked during one of their sessions, looking at her through his "invisible" framed spectacles that magnified his eyes to five times their normal size – quite terrifying.

It was hard to concentrate when all she could think was how he'd benefit immensely from a more substantial frame.

"I *can* see you're wearing glasses, Dr Wilson," she wanted to scream. "You're fooling no one."

"Well, Olive. Do you think that's what you're doing?"

he'd repeated, the eyes nearly touching her face now, in anticipation of her response to his pathetic revelation.

"Yes, that's precisely what I'm doing," Olive tutted impatiently, growing tired of Dr Wilson and his bug-eyes.

What was the point in wearing glasses, trying to pretend you're not wearing glasses? And, indeed, what was the point in seeing a therapist if you couldn't tell them the one thing you knew was the root of everything? There was nothing Dr Wilson could uncover, no matter how hard he looked at her with his abnormally large eyes, that she didn't already know. But it was a weekly appointment to attend, a purpose, something to do.

After their session, she'd headed straight to Grafton Street, Dublin, to one of the department stores, for the only therapy that made her feel alive – for a few hours, anyway.

"Olive." She heard Eugene calling her. "Olive . . ."

Olive sank further into the chair. What did he want now? Continually trailing after her around the house, wondering what she was up to, what were they doing now. *Be careful what you wish for.*

It was all she'd wanted for years. Eugene and her together, sharing a life, sharing a home. Sometimes she wished she'd packed him off to The Slut in Dublin. The Slut walked away with a house, an allowance for the child and no Eugene to follow her like a lost puppy. The Slut was clever.

The Slut had won.

At least Mark would be a good distraction for the weekend. It would give her time to . . . what, spend time with Jessica? Even the thought of Jessica made her chest tighten. It was Jessica who needed therapy. Perhaps Dr

Wilson would be able to fix her. But who knew what Jessica would say. It was far too risky.

Yes, Olive Dempsey was bored. So bored that she couldn't think of one thing to do. So far, she'd kept out of town, avoided meeting the neighbours. Once bitten, twice shy. Instead, she'd watched life go past from her window. She often wondered who else had once sat here, staring out at Knockmore from the oriel bay window. She knew so little about the history of the house – nothing, in fact.

It was almost too grand for the town, perched on the hill looking down. It would suit it even less after the refurbishment. Olive knew she could trust Mark to make it happen. Her Mark, the apple of her eye. What she wouldn't do to see him settle down and produce grandchildren. Now that would give her a new lease of life. She'd heard that – that grandchildren give you a second chance to do things right, to amend your mistakes, fill the space in your heart.

Olive heard the gravel crunch in the driveway and stood again.

"Mark," she called through the window and then rushed to greet him, grabbing the plans for the house off the hall table. She'd catch him while he was still in work mode. "Darling," she called as she saw him approach.

Olive turned back towards the study just in time to miss Mark roll his eyes and slowly shake his head with dread.

CHAPTER ELEVEN

Ann shielded her eyes against the evening sun, looking out at the grass where the children were running up and down barefoot, drenching each other with oversized water pistols the size of bazookas. She was thinking how much it had changed from her day, when the tiny water pistols would deliver nothing more than a dribble, when she saw the car pull up. The driver pushed her enormous black sunglasses up onto her chestnut mane, clapped her hands together in excitement and gave a frenzied wave.

"Oh my God! Look at you!" Sophie squealed, falling from the car and losing a ballet pump in the dash to reach her friend.

Ann was up the path and out of the gate before Sophie managed to retrieve her shoe, flinging her arms around her.

"I can't believe you're here at last!" Ann gushed back. "It's so good to see you. I missed you. It feels like I haven't seen you in years." Ann was suddenly so overcome with emotion that she burst out crying.

"Hey. Don't do that. You'll start me off. I'm here now." Sophie patted Ann's arm and then looked over her shoulder at the Knockmore Estates. "So, this is where you've been hiding – the home of mystery, intrigue and all-out Irish scandal."

Sophie looked at the houses, bunched in a line, snaking their way round the corner. They were all more or less the same – some painted, some with the original façade. Most had different-coloured doors, some with hanging baskets, bursting with overhanging greenery. One or two had added a porch at the front. "The posh ones," Denise would say. A few had Velux windows in the roof, where they'd been forced to make an attic room to allow for their growing families. "The ones who didn't know when to stop."

"It's nice," Sophie said approvingly. "Really nice. Not what I expected at all."

"What did you expect?" Ann laughed, taking Sophie's weekend bag from the passenger seat.

"Well, I suppose I pictured it from the story you told me about Mad Margot trying to escape certain poverty." Sophie made a face.

"I loved it here as a kid. I thought we were rich."

"I think most kids think that and hey, what's the harm? You find out quick enough how expensive everything is and how impossible it actually is to buy a house."

"Oh," Ann nudged her. "Are you in the market?"

"Well . . ." Sophie hesitated before producing her left hand from behind her back and thrusting it forwards with a smile.

It took Ann a moment to understand what she was looking at, at first thinking Sophie was showing her another one of her crazy manicures. Ann glanced beyond the watermelon-coloured nails and settled on the glinting diamond.

"Sophie!" Ann shrieked. "You didn't! When?"

"Wednesday! Jack took me to that insanely overpriced French restaurant in Dublin. You know, the one you used to go to with Dom."

"Jacques?" Ann laughed, remembering how often she'd frequented it with Dom and his annoying friends for what, to them, was a standard night out. Ann took Sophie's hand to examine the delicate emerald-and-diamond ring. "It's beautiful," she whispered, squeezing Sophie's hand.

"I know. I had a sneaking suspicion when Jack said where we were going. I mean, Jack's more American diner than fine French dining, let's face it. I nearly fell off the chair when he got down on one knee in the middle of the restaurant." Sophie's eyes were glistening. "And then we were forced to eat all sorts of quail egg creations covered in foam before we could leave. Never again! I mean, I wasn't sure if I was eating a pig's anus or a mushroom at one stage. And guess where we ended up going afterwards? For burgers! We were starving."

"I'm thrilled for you. Jack is perfect, as are you." Ann felt the tears smart her eyes again, coupled with another emotion.

"I wanted to tell you in person." Sophie looked unsurely at Ann. "I was going to wait until after this weekend, but there's no way I could keep it in."

"No." Ann shook her head, trying to swallow the tears. "You shouldn't have to keep it in. This is your news to shout. I'm sorry. I'm so happy for you, really, it's just . . ."

"I know." Sophie could read her thoughts. "Been there, done that, bought the T-shirt."

Ann grimaced. "It's not that entirely. I'm not anti-marriage. Well, if it's to the right person. And Jack is right for you. It's just . . . I don't know. I suppose I feel like I'm right back at the beginning, but with a load of future divorcee baggage around my neck."

"Do you think it's too fast? It's only been a year."

"No, Soph. When you know, you know. And a lot can happen in a year," Ann assured.

Except for her – not much had progressed in Ann's life, but for everyone else, life was moving on. Sometimes Ann felt she'd already lived an entire lifetime and was now some strange reincarnation of herself, having to go through it all again.

"Well, if I might say, you're rocking the divorcee look." Sophie stood back to admire her friend. "The running suits you, as does the country air. I didn't think you could look any better, but you look sensational." Sophie looked her up and down approvingly, taking in her lean, tanned limbs and almost Scandinavian blonde hair. "Believe me, at this rate, you won't be single for long. Any Knockmore stallion would be happy to have you."

"Well, there is someone . . ." Ann giggled, going on to tell her all about her randy 78-year-old admirer from Tea and Sympathy as they walked up the driveway to the house.

"Stop. I can't breathe," Sophie spluttered. "And the name of the place! Tea and Sympathy. Jesus Christ, is it honestly a funeral home, too?"

"Yes!" Ann was bent over laughing.

"Oh, God. Do you see the dead bodies coming through? Oh, Ann, I can't cope!"

"No. It's in the back, all separate," Ann explained. "I mean, we hardly store them in the fridges in the café. Can you imagine? I'll take a coffee and one of those cream buns at the side of Vera's leg!"

This set them off again.

"And are you serious that one of the undertakers does face painting on the side?" Sophie gasped for air.

"Yeah!"

"Do you think she ever gets mixed up and paints a tiger face on one of the stiffs?"

Ann buckled over again. "Stop! Ah, here, we haven't even had a drink yet. Come on, this calls for champagne. Well, actually, will prosecco do? I'm on a budget."

"What, no Dom?" Sophie raised an eyebrow.

Ann threw her eyes to heaven, remembering when Dom insisted on only drinking Dom Pérignon at their engagement party.

"No Dom in this house. Ever. Come on. Follow me."

"Look . . ." Sophie nudged her as they walked up the path to the front door. "Looks like we have an audience."

Ann glanced to the left to see Tracy standing at her living room window with one of the boys in her arms. Ann waved and Tracy lifted her hand then turned her back.

"Jesus! that face would stop a clock," Sophie giggled.

"Ah, she's harmless enough. Probably looking at the lads playing out on the green. Come on inside. Let's get that drink." There was nothing that could darken Ann's mood today.

While Sophie admired the freshly painted dusty-pink kitchen cupboards and dark wooden worktops, Ann poured them each a massive glass of fizzing prosecco and waited for the bubbles to stop spilling over the top.

"Cheers to my friend. To new beginnings for us both." Ann clinked her glass against Sophie's.

"To friendship. To you. To us. To Knockmore. To everything," Sophie replied, smiling broadly. "Now, show me around. I can't believe this is the same place. It's like a doll's house now. I love the girliness. From the before pictures you sent me, it was more . . . old lady musty."

Ann led Sophie out of the kitchen, through the hall and into the living room. The grey couch and matching footstool sat against the wall. There was a pink rug in the centre of the room, with lots of rose gold ornaments scattered here and there. Her dad's vintage leather jacket hung like a picture, perfectly contrasting against the softness of the room, next to the guitar sitting against the wall.

"Wow. It's like something out of an interiors magazine. What's with the guitar? Are you rediscovering your inner Sammy?"

"Something like that. Dad taught me to play when I was young. I hadn't touched a guitar in years, but I guess you're born with certain things in your blood," Ann blushed. "I've been practising one song in particular. If you get me drunk enough, I'll play it for you."

"Go, Ann!" Sophie did a fist-pump. "I can't wait. Maybe you can play at my wedding."

"Ah, here, Sophie, hold your horses."

Ann led her back to the hall and up the stairs. Sophie paused to look at the black-and-white photos that hung the length of the stairs, graduated on the wall in different frames. Aunt Lucie had saved some pictures from the house after her mam died and Ann had picked out her favourites.

"I got all the frames in the charity shop," Ann explained.

"It's like looking at stills from a movie." Sophie smiled at the vintage-style photos.

"Sometimes it hurts to look at them, but they deserve to be seen."

Ann watched Sophie reach out to touch the glass of each one.

"Ann!" Sophie gasped. "I had no idea. She's beautiful." Sophie's eyes rested on a picture of Felicity, sitting on the beach, her arms wrapped around her knees, staring out to sea. "It's you."

"I could never see it, but now I'm the age she was in some of these, I can . . . a little."

Sophie stopped and stared at the final one. "Their wedding day?"

Ann nodded as they stared at the picture of Sammy in his leather jacket, Felicity looking like a child in a communion dress. "Dad was twenty and Mam was eighteen." Ann wished she'd listened harder to the story of their wedding when she was younger. "They talked about it all the time. Well, Dad did . . . and I was always telling him to stop." Ann smiled sadly. "I guess you never really appreciate something until you can hear it or see it no more."

"Wow," Sophie said finally. "What you've done with the house, all by yourself. I'm so proud of you. Really. You're so lucky to have this place. I thought you were making a massive mistake moving back here. I was so worried, but I love it. And you look happy, Ann, do you know that? And you're allowed to be happy."

"I hope so. It took me a while, but I feel stronger." Ann smiled back, suddenly glad that Sophie hadn't been around to witness the initial months of bleakness.

"There's something about this house," Sophie continued. "I know there was lots of sadness here for you, but it has a nice vibe. You can feel it."

"I know what you mean," Ann agreed. "I thought about returning to Dublin so many times, but I sense it now, too. It feels . . . peaceful," Ann said, searching for the right word, laughing at her choice when she thought about the noise from Doyles next door.

"And one more thing . . ." Sophie looked at her seriously and then pointed towards the picture at the top of the stairs. "Your dad was hot."

CHAPTER TWELVE

Mark

Mark kicked off his shoes and threw himself on the bed, wondering how he'd found himself back at Knockmore for the second time in so many weeks. He didn't bother undressing, nor attempt to remove the mountain of cushions and throws from what should have been an inviting four-poster bed in the guest-room. It wasn't. Far from it. The new duvet cover – the creases still visible, unscathed, straight from the packet – crunched under him as he tried to get comfortable while avoiding suffocation from the plethora of scatter cushions. Contrary to their name, they were strategically positioned, ordered by size and, it appeared, fabric. Velvet, fur, wool. Velvet, fur, wool.

Mark slithered down low, away from the range of pillows, put his hands behind his head and sighed. He'd spent the entire evening trying to appease his mother, listen to what his father was trying to say over her verbal diarrhoea and keep an eye on his sister. It was worse than a bad sitcom. Evidently, avoiding his mother for several weeks had done nothing to deter her eagerness to plough on by injecting an extortionate amount of money into the house.

He'd thrown his eye over the plans for the house again. An orangery? What on earth was she thinking? He couldn't think of one reason why his parents would require an enormous glass structure at the back of their home. They never entertained. Mark didn't believe they had any friends left after oddly choosing to leave Wicklow and move to a place they'd never heard of before.

"The orangery will be big enough to host a wedding," Olive told him earlier.

Mark shuddered as the thought hit him – surely not! Surely his mother wasn't creating a venue for a fictitious wedding. Neither him, nor his sister, Jessica, were attached to anyone – or had any plans to be married soon, if ever. And glass walls inside an old house? What a bizarre choice.

Mark knew the look she was trying to achieve, but to him, it was more suited to an office building than a Georgian-style country home. Its charm was the elegance and character of classical architecture. It didn't need modernisation. At their age, weren't his parents meant to have lots of trinkets and embarrassing photographs bunched together on wallpapered walls? They should have been propped up in brown velvet armchairs, instead of living in something that a London stockbroker might aspire to reside in.

"These old houses are disasters waiting to happen. Are you sure about this, Mum? It's a huge job and do you love it around here? Are you sure you're going to stay? God only knows what problems we'll unearth when we start messing around with the original structure, tearing down walls and ripping up floors. Could we compromise and leave out the orangery?"

"Absolutely not. We might need it someday. Besides, I read in *Country Living* magazine that the current trend is mixing external classical features with internal modernity."

Mark rolled his eyes. It was the opposite of what his mother was. Nowadays, she was more modern externally and antiquated internally.

"Mark, I told you before. I'm simply adding to the value of the house. You should be pleased. All this . . ." She gestured with her hands, her diamond rings glinting as she did so. "It will be yours one day." Olive sat back in her high-back dining chair and picked up her glass. "Cheers," she chimed. "To new beginnings."

Jessica picked up her glass of red wine and sank the entire contents in one go.

"Scheers," she slurred.

It was the first thing Mark had heard his sister say all day. She'd barely lifted her head when she walked by him in the kitchen earlier, headphones in, hoodie up over her head like a sulky teenager. She'd hardly touched her meal, choosing instead to sip incessantly at the wine, refilling her glass every two minutes. Jessica looked worse than he felt. Wretched. Rail thin, unkempt, withdrawn, dressed in pyjamas.

In contrast, his mother had changed for dinner into a tight black dress, so low-cut that Mark spent the entire time averting his eyes. It confirmed his suspicions that his mother hadn't been at a health farm a month ago but was in fact under the knife.

"Besides," Olive continued, "I'm not getting any younger, in years at least, and I can't keep walking in and out to the dining room. It makes much more sense to have it all open-plan."

Mark glanced at her again and looked away quickly. Her oozing breasts appeared as if one might explode from her flesh and land with a thud in the centre of the table.

"We could have eaten in the kitchen," Mark answered. "It was good enough up until a few years ago. What's with all the sudden formality? I hardly recognise anyone at this table. Who are you all?"

He put his glass down with a bang and looked at Olive. She had so many rings stuffed on her fingers, it was a wonder she could even lift a fork, let alone use it. Her platinum hair barely moved, stiffened with hairspray that crunched if you brushed off it, and her face looked as though someone had pulled her imaginary plaits too tight. It was farcical.

His poor father, in contrast, was half the man he used to be, sitting opposite her, way down the other end of the table, his mouth drooped to one side, the left side of his body now more or less powerless. It reminded Mark of a comic strip, where Olive had used her husband as some sort of power source, feeding off him – the weaker he became, the more ridiculously plastic she did. Thank God Eugene was still able to walk – that was something.

It was a wonder Eugene hadn't woken up one day and started hobbling back to Wicklow with the aid of his stick, to escape any further parasitic torture. Instead, his father pottered in the garden, did the crossword, shuffled papers. He managed, but it still pained Mark to see his mother cutting up his food for him like a baby.

"Darn stroke," he'd often say. "My penance. For all the mistakes I made."

Mark would never forget his mother's words that day, when they'd received the diagnosis at the hospital – the news that Eugene Dempsey would never have the mobility he once had.

"He deserves it." She'd been staring ahead, motionless. "He bloody deserves it." Her teeth were gritted, her face gnarled. "But I don't. I looked after him all of his life and he betrayed me. Now, I'll spend the rest of my days with him like this: a burden. *She* got off lightly. I should have snipped him loose. The Slut probably wouldn't want him now, anyway."

You could almost taste her anger and it had shocked Mark to his core. His father would spend the rest of his days trying to make up for what he'd done and Olive would pass the rest of hers making him pay.

"I'm going for a schmoke." Jessica wobbled away from the table, opening the back door to sit on the step.

"I'll clean up," Mark offered, grateful to have an excuse to end the debacle of another family dinner.

At least it would give him a chance to gather his thoughts, the mundane task allowing his mind to rest from the stifling atmosphere of family time. Mark couldn't bear to be in the same room as Jessica. His once vivacious younger sister was a shadow of her former self. A far cry from the fun-loving girl, once the life and soul of the party, dazzling them all with her ludicrous fashion sense and ditsy attitude.

"Golden boy, back again?" she usually asked when he arrived for the weekend – not this time.

At one time they'd been close, but not any more. When they were teenagers, his friends were all mad about his younger sister, but they were all warned that Jessica Dempsey was off-limits. When she went to live in Dublin for college, she spent more time out partying than at lectures, but all that changed when she met her new boyfriend. From what Mark could remember, he'd been a bit older than her – an architect.

"Nicest person I've ever met. Handsome, great prospects. Mum and Dad are going to love him."

Jessica never got to introduce him to them. Mark didn't even know his name, but he often thought about him – the break-up from the perfect boyfriend that spiralled his sister out of control.

Mark yawned and stood up to look out of the bedroom window, staring beyond the pebbled driveway towards the road. It had been her all right, earlier on, at the gate. He was sure of it. His mother had mentioned at dinner that she'd seen some girl looking in at the house a few times. Mark had shrugged her off. What? Did his mum think that his father had yet another family out there? Then after dinner, he'd been chatting to his dad, when his mother had frantically summoned him.

"Mark. Quick."

"Mum?" He'd appeared immediately.

"There," his mother pointed. "There's that girl I was telling you about earlier. Except there's two of them now."

Mark looked out at where the two women were standing, their arms linked, staring in, and then immediately took a step back.

"It's no one, Mum. Just someone looking at the house," he'd said, leaving the room.

Of course, Mark had known straightaway who it was when he saw her standing there, with another woman. This time, though, it wasn't her aunt with her – a friend, perhaps. Mark had thought about Ann a lot recently, to the point where he wondered if he was ever *not* thinking of her. How was it possible to meet someone just a few times and for them to saturate your thoughts for months afterwards? What did that make him? *Pathetic.*

At least he'd had the sense to say nothing to his mother earlier and feign ignorance. The less his mother knew about *anything*, the better. He was surprised he'd been able to restrain himself from rushing out of the door and sprinting down the driveway towards her.

In truth, Mark had never met anyone like Ann. He'd been blown away instantly the two times he'd met her – so refreshingly unsure of herself as if she'd no idea how beautiful she really was. It was no act, either – she was different, he was sure of it. What was it she'd said to him that day?

"My life is currently under construction."

It seemed everything where Mark was concerned was under construction.

Mark thought he'd never see her again until she'd turned up at the doorstep with her aunt the next day. That time she'd told him more – the entire story of her mother, the real history of Knockmore House. Funny, through all of it, she'd barely talked about herself. All he knew was that she lived in Dublin. At the time, the facts hadn't seemed necessary. He was sure they'd connected that day, shared something special, and Mark had been confident she'd call. She hadn't. So, he'd tried to put her out of his mind, but somehow, she kept creeping her way back in.

And here she was again.

His mother said she'd seen her a few times looking at the house. Perhaps Ann would come back. He could hardly sit looking out of the window his entire life, like some reverse stalker, waiting for her to walk past again, much as he'd have liked. Mind you, someone like her was probably better off without someone like him and his twisted family. It sounded like she'd had enough heartache in her life, without him adding to it.

Mark lay on the bed again. Who was he fooling? He knew deep down that if the opportunity arose to see Ann Maguire again, wild horses couldn't keep him away.

CHAPTER THIRTEEN

"Happy birthday!" Sophie flung open the door, still dressed in pyjamas, and took a running jump, landing on the bed beside Ann. "God, I'm tired. I slept like a log until a band of thugs started shouting outside. Jesus! how do you put up with them? They're feral."

"Ah, the drone of the Doyles," Ann smiled, rubbing at her eyes. "I heard nothing this morning. Maybe I should drink a bottle of wine every night." She reached for the glass of water beside her bed, knocking it back in one.

"Make that four bottles."

"Oh, Christ. Really? What time did we get to bed?" Ann pulled another pillow behind her head and lay back.

"Last time I looked, it was two. And actually, it may have been more than four bottles – let's not mention it again." Sophie stretched out flat, wiggled her legs and then sat up again.

"My head! It feels like there's a drill bit lodged in my brain. What time is it now?" Ann grabbed her phone off the bedside table and squinted. "Nine thirty," she groaned, rubbing her temples.

"Come on. Get up. I'm on my holidays and . . . I have a surprise for you downstairs," Sophie grinned.

"I hate surprises – scarred for life."

The last surprise birthday Ann attended had gifted her

the revelation of a cheating husband, being gifted a birthday surprise of his own down the side passage of their house with Sabrina.

"I know. I know. But this is nice. Come on. Get up. Fear not, it isn't Dom hiding under the table."

"Don't even joke. I'll vomit." Ann pushed back the covers and edged out of bed.

Sophie was already bounding down the stairs. "Come down when you're ready."

Ann padded towards the bathroom and ran the tap, splashing cold water onto her face, then looked in the mirror. *Thirty years old*. She reached for the towel and patted her face dry before glancing up again at her reflection. Did she look thirty? She certainly felt it after last night.

"You promised you wouldn't let me drink last night. How are we going to manage tonight with Denise and Ian? I'm poisoned," she called down the stairs.

"Ah, shut up! You're only young once," she heard, along with lots of banging from the kitchen.

"Suppose it was worth it." It *was* the best evening she'd had in ages.

After their initial reunion, they'd walked up through the town so that she could show Sophie the sights.

"Cute houses, aren't they?" Sophie commented as they passed. "Well, except that one . . ." She pointed at the second last one. "Christ above, what even is that?"

They stopped to stare at an almost life-sized donkey and cart, placed precariously at the edge of a small pond, with a garden gnome sitting in the cart, clutching the reins.

"Sweetest divine. That's terrifying." Sophie began to giggle.

Ann must have passed it a thousand times, never paying it the attention it deserved.

"Look at those." Sophie pointed at the two giant stone German shepherds perched either side of the front door, adorned with red collars. It must have taken years to dab paint painstakingly on the bumpy surface of the pebble-dash walls of the house, in a confident declaration of dedication to a dubious shade of Pepto-Bismol pink.

"Look at the colour of the front door. It's like bile! I'm going to get a picture of you sitting in that cart before the weekend is through, it's my mission," Sophie promised. "Come on. My eyes are hurting."

They'd laughed their way up the road, Ann pointing out various milestones from her youth as they went. They walked past Tea and Sympathy, long closed for the evening, and the hardware store, where Ian was probably upstairs in his apartment enjoying a Pimm's with a dish of olives.

"So, let me get this straight," Sophie asked. "Your best friends are Denise, who's in her mid forties and is now your boss, and Ian, who's fifty, gay and runs a hardware store-cum-off-licence?"

"Yep. That just about sums it up," Ann laughed. "Can you imagine what all the heads back in Dublin would think?"

"You'd be excommunicated."

"Hah. Too late. I already am. It sounds strange, but I have more in common with these people than I ever did with that pack of snobs."

"Well, you know I never liked them."

Ann rolled her eyes. "I know. I know. You can call a person's true nature from twenty paces." Ann repeated one of Sophie's many tag lines.

"I'm sure I could have warned you that Tracy next door is cuckoo, too. Even through the window earlier, I could tell. Be careful you don't wake up one night with her standing over you, brushing your hair. You need to get better at judging people, Ann. You're far too nice. You always seem intent on picking up the crazy people."

"Don't I know it!" Ann pushed her. "Sure, I picked you."

"Touché! But seriously, enough now. I'll be letting you know tomorrow night how I feel about this Denise and Ian," Sophie added. "I'm not one bit happy that you've gone and made new friends." Sophie playfully nudged Ann.

"You're going to love them." Ann took Sophie's arm and dragged her up the hill. "They've been good to me."

Ann was so grateful for the unlikely duo, who'd arrived in her life precisely when she needed them. She didn't know what she'd do without Denise, and Ian was a bundle of energy.

"The only gay in the village," he'd often say. "And that's the way I like it. Knockmore isn't big enough for a second Pimm's-sipping, cravat-wearing, Vogue menthol-smoking hardware store owner."

Ian was flamboyant, friendly and utterly fabulous.

"The three Fs," he'd informed Ann early in their friendship. "But I can see you're a mystery, Ann Maguire."

To begin with, Ian had pushed her a little as to her sudden return to Knockmore, when they'd first started chatting far beyond the time it takes to purchase undercoat and pinkish-grey paint.

"I can wait," he told her patiently, noticing how reluctant she was to divulge any information. "A good mystery unfolds. You can tell me when you're ready. I won't judge. Sure, what right have I? I've been judged my whole life in this two-bit town, bullied growing up for being different. But I soon learned that people don't really care about you, or what you're doing. As long as you own who you are, they'll get over it.

"As soon as I stopped caring what people thought, they accepted me. I wished I'd learned it sooner," he'd smiled sadly. "But it's never too late to become who you should be," he'd winked, pushing the sleeves of his cashmere sweater up and resting his hands on the counter. "Has anyone ever told you there's something special about you, Ann?"

"There it is." Ann pointed at the gates of Knockmore House.

"Holy crap. It's massive. It makes the whole story real when you see the house. You can almost understand why that Margot one wanted to live here. With the reverend, though? Surely there was an easier way." Sophie looked at Ann. "You okay? You're in a trance."

"Sorry." Ann shook her head. "The house gives me the heebie-jeebies. I don't know what it is about it. I suppose I'm fascinated by it, weirdly. I wish I could see inside again. Maybe it would satisfy my curiosity."

"That's understandable." Sophie patted Ann's arm and then smirked. "If you want to see inside again, why not call—"

Ann reached over and clamped her fingers over Sophie's mouth. With all the recent progress she'd made, Ann didn't have room for anything, or anyone, else in her life, firmly deciding that it was the fantasy of Mark and not the reality that had ignited her imagination. Once you scratched through, she was sure Mark was just another "rich kid" – and that was something she cared never to repeat. Besides, there was a difference between being lonely and alone, and lately, being alone didn't seem as lonely as it once had.

"Not today, Soph. Not today."

"Play me something," Sophie said later, pointing towards the guitar after they returned home to open yet another bottle of wine.

Buoyed by the copious amounts of alcohol, Ann grabbed the guitar and sat in the centre of the rug. Closing her eyes, she began to strum the notes expertly, lost in the acoustic version of the song. When she'd finished, she opened her eyes to look up at Sophie.

"It's your parents' song," Sophie whispered, wiping her tears. "I've never heard it that way. Ann, that was beautiful. How did I not know you could do that? That was amazing. I'm in shock."

Ann put the guitar down and smiled. "I told you, Dad taught me. He was good. Mam said he could have made it big. Well, I suppose if I hadn't come along out of the blue . . ."

Sophie tilted her head to the side and shivered. "Sometimes, the best things come along when you're least expecting them. There's something on the horizon for you, Ann, I can feel it."

Ann picked up one of the grey furry cushions and threw it at her. "Stop that. There's been enough on my horizon to last me a lifetime." She lay back and smiled. "All I want now is a nice easy, uncomplicated life." Ann yawned, trying to ignore it – that niggling feeling that something was about to happen, one of excitement, a shift in the atmosphere – and it both excited her and terrified her all at once.

"Close your eyes!" Sophie shouted, hearing Ann descend the stairs.

"I'll kill myself."

"Here." Sophie covered her eyes and led her through the kitchen door. "Ready? Three, two, one. Ta-dah!" Sophie dropped her hand.

A huge number three and a zero helium balloon rested

in the centre of the kitchen as an enormous pink reminder that she'd safely passed the threshold into her fourth decade and wouldn't be allowed forget it. The kitchen table was laden with gifts.

"Where the hell did you hide them?" Ann asked, looking at the balloons.

"In the boot of the car. The three has gone a bit saggy, like your arse will in a few years!"

"Less of that, you! Ah, Sophie, I love it." She hugged her friend tightly. "Thank you for being here. It's exactly where I want to be."

"This one first . . ." Sophie thrust a tiny silver box at her, wrapped in a black bow.

"It's a pony. Isn't it?" Ann shook the box.

"It's the donkey from down the road. Your very own." Sophie watched Ann untie the ribbon and flip open the box.

"Oh, Sophie. It's beautiful." Ann touched the delicate gold chain.

"The star is because you're a star, obviously." Sophie pointed at the pendants. "And the lightning bolt is because you're braver than you think, with much bigger balls! And, quite poetically, if I do say so myself, it's a reminder that lightning never strikes twice, so all the bad stuff is behind you."

Ann ran her hand over it, feeling the tears well. "It's perfect. Thank you."

"Now this one . . ." Sophie led her to the table. "Go. Open it."

"Now, what could this be?" The box was much bigger. "It's a German shepherd, I'm sure." Ann pulled the colourful wrapping from the box, throwing it in the air to reveal a vintage-style record player. "Oh my God! I was forever scratching the needle on Dad's one. I wonder what happened to it."

"There's no sound on earth like that of a record starting. It can throw you right back into a forgotten moment," Sammy used to say.

Ann clapped her hands together. "I love it. Lucie gave me a box of Dad's records. I have them in the attic. Now I can play them. Sophie, this is all too much. Thank you."

"Stop that!" Sophie swiped the air. "If *I* can't spoil you, who can? There's one last one. It was Jack's idea, would you believe? We came across it in one of those horrible musty shops in town. I had to put my scarf over my face for fear of inhaling consumption," Sophie grinned. "You might understand now why I was so blown away by your song last night." Sophie handed Ann the final gift.

Ann hugged the package, knowing what it would be and realising as soon as she opened it that there'd be nothing she could do to stop the tears. She took a breath and peeled back the paper to reveal the 12-inch vinyl version of the song that changed her parents' lives – and started hers. A face so like her father's stared back at her from the sleeve of the record.

"Do you believe in destiny, Sophie?" Ann couldn't take her eyes off the gift.

"What do I keep telling you?" Sophie put her arm around Ann and kissed her cheek. "You, my friend, are destined for something. What it is, I don't know, but I do know one thing. Whatever's coming, there's feck all we can do to stop it."

CHAPTER FOURTEEN

"I can't wear this," Ann shouted down the stairs, shaking her head. "I'm not sure you understand Knockmore style."

"I'll be the judge of that." Sophie bounded up the stairs two at a time and stood in the doorway smiling approvingly. "You're fabulous, look!" Sophie walked in and swivelled Ann towards the mirror, forcing her to look at herself.

"It's too much, Soph."

"No. This . . ." Sophie gestured towards her own outfit, "is too much. That . . ." she pointed at Ann again, "is perfect."

Ann looked at Sophie, who was casually sporting a pair of soft black leather shorts, gathered at the waist, teamed with a black fitted top with enormous balloon sleeves, complete with orange-and-pink lining that puffed out around her narrow shoulders like colourful clouds. Sophie pointed her foot to highlight a pair of fluorescent pink suede stilettos, perfectly elongating her tiny frame. Her brown hair hung in loose waves, flashes from some orange tassel earrings visible amid them.

"Sophie, you're every inch the Dublin blow-in and I love it," Ann smiled, admiring her friend's daring choice. "Knockmore won't know what hit it, but I can't wear this."

"Will you ever cop on? It's stunning! And look! We match."

Ann observed their reflection in the mirror. It was like a double act in some sort of eighties Olympic dance team.

Sophie was grinning from ear to ear. "Besides, I promised Lucie I'd get loads of pictures of you in the dress, so you have no choice," she finished triumphantly.

"I should have known better than to give you Lucie's email address. You lied."

Sophie had made a big deal of getting Lucie's contact details under the pretence of asking her some advice for her cousin, who was allegedly planning to spend a year in Australia. In truth, Sophie had wanted to see if Lucie might be coming back to Knockmore to surprise Ann for her birthday, but it hadn't worked out, so instead, they'd coordinated the presents.

"There is no cousin. You got me and you're wearing the dress."

Earlier, after a lazy breakfast and a walk up town, where Ann introduced Sophie to Denise and Ian, the pair had returned home to have a lie down before getting ready for the evening festivities.

"Get your beauty sleep, girls. You look greyer than the corpses out back. I've reserved a table in Lennon's for later," Denise told them, pushing them out of the door of Tea and Sympathy.

"Is it really where your parents met?" Sophie had asked.

"Sure is. Lennon's is a Knockmore treasure. I haven't set foot in the place since I was about fourteen. Dad still played there up until . . . well, you know."

"Well, it sounds like the perfect place to celebrate. And my new best friend, Ian, says the band playing tonight are quite good."

Ann had been right about one thing – Sophie and Ian had hit it off straightaway, instantly teasing each other and giggling like schoolgirls.

"Which reminds me . . . I almost forgot." Sophie jumped off the bed and bounded out of the room, returning a moment later with a big gift bag.

"What? *More* presents? Sophie, I'll kill you."

"This one's from Lucie. She sent it to me weeks ago. Said I was to give it to you before you got ready to go out."

Ann took the bag and sat up. She took out the card first, laughing at the high-pitched *Happy Birthday* song that started to play as soon as she opened it.

"To my Annie," she read aloud. "Happy thirtieth. I feel so old right now. Love always, Lucie."

Ann picked up the piece of paper that fell out of it, closing the card.

"I'll give you a minute," Sophie smiled and left the room.

Dear Ann,

I couldn't possibly write what I want listening to that dreadful card. You can thank Declan and Bella, your little Aussie cousins, for picking out that musical nightmare. Instead, I find myself sitting here in Sydney, so far away from you, writing everything I want to say.

First, I can't tell you how proud I am of you and how happy I am to have found you again. I can never forgive myself for leaving you alone all those years. I should have come sooner. I had my reasons. Someday I'll tell you all about it, in person!

Anyway, the past is the past and all we have now is the future.

I know from our chats on the phone that you feel

as if your life has turned full circle. I want you to know how brave I think you are for walking away from a life that wasn't right for you and starting again. I'm not sure I could do it. I know that wherever you go, Ann, you'll always find your way. You have the pizazz of Sammy and the strength of Felicity running through your veins. Your parents loved you so much, Annie, please know that, and they'd be bursting with pride right now.

You have your whole life ahead of you and I know that your second attempt at it is going to be fantastic. Felicity once told me never to let a moment of life pass you by. Don't waste it. Seize it, because one day, it could be over. Forget the past. I've thought a lot about everything lately – you, Fliss, Sammy, myself even – and I believe that sometimes it's not about trying to mend a broken past but instead starting over and creating something better.

I suppose the present you're about to open may not match that message, but when I saw it all I could think of was you and your mam. You're so like her, in every way. As long as I have you in my life, I'll never feel as if they're gone.

Wear it tonight. Throw your shoulders back and walk into Lennon's like you own the place. I wish I were there by your side, as I once was with Felicity, in that same place. God, we were young!

There are three presents in the bag. My inner control freak has them labelled. Open them in sequence.

Love always,

L

xxx

Ann could barely see the bag in front of her through the tears. She reached in and took out the three parcels. The first was small. She opened the paper, feeling the tissue rustle in her hands. It was a silver photo frame, a Post-it note concealing the picture.

> *I found it the day before I bought present two. I thought I'd lost it. This was* the *night.*

Ann pulled the Post-it note from the glass and felt her heart swell. It was a grainy Polaroid picture of Felicity and Lucie. Lucie had her arm around Felicity's waist and they were standing in the kitchen of the very house she was in now – the house where her father, Sammy, and Aunt Lucie had grown up, and where Ann would spend her latter childhood years with her parents. This was the night her parents had met – the night Felicity had sneaked out with Lucie and ended up staying the night at the Maguires' house.

Her mother was wearing the black dress her father often spoke of so fondly, with a shiny red belt around her tiny waist. Lucie's hair was like a red mop as she giggled in the photo, while Mam looked straight ahead, poised and elegant. Wow. How had Ann never seen this photo before now?

Ann wondered if this was the night she'd been conceived. How innocent they looked in the photo, how unaware that after that night everything would change. How Sammy and Felicity, her parents, would end up with her, a baby, married and living in this house. How Lucie would one day emigrate to Australia. How Ann's parents would end up dying so young and how Ann would end up back living here, in the house her mother had left Lucie to manage for all those years. Ann wiped her tears and opened the second parcel. There was another note inside.

Maybe this will make sense now. Same but different. Leather in place of plastic and pink instead of red, and a teeny bit more expensive!

Ann unravelled the tissue paper to reveal a fitted black dress with a metallic shocking pink soft leather sash belt. Jumping off the bed, she held the dress up to herself and looked in the mirror. The resemblance was uncanny. Ann looked at the tag. She remembered hearing Sophie bang on about that Australian fashion label. It must have cost a fortune.

Ann picked up the third gift – an envelope with a note stuck to the front.

Whenever you need me, I'm right here.

Inside was an open-ended return flight to Australia.

"Can I wear flat shoes?" Ann asked hopefully.

"Only because you have those darned amazing legs." Sophie reached into the wardrobe and pulled out a pair of pointed black Jimmy Choos, throwing them at Ann. "At least short-arse left you with a decent wardrobe," Sophie said as Ann slipped them on. Sophie fixed Ann's hair and smiled. "I mean, if it were me, there'd be a little more make-up for such a momentous night, but I have to admit, your mediocre attempt at glamour seems to have paid off. Close your eyes." Once more, Sophie turned Ann towards the mirror. "Now, open them."

There she was. Felicity stared back, smiling broadly at Ann, who could still hear her words.

"This is life. It's not a dress rehearsal. It's not a practise run, Annie. Live it."

Perhaps it was time to throw her shoulders back and see where the wind blew her. Hadn't she been cautious for long enough?

CHAPTER FIFTEEN

Mark

"Are you ready, Dad?" Mark called from the hallway as his voice echoed off the high ceilings.

"Fancy a few pints this weekend, son?" his father had asked the day before while his mother gesticulated around the garden.

"Sure, Dad." Mark almost felt sorry for him. He'd done the crime and now he was doing time.

"There's a nice place a mile down the road. Does a nice Guinness."

"Sounds good."

Saturday had been a quieter day. Mark had slept well in the end, in the oversized bed, falling asleep with images of Ann's face swirling as his breathing deepened and he gave in to the exhaustion. He'd woken still thinking about her, unable to understand why he couldn't get her out of his thoughts. Perhaps it was the idea of her, her connection to this house – the fantasy more enchanting than the reality. Well, that and the fact she was gorgeous.

He'd had girlfriends before – one or two who'd even managed to get past the six-month stage – but ever since his family had started to crumble around him, Mark wasn't inclined to allow anyone to get too close. At least he told himself that was it, knowing deep down that if the right person came along, there was no complication too significant to overcome.

"Too darned good-looking. Too darned cagey," the last girl he was seeing told him when he'd said he wasn't looking for something serious.

"Too darned busy," he'd replied, trying to remove himself from where she'd wrapped herself around him.

"Let me in, Mark. Don't fight it. Give in to me. Take my breath away. Let me mend your broken wings."

While she'd regurgitated one-liners from love songs, he'd stared into space, bored senseless, feeling suffocated, attempting to release himself from the spaghetti arms pawing at his chest and then under the covers, trying to entice him.

"Do you like that, baby?" she'd asked, not reading the signs, straddling him, rubbing at her breasts and moaning like a cheap porn star.

"Not particularly."

Mark had lifted her off and walked towards the bathroom, naked. He didn't trust himself to stay there any longer, afraid he might insult her further.

"You know what your problem is?" she said when he'd returned a few minutes later with a towel hanging from his waist, displaying that V-shaped muscle that no woman can resist.

"What's that?"

He didn't look up, still trying to figure out why women always insisted on doing a relationship post-mortem when nothing could bring back to life something already dead. He ran his hand through his wet sandy hair, pushing it away from his face as he waited.

"You're never going to find what you're looking for. What you're looking for doesn't exist," she'd spat before picking up her bag and heading for the door. "One more thing. You're *not* that good-looking."

It sounded like what a teenager might say in a reverse psychology battle. Perhaps she was right. Maybe what he was searching for didn't exist. Mark wasn't even quite sure what it was, or if he was looking for anything at all. He wasn't an arsehole, much as his friends and their wives liked to tease him.

"Another one bites the dust, Marky Mark. What did you do this time?"

Nothing. Mark never did anything – perhaps that was the problem. He didn't mistreat women. Mark was mostly polite, well-mannered, generous. There just hadn't been anyone who could hold his attention for any length of time. They all tried too hard, appeared too desperate. Was it his looks? There was nothing he could do about that. He wasn't vain. He was tall. He worked out, there was nothing irregular about his features, he had all of his hair.

"When you know, you know. When it happens, it happens and you'll cross rivers to be with her," Dad had said a while back.

Mark didn't need to ask his father to whom he was referring. His father had pined for *her*. Grieved until he'd suffered that darned stroke. And when he could brood no more, he'd resigned himself to this new life, in Knockmore.

"She's too young to be looking after a cripple, anyway."

Mark had pretended not to hear. It wasn't what his father had said, more the way he'd said it that made Mark think it was one of the saddest things he'd ever heard. His father *had* loved her: the other woman. But crossing rivers for her was impossible – his mother had made sure of that.

"Not a bad old place." Mark looked around him now. "Not very Knockmore."

They were propped up at the bar, two ice-cold pints in front of them, admiring the setting.

"Make sure you face Eugene's good side out," his mother whispered into Mark's ear before they left. "For himself. Don't want anyone staring. And have him home nice and early, all right?"

Mark knew it was for his mother and not for his father, but nonetheless, he'd sat him with his left side against the bar, away from the door, where they could chat easily over the lively Saturday night atmosphere.

"Oh yeah, Lennon's is a fine spot. I was chatting to a fella who often walks his dogs past the house and he was telling me all about it. Not that I'd get to come here without you. I can't see this being Olive's cup of tea."

"No." Mark shook his head. "There's not much that's Mum's cup of tea around here, except the house, I suppose." Mark gulped his pint and set it back down on the bar. "What do you think about the building job, Dad? I'm still not sure I have the time to oversee it. Bit excessive. No?" Mark was still hoping he could talk them out of it.

"It's not as big as you might imagine. That conservatory or whatever she's calling it comes in a pack from France. So once the foundations are in and the internal work is done, it'll fly up. As long as we're not touching external walls too much, there shouldn't be a problem. If I were able, I'd have it done in a few months. But sure, look . . ." He pointed towards his limp arm.

"But the internal plans don't suit the house."

Eugene held up his hand. "Son, I learned a long time ago not to give my opinion on what people want in their houses. Do the job. Do what you're asked. That was my motto and it didn't see me far wrong. Besides, Olive's mind is made up and the funds are there, so what harm? She has her plate full with Jessica – and me, I suppose – and it gives her mind a focus, so leave her be." Eugene wiped some of the foam from his pint from his moustache. "I wanted to ask you about Jessica. Not normal, is it? What is it with her?" Eugene looked concerned.

"I don't know, Dad. I'm sure she'll be okay. A rough patch, maybe." Mark tried to avoid his father's glare.

"Three years is more than a rough patch, son. At first, I thought it was the business with your mother and me. I know she's angry with me, has never really forgiven me, but she's an adult. Then I thought it was that boyfriend she broke up with, that architect one. She was all talk about him and then I never heard him mentioned again. I know I was sick around that time. Your mother says she's wallowing, has herself stuck in a rut. Did I miss something?"

"No, Dad. You didn't miss anything." There was no way he was going to worry his dad any more than necessary. "Jessica suffers from depression, Dad. Plain and simple. Mum doesn't seem to want to admit it. She drinks too much, doesn't eat right, doesn't leave the house. I'll talk to Mum. Maybe Jessica should go and talk to someone – a professional. I think the time away in Spain will do her good," Mark tried to reassure him.

"I'd appreciate that, son. You're a good kid, Mark. I'm sorry we all drag it out of you."

"It's okay, Dad." Mark placed his hand on his dad's, feeling the papery skin under his own. "Another pint, Dad?"

"Sure. My quota is three. Let's drink as slowly as possible. Make the most of being out," Eugene winked. "Makes me feel young again sitting here. You should be in among that crowd inside, instead of sitting here with me." He gestured towards the lounge area and packed seats near the stage.

Mark didn't bother to turn round. "Ah, I'm happy here with you, Dad," he said, focusing his attention on his father.

"Did I ever tell you about that office development in Dublin?" Eugene began.

Mark smiled. It was great to be here with his dad. He'd missed out on it as a kid, but there was still time to make amends. There was always time, wasn't there?

CHAPTER SIXTEEN

"Let's just walk." Sophie was chomping at the bit to get the night under way. "It can't be that far."

"In those shoes! Are you mad?" Ann looked down at Sophie's impossibly high heels. "You'll need corrective surgery by the time we get there."

"We could see if the donkey and cart up the road will give us a ride. I told you I wanted a picture of you in it!" Sophie suggested, giggling.

"I'm not sure he'd make it." Ann was too nervous to laugh, her earlier enthusiasm suddenly waning. "Ian will be here in a minute. He said half past. He's going to leave his car there for the night. Look, here he is now."

They looked out of the window to where a white convertible BMW, complete with a pink ribbon tied across the bonnet like a wedding car, had just pulled up, Ian waving his arm frantically at them. A band of kids had gathered around the vehicle.

"Give us a go in your car, mister," one shouted while Ian shooed them away from the balloons he'd attached to the headrest.

"Oh, sweetest Jesus, the ribbon!" Ann rolled her eyes. "You're going to make a holy show out of me, aren't you?"

"Yep, we sure are."

"It's not my hen night," Ann said apprehensively,

wondering what else they had in store.

"No, thank God. This is your coming-out party! Whose idea was it again to go for afternoon tea and flower arranging for your hen? Oh, yes. The one who never ate, with the keto breath, who used to get blotto after two drinks. If you'd let me arrange it, it would have been willy pasta, willy straws, willy hats, all the way. Oh, and a banner saying 'Same Willy Forever', although that's not true any more," Sophie sang, raising her eyebrows. "Maybe tonight you'll get to see a second one."

"There will be no willies, thank you very much, and that's exactly why I didn't let you arrange it. Come on, before Ian has every child from the Estates hanging on to the back of the car."

Ann grabbed her leather jacket and threw her bag over her shoulder. Sophie was already running out of the door, waving at Ian.

"Big night?"

Ann jumped when she saw Tracy standing at her door, arms crossed, looking at the car, face like curdled milk.

"Hi, Tracy. I didn't see you there."

"No, I suppose you didn't. Fancy dress, is it?" She gestured towards Sophie, who was twirling and pirouetting for Ian while he applauded.

"Not quite." Ann furrowed her brow.

"No, I suppose not."

"Okay, Tracy. Nice talking to you." Ann turned to leave.

"I haven't seen you in a while," Tracy said suddenly. "Too busy for us? Must still be a big change from Dublin."

"Well, actually, I never said before, but I grew up in this house, right here. It was my grandparents' and then my parents' . . . well, before they died."

"Is that right? Dark horse, you are." Tracy paused. "Still, makes me wonder why you'd come back here, when clearly you're more suited to Dublin. Is there more to it, Ann? You're not part of the witness protection programme, are you?" Tracy looked deranged, her eyes narrowed like a detective.

"Hardly. Ah, we all have a story," Ann said calmly. "I imagine you must have one too, Tracy. Where did you blow in from originally?" Ann was beginning to lose her patience. It looked like Tracy's gloves had finally come off.

"Next town over. Not that you've bothered to ask. Keeping yourself to yourself. I was born and bred in this neck of the woods, with every right to be here. Not like some." She gestured again towards the car, where Sophie and Ian were getting restless.

"Like me, so. I'm Knockmore through and through. And don't worry about Sophie. She's just here for the weekend, so no need to lock up the husbands – and she's engaged. You should see him! Fabulous." Ann stopped then, remembering herself and not wanting to let anything spoil her mood. "Look, Tracy, you're welcome to join us for a drink," Ann offered half-heartedly. "It's my birthday."

For a moment, Tracy looked as though she might say yes.

"No babysitter."

"Next time," Ann smiled before leaving.

"Oh my!" Sophie exclaimed, looking at the thunder-like face watching them as Ann hopped into the passenger seat. "Looks like you've made a frenemy there, Ann."

"Feck her," Ann replied. "I've enough people in my life to be worrying about the likes of her. Good riddance."

And they were off, speeding up the road, music blaring and Ian beeping the horn at passers-by.

Driving out towards Lennon's, the wind blowing through her hair, Ann was transported back to her childhood, riding in the front of her father's van, music blaring and him singing along. Dad knew the words to every song that came on the radio. Old and new hits, he was always singing away, tapping his hand against the steering wheel to the beat, glancing over at Ann, smiling that smile.

It was hard to believe he was only thirty-four when he died. Not that much older than Ann was now. He'd packed a lot into those years, always making the most of life, relishing every minute he had on this earth. If Mam had been right and our lives were already mapped out for us, then perhaps it had always been secretly ingrained into him, that his timeline would be short, making him appreciative and positive, where others failed to be. Sammy would have loved to be celebrating with Ann tonight, heading to his favourite haunt. Wild horses wouldn't have kept Dad from hopping up on the stage in Lennon's and singing to her if he'd been here. Ann smiled.

Looking out of the window now and remembering the great times was progress, Ann was sure of that. Perhaps being back here *had* helped to fill the vacant piece of her soul that she'd fought against in Dublin. Bit by bit, she was gathering an army of people who had her back and appreciated her for who she was, not the version she'd tried to be when she was married, and it felt like home, it felt real.

"Here we are," Ian shouted over the music as he pulled into the car park, swinging the car round and parking it in front of a low wall overlooking the road.

"Oh, it's cool." Sophie looked over her shoulder.

It hadn't changed that much, but it was enough to bring it up to date. It was a huge house, built in the middle of a sprawling car park that saw buses of people come in at the weekend from surrounding towns to enjoy the nightlife that Lennon's had provided for the last fifty years. The one-time yellow paintwork was now replaced with a steely grey façade, in striking contrast to the red-painted windows and doors. There were several picnic benches outside on a patio area, with matching red umbrellas and outdoor heaters scattered here and there, where a few families sat enjoying baskets of fish and chips in the early evening sunshine.

"Now, that's a green-grey." Ian looked up at the pub. "Don't you think, Ann?" he said with a wink.

"You and your colours, Ian! But the place looks amazing, well done."

Ian had helped the owners with a new exteriors and interiors project, sweating for weeks trying to select the best colours.

"Wait till you see inside. You won't recognise it."

Ann and Sophie waited while Ian wrestled with the roof on the BMW and then linked both of their arms in preparation for their grand entrance.

"Come on, girls, let's go make a holy show of ourselves. I never got to do the whole Lennon's on Saturday night thing when I was growing up here. I was hiding at home under the duvet, terrified anyone would catch me looking at the boys instead of the girls."

"Well, then it's high time Knockmore got a taste of Ian, in all his glory." Ann reached over and adjusted his cravat.

"How do I look, Sophie?" He stood back to show off his light beige trousers, turned up to reveal bronzed ankles and snakeskin loafers.

"My, my, Ian, I think I spy Gucci," Sophie whistled. "I approve."

Ian pulled open the door of Lennon's and they stepped inside.

"Wow." Ann took in the grey leather couches, dark wooden tables and a deluge of velvet cushions in every colour under the sun strewn across the chairs.

The light fittings were gigantic glass balls, filled with fairy lights, glistening above them like stars. Dotted throughout the pub were antique typewriters, stag antlers, bookshelves with stacks of old books. Large vintage signs hung on the walls with lights all around them. Ann looked at the one ahead of her, feeling the hairs on her arms stand on end.

Happiness is Not a Destination. It's a Way of Life.

"Ian. It's beautiful. Well done you."

Ian took a little bow, unable to hide his delight. "Do you like it?"

"Yeah," Sophie assured him. "This is far nicer than any of the big, trendy new bars in Dublin."

"Well, I'm honoured. What I was going for was . . . just gay enough," Ian grinned. "Come on, let's find Denise."

Ann spotted Denise standing up and waving to them on the far side of the pub, looking youthful, dressed in a silver sequin blazer, black skinny jeans and a black T-shirt – not a floral pinny or hairnet in sight. She'd had her hair blow-dried and her make-up done for the occasion, and Ann had never seen her look better.

"I'll have to go all out to keep up with you young ones. Come Saturday night, I'll be more Gin and Frolics than Tea and Sympathy."

Their table was in prime position in front of the stage. It was the one thing untouched in the refurbishments, Mr

Lennon Junior rebuking Ian's suggestion to rip it out and start again.

"This stage is an institution," he'd said, banging it with the palm of his hand, appalled by the idea. "My grandfather built it with his bare hands. Nothing you can do could convince me to change it. You're barking up the wrong tree. My father would turn in his grave, Ian. Now I accept the other changes, but the stage stays."

Ann was glad Mr Lennon had stood his ground as her eyes travelled across the stage, conjuring images of stories long told.

"Come on, hurry up," Denise beckoned.

Ann walked towards her, oblivious that several pairs of eyes had turned to watch the approach of the girl in the black dress with the shocking pink belt, her leather jacket slung over her shoulders, her blonde hair loose around her face. There were no jewels to accompany the simple yet exquisite dress, no impossibly high heels that she couldn't walk in. No fluttering fake eyelashes, winged eyeliner, kohl-lined eyes nor sticky lip gloss to distract from the canvas.

As she came near, Denise stood and threw a handful of confetti in the air. Ann smiled up at the rainbow of colour above her, feeling the same anticipation for the night ahead that her mother, Felicity Montgomery, had once experienced more than thirty years before.

CHAPTER SEVENTEEN

Ann could hear her own breathing, her heart hammering in her chest. Her palms were moist, her hands trembling as she sat, staring ahead, unable to see anything beyond the blinding lights. Raising her hand to shield her eyes, Ann tried to pick out Sophie from the crowd as a sudden hush descended on the room. The walls appeared to be closing in around her, the buzz of earlier now flat, sober.

How had she let Sophie talk her into this?

It was Sophie who craved the limelight, not Ann, and she'd already had far too much to drink. Her stomach heaved unexpectedly. Damn Sophie, always trying to push her outside her comfort zone, not realising Ann was happy being one of the ones who clapped along, cheering from the sidelines. You don't have to do this, she told herself. Stand up. Walk away. Her body remained motionless, glued to the seat, immobile, staring over their heads, with no escape route.

So far this evening, Ann had laughed until her sides hurt, the combination of Sophie, Ian and Denise the perfect cocktail of giddiness. They were all as loud as each other, sure of themselves, taking no notice of those on the other tables glancing across, interrupted by squeals of delight coming from the party of four.

"We'll be thrown out!"

"No one's ever been thrown out of Lennon's for having

a good time." Denise smacked Ann's arm playfully. "Gosh, love, when I saw you walk towards me this evening, I thought I'd been catapulted right back to the eighties."

Ann looked down self-consciously at her dress. "Oh, Christ. Do I look like an eighties throwback?"

Denise laughed and shook her head. "No, you great big eejit. You look like someone I remember from the eighties," Denise told her, softening. "You look so like your mam tonight, Ann. The walking image of her. That dress. It's perfect. You look incredible." Denise placed her arm around Ann's shoulder and squeezed her. "All we need now is a Sammy for you!" Denise turned towards Sophie. "Wait till I tell you about Sammy. Jesus, I tried to get him round the back of Lennon's more times than I've had a rub of the relic with my fella."

They all burst out laughing at the description.

"Is that what they call it?" Ian chimed in. "If only I'd known."

"Guys, that's my dad you're talking about!" Ann couldn't help laughing.

"Christ! and I could have been your mother if he'd let me." Denise's hand flew to her mouth.

By the time the band came on they were already in high spirits, having covered every topic from ex-husbands, future husbands, current ones and Ian's Italian boyfriend, who arrived twice a year for two weeks of heaven.

"Just the way I like it before we start killing each other."

There was much discussion about Sophie's upcoming wedding, even though there was no date set nor money put aside.

"If you continue to buy flashy little leather shorts, you'll be my age before you're married," Ian joked.

"I love this one," Ann said, listening to a familiar song and humming along.

"Oh, I remember this one well," Denise agreed. "Go West, isn't it?"

"That's the one," Ian added. "'King of Wishful Thinking'. It was in the film *Pretty Woman*. Classic tune."

"You guys have the worst taste in music. You should see her playlist," Sophie giggled, pointing at Ann. "Eighties central."

"I can't help it. I was reared on the classics."

"And classics they are," Denise agreed. "I can't believe I'm going to say this, but they don't make them like they used to. I'm showing my age now."

As the song finished, the lead singer stepped away from the mic to take a drink of water before walking back.

"How's everyone doin' tonight?" he asked in his best DJ voice, pronouncing it as *tznight*.

The crowd gave a cheer.

"We're gonna be tzaking a tziny break before my favourite part of the evening. I know we have some singers out there tznight. Who's gonna give us a tzune?" He shielded his eyes and looked into the crowd. "Is that a birthday? What do those balloons say? Tzirty? Will we do tzirty kisses? We'll see you in five."

Ann ducked under the table as Sophie let out a howl. There was no way Ann was going to let herself be dragged on the stage to be licked by thirty unfamiliar mouths.

"Ann." Sophie leaned across the table to grab her hand, ready to throw it in the air. "You have to sing."

"Don't, Sophie, please." She grabbed her hand away.

"Ann, you listen to me and listen well." Ann watched her friend's face turn serious. "What I heard you do last night was incredible. Out of this world."

Ann tried to look away.

"Look at me," Sophie said through gritted teeth. "Now, I'm not one for soppy shite, but this is what I was talking about – something's in the air, and you need to reach out and grab it by the balls." Sophie reached out in front and mimicked grabbing something rather sizeable and pulling it into her chest. "I wouldn't let you get up there if I thought you were going to sound like a bag of drowning cats. You have talent. Real talent. Please, Ann. Today's special. Don't do it for me . . ." she paused, but Ann knew what was coming. "Do it for yourself," Sophie finished as they heard the lead singer ask again.

"So, who's gonna give me a tzune?"

"I'll do it."

It was out of her mouth before she could stop herself. A reflex. A knee-jerk reaction. As soon as she'd said it, she wished she hadn't. The chatter stopped and everyone turned to see where the voice had come from, their eyes gradually settling on her. Ann swallowed.

"Jesus, Mary and Joseph. Are you messing?" Denise sniggered, leaning forwards.

Sophie turned to her and put her finger to her lips. "Shush. She's got this."

Denise held her hands up, made a face and sat back.

"Do it, Ann," Ian whispered. "Sophie told me about your singing earlier. Do it!"

"I'll do it," she repeated, standing up as if volunteering for war, bravely throwing herself forwards to the front line, when no one else would.

A round of applause swept across Lennon's as she made her way to the stage.

"What's it gonna be, sweetheart?" the lead singer grinned,

thrilled that it wasn't some mammy intent on singing a Celine Dion number. "How about a dzuet?" he chuckled into the microphone.

Ann leaned over to whisper something in his ear. His head jerked back and he smirked, wondering if this was one of the moments where he'd have to turn down her microphone and sing louder to drown her out.

"The acoustic version," she nodded, nonplussed. "Just me on guitar."

He shrugged his shoulders, disappointed not be included, and gestured at the other lads, who sat down either side of the stage, delighted with the break.

"What's your name, sweetheart?"

"It's Ann. Ann Maguire," she said into the mic, jumping back from the feedback.

Ann stood with her back to the audience, tuning the guitar before sitting down at the mic. She rested the guitar on her legs, which had started to shake.

Do it for yourself.

"Could you turn the lights down a little?"

The leader singer rolled his eyes and dimmed the spotlight slightly.

"Come on. You can do it."

Denise's voice reached her from the audience as Ann began to pluck at the strings. Then she squinted at the audience one more time, closed her eyes, inhaled and opened them.

Then she saw him.

He was watching her so intently that she stared back curiously. He nodded his head once, barely a movement, and she nodded back, smiled, looked down and started to play.

You could hear a pin drop in the room as she began to

sing, keeping her eyes on the floor at first, trying to level her breathing, remember the words. Reaching the climax of the song, Ann finally found the confidence to look up again, her eyes immediately meeting his once more. He was all she could see in the sea of people, as if everyone else had suddenly disappeared, floated away, and they were alone in the crowded room together.

"Find a person in the room and sing to them." She could hear her father's words.

Ann's eyes settled on his and a slow smile lifted his features as he watched her perform. Every nerve ending in her body came to life as she looked back, unable to stifle her grin, unable to tear her eyes away from his. You could hear the emotion in her voice, now on autopilot, coming from deep within her soul. Ann forgot everything but here and now as her voice rose and fell towards the end of the song.

He remained still, one arm resting on the bar, the other in his pocket, his eyes never leaving hers, buoying her along. As she sang the final note, the lead singer reached over and turned up the spotlight, instantly illuminating her. The lights dazzled her and she stumbled slightly. The silence reverberated in her ears as she tried to look out over the sea of people. And then an explosion as almost every person in Lennon's rose to their feet with thunderous applause.

"Ann."

Ann felt Sophie's arms around her.

"Oh my God. That was unbelievable. *You* are unbelievable."

Ann made her way off the stage, pushing through the crowd.

"Sophie, did you see . . .? There was a man right there . . ." She pointed towards the bar, an empty beer bottle left sitting where he'd been.

"No. Ann? Are you okay?"

"Yeah. Great. I'll be back in a minute." Ann rushed past her towards the door.

Her heart was pounding as she pushed her way outside, her head darting from side to side. There was no one there. Just a few couples pressed against the walls of the pub, the odd smoker sitting on the wall. Ann shook her head. He'd been right there and then Ann thought she'd seen him walk towards the door. Was it her mind playing tricks with her? She'd never felt anything like that in her life. Had she imagined it, the story of her parents setting eyes on each other to that same song, creating a fantasy in her mind?

She looked around once more, squinting across the car park. Then she took a deep breath and shivered, still unable to believe that she'd just sung on stage and unable to fathom that she'd only imagined the most sensual moment of her entire life. What just happened?

CHAPTER EIGHTEEN

Nathan

What the hell just happened?

Nathan put his head back against the headrest of the truck and ran his fingers through his hair, massaging his scalp. Rubbing his hand down his face, he exhaled loudly through his fingers. The stubble felt sharp against his skin, sobering. His jaw felt welded together with tension. Always tension – except for those few minutes.

Nathan closed his eyes, trying to capture the moment like a photograph and relive it, hold on to the look on her beautiful face. It was the first time in what felt like years that he'd felt present in the moment, his mind free of everything. Up until then, he'd been lost in thought, standing there, not paying attention to what was going on around him. It was how he was nowadays: withdrawn, aloof, unapproachable – how he coped. The only way to survive was head down, keep yourself to yourself. Don't get involved. He was good at it, too. Existing – drifting from place to place, doing the odd job here, making a bit of money there, staying long enough to finish a project before moving on, never looking back.

Nathan never had trouble picking up a bit of work. People trusted him – his no-frills attitude, his quiet confidence. "Well-spoken, mannerly," that's what they said about him, his exterior not quite matching his voice.

People were often shocked to hear his accent on seeing him pull up in the ex-corporation blue truck, a large red metal container strapped to the back containing his tools – just about everything he needed to complete most jobs. Whatever he didn't have, or couldn't carry with him, he rented. He preferred the smaller jobs. In and out. Get it finished, get paid, move on. Simple.

It was so different to how life once was, when he'd had the world at his feet, patiently and meticulously trying to rise to the peak of his profession. Plenty of friends, someone to love, a family. How life can change!

Nowadays, he existed like a ghost. Here but not here. It didn't have to be that way, he supposed, but it was the only way he could get through each day, each week, each month. It was the decision he'd made when he'd checked out of his previous life. Was that how he'd describe it? Pushed out – that seemed more apt. He missed it – what life had once been, who he'd once been – but it hurt too much to ponder on it.

Tempted by money, once or twice Nathan forgot himself, undertook a total refurb or an extension that kept on extending, tying him there for months past when he was ready to leave. Afterwards, he'd reminded himself why he preferred the smaller gigs. People started to get comfortable with you, began asking questions, wanting to be friends, get under your skin. Where are you from originally? Do you have kids? Are you married? Do you live nearby? Where did you go to school?

It wasn't the jobs he minded. It was the people. Nathan rather enjoyed seeing a building transform, using his hands, the skills he'd picked up to make something better. He had an excellent team of lads, too. Fellas he could rely on: a roofer, a brickie, a plumber, a sparkie. Good guys. Honest guys. Guys with a past. Nathan was willing to take a chance on them when no one else would.

Who was he to judge?

It was often casual work, but his team were grateful for any job he could pass their way and they respected him.

"Odd as bejaysus but a decent skin. Just don't go asking him anything. There are clams more open than Nathan. You won't be asked back," one of his team would whisper in a warning to any new lad taken on for a contract job.

Nonetheless, the lads all adored him, were able to see through the cool outer façade he'd built around himself for protection. Behind it, there was a softer side. It wasn't always visible, but at times the dense wall would slip, revealing a man who was so broken that you could almost see the cracks on his face. By what? None of them knew. Well, no one but Sully, his right-hand man, but Sully was even tougher to crack than Nathan. The lads would never know unless he chose to tell them, but they weren't going to hold their breath. Whatever it was that had changed Nathan into the stony version he now was must have been ruinous, but it hadn't fully succeeded – there was still a kindness to him that would seep through unexpectedly.

Nathan was always there in the morning before they arrived for work, was the last to leave, never needing to slip away in the day, nor leave early, rushing home to a wife and kids. The lads sometimes wondered if he slept on the job, but once or twice they'd seen the blue truck parked outside various B&Bs and guest-houses in the evenings. They never questioned it. Why would they?

The wages were always distributed every Friday afternoon, on time, never a second overdue. He treated them well. He was fair. He rarely lost his temper, even when mistakes were made. Nathan stayed to clean it up. He always had their back. Every house was left immaculate, finished to a standard you didn't get from most builders, not unless you wanted to pay through the nose.

Nathan O'Keefe was no cowboy, that's for sure, even if sometimes he played the hard man act. He was a gentleman, trying to act shifty – but the lads saw past the performance. Deep down, there was nothing dubious about him, except maybe something in his past. Then again, they all had a history. Didn't everyone?

"And a fine-lookin' man," the women whose kitchens he improved, walls he knocked through and bathrooms he transformed would describe him to their friends. "Better than fine, actually," they'd giggle. "Who doesn't love a bit of rough!"

Only, Nathan wasn't rough. Outwardly rugged, maybe, but as well-read as any of his employers, with brains to burn and a soft face, hidden under a scruffy beard.

"Those eyes! I might see if I can get the attic converted next. Be worth it. I could look into those eyes all day."

Nathan adjusted the rear-view mirror now and looked directly into *those eyes*.

"Arghhh!" He banged the steering wheel suddenly and ran his hand over his face again. His hand reached out automatically, pulled the door handle open and then slammed it closed just as quick. "No," he wrestled with himself.

More than anything, he wanted to get out of the truck and walk back inside Lennon's, but that wasn't why he was here. Most towns, Nathan floated into. Knockmore wasn't one of those towns. He'd known what he was doing when he turned the blue truck off the motorway and drove along the stretch of road towards it. He'd checked into a guest-house, then travelled the length and breadth of the town before he came across it.

"Well, knock me over with a feather."

Nathan peered up the driveway of Knockmore House. He hadn't been expecting that. It had thrown him. There was no plan as such – Nathan never planned much – but he'd thought about this a lot over the years. Indeed, he'd thought of little else when he was unable to fall asleep in the damp rooms of various guest-houses, when he'd spent evenings alone, staring blankly at the TV screen, seeing nothing. He'd obsessed over it. The pain never leaving him, the hurt was ever-present – the bruises to his heart still as fresh as the day they were inflicted on him.

That house, though, Knockmore House, threw him. Circumstances had changed for the Dempseys somewhat. Nathan was about to get out of the truck, walk up the drive, bang on the door, but something stopped him. He'd waited this long. What were another few days?

So he'd left, driven away, past the pubs on the main street and out along the road before coming across Lennon's. What he needed was a drink and it was far easier to keep to himself in these bigger pubs. Not like the smaller places, where he was always bothered by someone wondering what a rugged young man with haunted eyes was doing sitting alone at a bar on a Saturday night when he could have the pick of any woman. He'd heard it a thousand times.

Nathan had settled himself at the bar and ordered a bottle of beer. There was a good buzz in the place, aside from the awful band and the has-been singer with dyed hair playing throwbacks from the eighties. Every man in the place was silently groaning at the wannabe Michael Bolton performer shamelessly working the stage. You wouldn't trust someone like him with your mother, let alone your girlfriend or wife. Pure cheese and they were lapping it up. It almost made him smile. At one time, he'd have been joking with his friends, or his brother, slagging the singer, instead of standing here alone. All by choice, he kept telling himself. It was what he'd wanted – a new life.

When the singer asked for a volunteer to come up and sing, Nathan put his hand in his pocket to look for his keys. He'd enough troubles in his life without listening to some tone-deaf mammy trying to belt out a power ballad. His keys dropped to the floor and he bent to pick them up, ready to leave, when he saw a pair of legs stroll towards the stage.

The place went silent.

Nathan stood up in time to see her whisper something to the lead singer. Michael Bolton threw his eyes to heaven and turned to the drummer, making a lewd gesture behind her back. She didn't notice.

"Ann Maguire," he heard her say into the microphone and then startle at the painful sound that followed from the mic.

He watched as she settled herself on the stool, a brief look of terror flashing across her face. Was she going to bolt? She didn't. Instead, she started to pluck at the strings. There was something about the way she carried herself – self-conscious, hesitant. It felt familiar.

Then she looked up.

He nodded at her, briefly stunned, wondering what he was doing, but she nodded back – smiled. Nathan recognised the A-ha song straightaway. It was one usually reserved for the final songs at a wedding when everyone was well-on, ready to let loose, jump about with abandon, although he'd never heard it played this way. This version was different – slow, sad, haunting, filled with pain. Her pain? Or was it a performance? He couldn't tell.

At first, she was so quiet he had to strain to hear her. Gradually it grew, her voice almost breaking once or twice with emotion. It reminded him of Sinéad O'Connor singing that song – what was it called again? The one where she cries and it's so raw that it couldn't be anything but real. Nathan stared at her, her appearance not quite matching her demeanour. Christ! she was stunning. Her blonde hair hung down her face. Was she crying?

Played this way, it was one of the saddest things he'd ever heard. When she reached the second chorus, she looked up again and her eyes found his. His stomach twisted unexpectedly – a jolt. He wanted to look away, but he couldn't, his eyes glued to hers. He smiled, she smiled back, right at him, and Nathan felt the air leave his lungs. It was as if there was no one else in the room, just them. He and this girl. Nathan was mesmerised.

When she'd finished, that fool turned the spotlight on full blast and she looked as though she might fall over. A girl ran up and hugged her. Nathan looked up one more time. Her eyes were no longer able to find him, but she was looking, he was sure of it – searching over people's heads to see him.

He'd left, rushing from the bar, out of the door, to the safety of the blue truck, parked round the back out of the way. Nathan shook his head and pushed the rear-view mirror away. He didn't want to see his face, no longer recognising the person to whom those eyes belonged. In another life, Nathan would have hung around to introduce himself to that girl, who made him feel like the only man in the room. Then again, he wouldn't have been sitting in a truck at the back of a country nightclub.

In another life, when Ann Maguire sang the words, "*Take on me*", breathlessly, with her eyes focused on his, Nathan would have shouted yes, but that was another life and he'd never make that mistake again. Never.

CHAPTER NINETEEN

"Fair play to you."

"Well done."

"Great song."

A few people patted her arm as Ann made her way back inside, smiling politely in response, still shaking with adrenaline.

"Can you believe you just did that?" Sophie shrieked when she reached the table. "Where did you go?"

"I just needed some air. It was hot up there."

The whole experience of singing in public was so alien and yet, in a way, it felt as though she'd been born to it. Denise and Ian stood up, clapping loudly as she sat back down.

"Ann. That was amazing. Truly amazing." Denise was still wiping the tears from her face. "I mean, it was fantastic all by itself, but when you know the history behind it . . . ah, girl, you have my make-up ruined. Your folks would have been so proud of you."

"Agreed," Ian piped in. "That was special."

Ann smiled back at her strange little family, all here for her. She *was* proud of herself – shocked, in fact – but the whole experience had been overshadowed by something else: *him*. Ann couldn't make sense of it, not even knowing how to describe it. An encounter? A moment? A connection? When she'd first met Dom, it took weeks, months even, for him to make her feel anything akin to that. Eventually, he'd worn her down. She laughed at her choice of phrase now, knowing it wasn't how you should describe the man you ended up marrying.

It was so glaringly obvious now, how wrong she and Dom had been for each other, especially when a total stranger had just made her feel more than she'd ever felt with Dom. Was that actually possible in a few minutes? It couldn't be. It had to be the emotions of the night, that song, the thought of her parents. Perhaps the story of their meeting had influenced her more than she knew. Ann had heard similar stories of couples meeting in the same way their parents once had. It was Knockmore, after all, where the opportunities of finding romance were few and far between.

"Are you okay, Ann?" Ian asked, noticing her silence.

"Yes, great."

"I'm going to get more drinks." Ian stood up from the table. "Perk us all up again. The night is but a pup."

"I'll come with you," Denise suggested.

"And I need to pee. Will you be okay here?" Sophie asked.

"Of course."

Ann was grateful to have a few minutes to gather herself. There was no way she could tell them what had just happened, knowing how stupid it sounded. Besides, Sophie would be rushing around trying to find out who he was and Ian would be asking her so many questions that she didn't know how to answer.

Could something so simple as a look between two people make you feel like that? Was it just her? Had he felt it, too? Can you honestly communicate without exchanging a word? Her mind was spinning.

"It was a shared moment of contact with no contact,"

her father used to tell her, describing the moment he first saw her mother. "I looked down. I waited. I lifted my head and this time, she smiled at me. And I realised I was right – it wasn't just me." He'd clap his hands together loudly. "The moment of impact. Bang! Like a bolt of electricity, Ann. And I knew right then I'd set eyes on the one person who'd change the course of my life."

"Seriously, Dad? Pass the sick bag," Ann would say, secretly loving the story.

"When there's a connection, there's a connection. It doesn't always make sense. It's not always the person you expect it to be. But in that moment, Ann, you have to choose: head or heart." He always finished the same way. "Seeing her that night made that very moment one of possibility."

A moment of possibility. Is that what just happened? Ann shook herself back to reality. If it were a moment of opportunity, whoever he was would have stuck around, instead of vanishing into thin air. No. Ann felt sure what she'd just encountered was a moment of impossibility. Typical.

"Excuse me."

She heard a voice behind her.

Ann turned to see a young couple standing there. The man stood back from her, appearing as though he'd been dragged over.

"I'm so sorry to bother you," the girl began. "But we're getting married in four weeks and . . . well, we just loved your singing and we still don't have a church singer, so we were wondering, would you sing at our wedding?" the girl gushed.

Ann was about to decline politely, but remembering Sophie's words from earlier, instead she found herself nodding. This was her chance to see where life blew her.

"Eh. Well, I'm fairly new to this, but I suppose I could give it a go. Are you sure? It's not what I do."

"Absolutely sure. We loved it. Didn't we, Colm?" The girl turned to her fiancé.

"Yeah," he muttered. "Loved it. How much?"

Ann laughed. The poor man was probably already paying through the nose for the wedding, terrified of another bill.

Ann stood up. "Well. Since it's my first gig and I'm honoured to be asked, how about we say a hundred euros. That'll cover the cost of the sheet music and transport," Ann suggested.

He immediately broke into a smile. "Wow! Are you sure? Thank you."

He looked so relieved, Ann couldn't help smiling.

"Here's my number . . ." She took out a piece of paper and a pen from her bag and jotted it down. "Call me next week and we can work out all the details and pick the songs. That should give me plenty of time to have them perfect for you."

"I'm Martha." The girl stuck out her hand and Ann shook it. "Can you do that one you just did? I felt like you were singing it just for us." She smiled up at Colm, who smiled back in a way that Ann knew he was mad about her.

"That song makes a lot of people feel like that," Ann said, wondering if she had, in fact, experienced a moment of possibility – just not the one she'd hoped for.

"See, what did I tell you? Open yourself up, grab the universe." Sophie splayed her hands again as she'd done earlier in the pub and pulled them back in a grabbing motion.

Ann looked at Ian and Denise, who were both mimicking the action.

"You've brainwashed them. That's enough universe grabbing," Ann giggled.

"Not a bad result all the same," Ian nodded. "We now know that you're an outstandingly talented singer and you have your first paid performance lined up. At a knock-down Knockmore rate, mind." He gave Ann a reprimanding look. "I'm appointing myself as your manager. Do you have any idea what those singers normally charge?"

"No. I really don't," Ann grimaced. "But they were so cute and young. I just wanted to do them a favour. Besides, the thought of singing again has my stomach in knots already."

"Nonsense," Denise chimed in. "You have plenty of time to practise and, of course, I can give you the time off. This could be the answer to everything for you." Denise picked up her drink and took a sip.

They were sitting in Ann's garden, eating crisps and leftover birthday cake, sipping on prosecco. It had been Ian's idea to grab a taxi back, have a snack and discuss the evening.

"I think so, too," Sophie added. "It would be a shame to waste that talent. It's in your blood. You can call the shots. It's perfect. Imagine, in one day you've become a professional singer."

"Hardly professional, Sophie. But I did enjoy it – once I got over the feeling that I wasn't going to projectile vomit over the audience. I promised you all I'd try, so here I am, trying," Ann finished, wishing she could tell them what she'd actually experienced on that stage, staring into those dark eyes.

"And the singer from the band was all over you at the end of the night. I thought he was gorgeous. Might be time to consider dating again," Denise suggested.

"Eh, not him, that's for sure. Like you always say, Soph, one must never trust a blonde man. His hair had more highlights than my own – and skinny jeans on a man in his forties is never a good idea."

"Fifties! But agreed," Sophie spluttered. "His face was ten shades redder than it should have been and the arse of his jeans was down around his knees. Maybe you'll meet a dashing best man when you're singing at some posh wedding – not that you'd tell us if you did."

Ian nodded. "Exactly. You kept the singing a secret, didn't you? What else aren't you telling us?" He raised his eyebrow. "Closed people are the most complicated of all." He tipped the contents of his glass back quickly and then spluttered as the bubbles shot up his nose. "Oh, dear. Sorry, Ann. I think I've had enough now."

"One more for the road," Ann said, pouring the last of the bottle into their glasses. "Actually, you're right. Maybe I am a little closed. I wasn't always, you know. How about a bedtime story?" Perhaps it was time to offload a little baggage. "I haven't told you everything."

There wasn't a sound as Ann relayed her story. Not a movement as she filled in the gaps of her mother's life. The secret that her mother was a stolen baby, ripped from the arms of a teenage girl in the Estates and destined for a tragic childhood at the hands of the evil wife of the reverend, Margot Montgomery. None of them moved as Ann told them of her mother, Felicity, meeting Sammy Maguire, the teenage pregnancy that followed, her attempted suicide, Sammy rescuing her.

"And the part that kills me. Margot threatened to get custody of me before my mam died. Mam was so scared that she sent me away, made me leave Knockmore. And then I was alone. Lucie didn't know where I was, as she was in Australia. I don't think Margot ever had any intention of getting custody. She just wanted to hurt Mam. Until the day she died, she just wanted to hurt her."

Three sets of eyes watched as she spoke, revealing her almost unbelievable story, and four sets of ears listened. Sophie, Ian, Denise and another set of ears tucked out of sight behind the wall heard it all – her sorrow, her despair, her truth.

When she finished, they were all wiping the tears from their eyes. There was only one member of the audience who smiled smugly to herself, delighted to have been in the right place at the right time and to be privy to such invaluable information about her prissy next-door neighbour.

Up until now, Tracy Doyle hadn't managed to discover everything there was to know about Ann Maguire, but she was glad she'd uncovered it now, hidden behind the garden fence. Tracy had tried welcoming Ann, inviting her for coffee, asking her to go for a run with her – all offers refused. She'd even included Ann in the night out with the girls, going above and beyond what she believed was the standard neighbourly duty.

Tracy had watched Ann that night in the Italian restaurant, knowing Ann thought she was too good for them all. She hadn't even bothered to get dressed up – not like she looked tonight, done up like a dog's dinner with her Dublin friend and heading off to Lennon's like a teenager. Tracy hadn't been there in years. She'd have loved a night out. Ann could have asked her before she was getting into the car, given her a bit of time to get ready. Tracy had more style than that brunette friend of Ann's, who was dressed like a clown. And Tracy was sure

Ann hadn't refused drinks all night, like she had when she was out with them, nursing the same glass of red wine for the evening and picking at her food, escaping at the first opportunity.

Tracy had been furious with her and then after Ann left, the other women had been all talk.

"Did you see her shoes?" one of them said after Ann scurried off early. "Christian Louboutin, I'm sure of it."

Tracy had always wanted a pair of designer shoes with the infamous red soles. She'd even bought a pair of press-on red stickers off the internet to attach to the soles of her black high heels, in an attempt at making do. One sticker had ended up on the floor of the restaurant and the other half stuck to the back of her jeans, from where she'd had her legs crossed.

"Overrated," Tracy had responded that night. "Sure, what's the point in having flat designer shoes. Boring! You can get shoes like that for next to nothing online."

"And the figure! You'd know she hasn't squeezed out any kids yet."

"Sure, we'd all look like that if we hadn't been ripped sideways giving birth," Tracy argued. "Bit scrawny."

"Gorgeous-looking," another issued. "And not a screed of make-up on. Not like us, who have to trowel it on nowadays."

"I can't see it. She's as plain as flour," Tracy had answered dryly as the other women raised their eyebrows at the catty comment.

What kind of a woman goes to a girls' night with a bare face? Tracy had thought afterwards. The type who couldn't be bothered with the likes of them, that's who.

Well, Tracy knew the truth at last, and it wasn't pretty.

It was no wonder Ann had been avoiding Tracy like the plague. Tracy supposed she was relieved. It wasn't Tracy, after all, who Ann was hiding from but the truth. Still, Tracy had more of a reason than ever to dislike Ann now, with her ever so shady past. She'd known all along there was something funny about that girl.

And what was it her own mother said? "Eventually, it always comes out." That Mam had been talking about the time she ate three slices of rich fruit cake and spent the evening on the toilet was neither here nor there. Tracy was glad, for once, that what had come out tonight was infinitely more interesting than her mam's daily health update. Now, this was something the girls would love to hear about. This would show them that Tracy had been right to be suspicious of squeaky-clean Ann.

"I'm Knockmore through and through," Ann had said earlier. If Ann wanted to be more Knockmore, well, then the others had a right to know about her – that's how it worked around here. That was the Knockmore Tracy knew.

CHAPTER TWENTY

Olive

Of everything she'd changed, there was one thing Olive never compromised on. She was sure Eugene's bit of fluff must have tantalised him, ignited his senses with all sorts of flimsy contraption-like gauzy undergarments – pieces missing, straps and ribbons in the wrong places. Still, for Olive, a staple nude underwired bra and a pair of full-sized white cotton knickers were the only options – even if nowadays what covered her sensible briefs was far more sophisticated than what had previously concealed them. It gave her an element of comfort and stability to know she'd retained a little piece of Ordinary Olive under her finery, all for herself. Not just any ordinary knickers, either – great big ones, grand and full, reaching right up to her bra.

"You could sail a ship with them, Olive," Eugene used to joke with her years ago.

Olive hadn't found it amusing, especially since by that time, the ship had, indeed, already sailed. Besides, back then it would have been far too frivolous for Olive to spend money on herself, on something as wholly unnecessary as fancy underwear.

It was difficult to imagine now, with them living the high life. Olive had spent much of their married life worrying about money, fearing the worst was yet to come. Sometimes waking in the night, tapping Eugene on the shoulder to ask was everything all right and did they have enough to see them through.

"All under control, Olive, nothing to worry about," he'd say, rolling onto his back and settling into a worry-free sleep.

It was funny, though, she thought afterwards. Eugene had never taken the time to reveal to her just how under control everything was. Keeping his level of success a secret was, after all, what had enabled him to lead his sordid double life for so long. It wasn't until Olive took control of the money that it dawned on her how much of her life she'd wasted worrying about nothing, fretting about the wrong things all along. The day she started to dig about in their accounts, to uncover the wealth her cheating husband had amassed, she swore there and then never to waste another minute of her life worrying about finances.

At first, it was liberating. Olive felt drunk on the information, wanting to scream it from the rooftops, rejoice – it didn't last long. Sooner rather than later, she'd crashed back down to earth, her one-time worries replaced by far greater ones. Olive would never have to worry about money again. Instead, she'd spend the rest of her days worrying about everything but money. How wonderful it would be if that were still her greatest fear. No. Olive could have whatever her heart desired, except for peace of mind – and the knickers. The knickers stayed.

Not that Eugene would have noticed anyway. They'd opted for separate bedrooms when they'd moved to Knockmore, all *that business* tucked away safely in the past, especially after his stroke. He was still able to "perform", the doctors told her, as if she should be thrilled by the prospect. Olive had never relished the "performance" much, anyway. She'd done her part. That's what marriage was about in her day.

"It's a wife's duty," her mother told her when she first married. "Use the time to make a list in your head of what needs to be done for the week ahead."

It wasn't entirely "lay back and think of your country" – it was more clean the skirting boards, wash the net curtains, polish the brasses.

She wondered, did the bit of fluff used to do the same? She doubted it. More than a few times, Olive found herself imagining Eugene with *her*, doing what he used to do to Olive. In one way, she sincerely hoped her husband made more of an effort with *her*. Otherwise, what had been the point of it all? Perhaps *she* had put in the effort, replacing her giant cotton briefs with some colourful bits of dental floss. Would Eugene have looked elsewhere if Olive had done the same?

Olive slipped off her silk dressing gown and put on her pants and bra. She always laid out what she going to wear the next day the night before as part of her bedtime routine. Hairnet on. Expensive creams applied to her face. Select outfit from her now enormous wardrobe. Of course, she didn't have anywhere to go today that would require a beige pencil skirt, white silk camisole and cashmere sweater, but it was nice to look beautiful, to feel as if she'd achieved something.

"Off out somewhere, Olive?" Eugene would ask when she emerged from her bedroom each day, looking as though she were going to a luncheon.

"Oh, shut up, Eugene," she'd reply impatiently, knowing he was trying to rile her.

Her husband hadn't seemed to notice any change in

her appearance over the years, although surely he must have. Hair and make-up perfect, skin smooth from various treatments and visits to a dermatologist in Dublin. It was fascinating what they could do nowadays: Botox, fillers – she'd had it all. The first time she'd had her lips done, the doctor had plumped them up so that her top lip curled up and over, making it possible to rest a pen there comfortably. The next time he'd done better – now, she was featured on his website as an example of success, with her eyes blacked out, annoyingly, but Olive knew it was her. Imagine! Olive, a model!

And yet, none of her family ever said anything, never passed comment. It irritated Olive, almost making her want to do more, change more, be better. She'd caught Mark looking at her curiously once or twice. As for Jessica, Olive could have come down the stairs in a PVC catsuit, platforms and a black wig and Jessica wouldn't have noticed.

None of them noticed her. Aside from the time Eugene had called her "Ostentatious Olive" in an attempt to be smart after she'd returned home from a day in Dublin, carrying more bags than was humanly possible for someone under five foot tall. It had cut like a knife.

"Who are you making the physical adjustments for?" Dr Wilson had pressed her, scrutinising her soul through his bifocals.

Olive had watched enough episodes of American chat shows to know what to say.

"Solely for me. All for me. No one else. Just me. I do it for myself."

He hadn't questioned her further. Olive had obviously answered correctly.

Olive finished dressing and stood back to study her reflection in the mirror, turning to the side, smoothing out her skirt, ensuring that no panty line was visible. It wasn't. Good. Now what? Coffee? No. Maybe she should go somewhere. There was a lovely new florist in town. She could go and get some fresh flowers. Should she ask Jessica to come along? Get some fresh air. Olive exhaled. What was the point? Even when Olive offered to take Jessica to Dublin for the day, she refused.

"Come on. I'll buy you some new clothes," Olive would ask hopefully. "We can go for some lunch. Get our hair done."

"No." Jessica didn't bother to look up.

"Come on. It'll do you good."

"Piss off, Mother," she'd shouted the last time. "Just piss off and leave me alone."

It was the first and last time Jessica hit Olive. She came at her so fast that Olive couldn't extract herself in time.

"You ruined my life!" Jessica screamed, striking Olive across the face. "You ruined my fucking life."

Olive's hand shot to her face, the heat from her cheek burning her hand.

"Don't ever, *ever* say that again. Don't ever raise your hand to me again, Jessica. Do you hear me? You'll be sorry."

Jessica had left the room crying and Olive had sat on the end of the bed, her hand still cupping her face.

"I saved your life," she whispered to no one. "I was saving your life."

Yes. Olive's underwear was the only thing about her that was still recognisable from the past. She'd never have admitted it, not to anyone, not even to a therapist, bound by confidentiality. Olive Dempsey made herself *look* different because she *felt* so very different. And in truth, she'd have done anything to be ordinary again.

Perhaps it was the same with the house. It was a beautiful home. It should have made her content, but as yet, it hadn't delivered on eradicating her hurt or concealing her secrets. Olive was sure that when it was altered, brought into this century, that she'd have everything she'd always wanted. Outward perfection would eventually seep through to the inside – she was just helping it along.

"I'm going for a walk, Eugene, into town."

"Really? Why?"

"What do you mean, why? What a stupid question. I'm taking a walk."

"But you never go into town."

Olive rolled her eyes. "Well I am today, for God's sake. It's like the Spanish Inquisition."

"Shall I come with you?"

"No, Eugene. It'll take too long with you hobbling along beside me."

"Oh. Yes. Of course. Okay, so. Enjoy. There's a bit of racing on the TV I can watch." He returned to the sitting room.

Olive ambled along admiring the other houses as she went, nodding politely at passers-by, enjoying the anonymity. She'd been right to keep out of village life, even though at times she craved recognition, the odd chat.

"Nice day." A young mother passed her, pushing a buggy, shopping bags hanging from the handles, and then stopped for a break.

"Lovely day."

"You look nice," she told Olive. The woman blew her hair from her face and placed her hands on her hips.

"Thank you, dear. I suppose at my age you have to make an effort. Don't be saving it for a rainy day – wear it now," Olive replied. She'd heard someone say it once and had liked the sound of it.

"Isn't that true!" The younger lady pointed at the buggy. "Not much chance with a new baby, mind."

"No. I suppose not. I do remember. It goes by very fast. Enjoy it while you can." Olive stared into the buggy. "Someday that adorable little girl there is going to despise you and the air you breathe more than you could ever imagine." Olive smiled broadly and continued down the hill, leaving the woman looking aghast.

If Olive had stopped to talk more with that new mother, she might have missed what came next just as she stopped outside the flower shop.

"Knockmore House? Are you sure?"

"Yes. Do you remember the Maguires? Well, Felicity was the reverend's daughter. She passed away young, God rest her, but rumour has it that her daughter, Ann, is back in Knockmore and she found out that Felicity was one of those stolen babies you read about all the time. You know, when the creepy parish priest gets involved. I tell you, it was all going on up in that house all those years ago. I can't remember the wife's name. Was it Muriel or something? Anyway, Ann's working over at Tea and Sympathy . . ."

Olive moved closer, her eyes round with surprise as the two women slowly edged away, hushing their voices.

Well, now, Olive thought to herself. There was an element of relief, she supposed, to know she wasn't the only one around here with secrets and that Knockmore House was already filled with them.

CHAPTER TWENTY-ONE

Nathan

Something seized Nathan's attention in the rear-view mirror and he sat up, watching her approach, recognition instantly flooding his senses. She looked different, dressed from head to toe in black, her hair tied back off her flushed face, but it was her. The familiarity of her features shocked him – that face, so familiar and yet unknown.

She veered out onto the road to pass the truck, but she didn't look in, remaining focused on the road ahead as she climbed the hill. It took all of his willpower not to turn his head and stare out of the window as she went. The muscles in her legs tightened as she made the ascent, her chest rising and falling with the effort. He was sure she'd keep going when she reached the top, but her pace slowed and she turned quickly, breaking into a sprint towards him.

Nathan grabbed his cap on the passenger seat and pulled it down over his face, slumping into the car seat as far as he could as her feet thumped by. When he was sure she'd passed, he edged up, adjusting the mirror, in time to see her descend the hill and round the corner at the end until she was out of sight.

Nathan stared ahead again. He hadn't expected to see Ann a second time, the woman who'd filled his thoughts for the weekend. Nathan wasn't even sure what he was still doing in Knockmore. After Saturday evening, he'd slept fitfully, past and present demons haunting him, keeping him awake past the time when he was no longer tired, just numb.

On Sunday, he'd gone back to Lennon's and had something to eat. It was a different place from the night before, packed full of families enjoying a big carvery lunch from the enormous catering stations that had miraculously appeared from nowhere. He'd stayed for a few hours, observing other people's lives, watching ordinary people interact, wondering how it would feel to be sitting at a table with a family, ensconced in the normality he'd once known and loved.

He didn't allow himself to ponder for too long on what he was missing, afraid to let himself feel anything other than the focus that kept him moving. Had he hoped to see Ann again? Maybe. Would he have done anything differently if he had? Probably not.

Seeing her again like this aroused those same feelings, making him feel jittery, preventing him from thinking straight. What the hell was wrong with him? He had nothing to offer anyone any more, certainly not the someone he imagined this perfect stranger to be. All he knew about her was her name, for Christ's sake, nothing else. She was just a girl, singing a song in a crowded bar, who'd momentarily puffed life into his damaged heart.

Had he heard something in her voice? Nathan was sure he had, some story she needed to tell, something more than the lyrics of a song. Ah! he was romantic. Perhaps he'd been listening too intently. Still, one part of him – the bit that hadn't been totally tarnished by the past – couldn't help thinking there was a reason he'd encountered her, and her, him.

Nathan shook his head again. Nah. Stop that – all wishful thinking, all notions. Besides, he gave up believing in destiny a long time ago. Destiny was for other people. Destiny was a choice and he hadn't always made the best choices in the past.

He shouldn't have stayed an extra night here. He had a job to finish on Monday in Dublin, but for the first time, he rang his clients to tell them something had come up and he'd be back on Tuesday. He hadn't slept again last night, holed up in the B&B, with the red crucifix attached to a picture of Jesus Christ, blinking and buzzing over his head, the floral wallpaper and curtains swirling and meshing, forming images in the dark – pictures of her . . . and someone else. He couldn't bear it.

Should he get the hell out of here? Forget it all. Nothing could change history. Much as he didn't want to admit it, this girl, this total stranger, awakened something that had lain dormant inside him for so long. Was it the idea that he might still deserve peace of mind? The recognition that it was him who'd been wronged? Perhaps he did have a future, if he allowed himself. Perhaps he didn't need to move around aimlessly from town to town for the rest of his life, unattached. Hadn't he lost enough? Not enough, he thought, before he could stop himself. Never enough.

Nathan started the engine as a glint of desire formed and gathered. Maybe he could leave the past behind and construct a new start. Yes, that's what he'd do – he could call his brother, perhaps even his mother. Maybe it was time to move on, to stop punishing himself. He could clean himself up, turn up again at Lennon's and meet Ann Maguire in person this time. Have the opportunity just to be Nathan – to walk up to her and say something ordinary like, "That was great. Fancy a drink?"

He'd wasted enough time on all this. Nathan was

ready to let go. He took one last glance at Knockmore House, preparing to leave, and then stopped.

It was Olive, walking out of the gate of the house, wobbling down the road, oblivious. As she neared the truck, he once again pulled his cap down, enough so he could still see her.

She didn't look in. Instead, she turned to the side and inched past the truck like a crab. If only for her height, he might not have known who she was. Even though he'd only come face to face with her three times, it had been enough for him never to forget Olive Dempsey.

She looked different. Well. Not a care in the world. She'd had a little work done, by the looks of it. Even her hair had changed, set into a short blonde hairstyle, shorter at the back, a feathery fringe almost to her eyes. When Nathan first met her, she was a meek-looking thing, standing there, shivering against the cold, shaking as she spoke, shock written all over her timid little face. The next time, she was more self-assured. And the last time he'd encountered her, he hoped he'd never set eyes on her again as she sat across from him, her hands resting on her lap, speaking measuredly – a reminder never to judge a book by its cover.

He'd been so crippled that day, so hurt, so afraid – unable to believe what he was hearing, nor comprehend it, as she'd delivered the final blow.

"Don't *ever* contact us again or you'll be sorry. Do you hear me, young man? I'll make your life hell."

If only he could have his time over. What would he do differently? Everything. It had been a snap decision, made out of trying to do the right thing. It was how he'd been raised – always to think of others first. To act out of kindness. It was hard to believe that one choice, one action, could alter your entire existence, making everything change in an instant. It made Nathan terrified to breathe, frightened not to scrutinise every future action.

Thinking of it made him want to jump out of the truck and grab Olive Dempsey around the neck, lift her off the ground, threaten her the way she'd threatened him – worse. He closed his eyes, trying to control his ragged breathing. Just breathe. Count to ten. Breathe. He needed to get out of here before he did something he'd regret.

He'd come back to Knockmore, though. Seeing her like this, living in that big house, all spruced up – it wasn't right. Not when other people were suffering. Not when other lives had changed irreparably. It wasn't right.

He was naïve to think that an encounter with a beautiful stranger could unlock the real him again. That version of Nathan was as vanished as the lives Olive had ruined. This wasn't about revenge . . . well, it hadn't been until he saw her face again. No, this was bigger than personal feelings. It was about doing what was right.

Nathan put the truck into gear and made his way out of Knockmore, sure that the next time he returned, he'd finish what he came to do.

CHAPTER TWENTY-TWO

"Sorry, I'm late." Ann made her way around the counter, hung her coat on the hook, grabbed an apron and tied it around herself. "How are you feeling?" she called through to the kitchen. "Thanks for giving me yesterday off, although I almost wish you hadn't," she babbled, switching on various appliances and taking the lid off the big butter container, ready to scoop some into the little spotty dishes.

"I had a dreadful sleep on Sunday night. I figured I comprised of five per cent water, forty per cent prosecco, thirty per cent gin and twenty-five per cent crisps. Have I done the percentages right?" Ann went on.

"I went for a run to try to sweat it out – my usual route, up the hill. Must have had alcohol-induced fear. I was convinced everyone was staring at me – totally paranoid. Mind you, I'd never drank so much in one weekend before. Then I started thinking, maybe I was drunker than I remembered on Saturday and made a holy show of myself in Lennon's."

Ann had planned to stay in bed for the day on Monday, catching up on well-needed rest after the weekend. But instead, she'd lain awake much of Sunday night, thinking of everything. It felt as if Sophie had been there with her for weeks, instead of just the weekend, and Ann had found it difficult to say goodbye.

"I don't want you to leave." Ann hugged her tightly. "I might lock you in the room upstairs."

"I wanted to do the same thing when you were leaving Dublin. I even asked Jack could he get his hands on a mild sedative – not enough to take you down, just enough to keep you pliable."

"Well, I know how you feel now." Ann hugged Sophie again. "Thank you for making it the best weekend of my life. From start to finish, it was perfect."

On Monday, Ann lay on the couch, wrapping the soft blanket around her, staring at the ceiling for hours, thinking of *him*. It was amazing how one encounter with a stranger had almost eradicated thoughts of Dom and the fictious Mark from her mind. Could the universe be so cruel as to throw someone in front of you for a few minutes and then grasp them back? Perhaps the encounter in Lennon's had been nothing more than a cosmic demonstration that she could still feel attracted to someone, show her that maybe she did want a relationship again, someday. She did want to be loved again, of course she did. It had taken that moment to make her realise it, to know that her heart could still function.

"There's someone for everyone, Ann," Ian had told her on Saturday night. "If you don't want to be alone, you don't have to be. I truly believe that."

Ann was starting to believe it, bit by bit, and maybe she *was* prepared to try. She laughed suddenly, realising how incredible it would have been if whoever *he* was had hung around on Saturday night. Imagine them telling their kids someday that they'd locked on eyes on each other in precisely the same manner that her parents had met. Hah.

"I didn't, did I?" Ann looked up now to see Denise standing at the kitchen door, a serious expression on her face.

"What?"

"Make a holy show of myself in Lennon's. Denise . . . what's wrong?"

"Ann, I think you'd better sit down."

"What's happened?" Ann grabbed the counter to steady herself.

"No, love, it's nothing too bad," Denise added quickly, seeing the colour drain from Ann's face and realising that someone who'd been dealt lousy luck her entire life was always somehow expecting the worst. "Well, it's not bad, but it's not great."

Ann walked around the counter and plonked herself down on one of the high stools.

"Denise, for Christ's sake, spit it out," Ann pleaded, holding her stomach as if going to be sick.

"Well, it's everywhere. Everyone knows," Denise began. "Well, at least I've heard four different versions so far. Some better than others, mind, but it's out there. And you know what they say once it's out – it's hard to put it back in. Better out than in." She tried to smile encouragingly. "Maybe not that last quote. I think that refers to flatulence, but you know what I mean. Yes?" She nodded at Ann, a huge, stiff smile plastered across her face.

Ann stared back. "Denise. I have no idea what you're talking about. None whatsoever. You're going to have to start again. You're scaring me. What's out?" Her heart was pounding.

"Sorry, love." Denise sat opposite her. "This happens to me sometimes. My thoughts can't quite keep up with my words. Coffee?" She handed Ann a takeaway cup from the new coffee chain in the shopping centre. "I went especially for you on my way here. It's your favourite. A soya cappuccino, extra shot. You might need to give it a blast in the microwave."

Ann took the coffee cup and gulped the bubbly liquid. It was still warm.

"It must be bad if you ventured into the competition," Ann almost smiled.

Denise took a deep breath. "Well, it all started yesterday morning when Una Dealy came in. I mean, I should have known when I saw her coming. She hasn't set foot in here since the day we opened. Too tight ever to go for a coffee – 'Sure, what would I be doing paying for a coffee when I make a perfectly good cup at home . . .?'" Denise glanced at Ann, who rolled her eyes.

"Sorry. Anyway, in she comes. 'Is Ann here?' she says. I say, 'No. Ann's on a day off and sure, what would you be wanting with Ann, anyway? Sure, you hardly know her.' So she tells me that she was in the pub on Sunday night and the next thing, she's standing at the bar when she hears Mary D and Susy F – you don't know them, nosy arseholes." Denise took a quick breath. "Anyhow, they were talking about some story they'd heard at the kids' football training on Sunday morning about the girl who works for me whose mother was stolen from a pregnant girl in the Estates." She paused. "And, wait for it, got pregnant herself and then jumped off the roof of the community centre. I said, 'For Christ's sake, Una. Are you as thick as you look? If she'd jumped off the roof of the community, 'the daughter would hardly be working here with me now, would she?'"

"Oh, sweet Jesus." Ann rested her head on the counter. "Oh, Christ."

"Anyway, that wasn't the worst of it. Someone else

came in and asked to see the mother of the stolen baby. Another was wondering if it was you who stole a baby."

"Oh, no." Ann banged her head down on the counter a few times before lifting her head. "But how, Denise? Did you tell anyone?"

"I'm insulted you even have to ask. What you tell me goes to the grave." Denise stuck her nose in the air and tutted.

"Well, then who? Ian? I can't see Ian telling anyone. He's the farthest thing from a gossip I know. Especially since he was a victim of it for so long."

"And yet you point the finger at me?" Denise looked hurt.

"No, Denise. I'm just trying to figure it out."

"Well, there's one thing for sure. Whoever it came from has it all arse ways, but that's the way news travels around here. One person gets a hold of it and the next thing, it's sprouting legs and arms – and in this case, a tail." Denise placed her hand on Ann's. "Listen, those who remember Sammy and Fliss and you as a child, they won't go believing backward tales about you. Everyone else, I've told them it's all a rumour and to buy something or get out."

"Was there anything else?" Ann asked. "Did they mention Knockmore House?"

Denise nodded. "Yes. I'm afraid they did. The local paper was here yesterday wanting to talk to you. Apparently, the new owners of Knockmore House contacted them. They wanted to do a bit of research into it all before people start knocking on their door looking for answers. I just put my hand up and said, 'No comment!' I've seen that in a few movies. It seemed like the right thing to say. Did I do okay?"

"Oh, Denise. What am I going to do? The last thing I want to be is the centre of attention. I'm so sick of being judged and gossiped about. It was the same before I left

Dublin. Everyone talking about Dom and the stupid divorce.

"I was just starting to feel settled and I was so hopeful after the weekend. Why can't everyone leave me be?" Ann threw her hands up. "The more I try to keep my head down and get on with things, the more people want a piece of me. It's the same with bloody Tracy . . ." She paused. "Why didn't you tell me yesterday?"

"Ah, I thought it might go away and I guessed you might be tired after the weekend. I'm sorry, love, but you listen to me, Ann Maguire. This changes nothing. How far you've come stays the same. People have nothing better to be doing than sticking their noses into other people's business. Half of them are curious and the other half are just arseholes."

"So I was right, everyone *was* staring at me?"

"Yes. I suppose they were. But listen, you grew up in a small town. You know as well as I do that haters will always hate and rumours are only accepted by fools. Those people don't matter, Ann. And *you* know the truth."

Ann nodded sadly. It was hard to think that after three generations, one woman's ambition of having a child at whatever cost was still hurting people.

"Should I go to Knockmore House myself? Explain the story," Ann asked.

It was really none of their business. You didn't own the rights to the history of a house just because you bought it. Ann couldn't think straight. She needed to talk to Ian and find out who'd told her story. It wasn't theirs to tell.

"Mark Dempsey."

It suddenly dawned on her as she said his name. What was it with this Mark? She didn't even know him and yet he seemed destined to be in her life somehow – and now, not in a good way.

"That guy from Knockmore House. He knew. It must have been him."

Maybe she'd been wrong about him. She hadn't always been the perfect judge of character, had she?

"Do you want to go home for the day, Ann?"

Ann shook her head. "No. I'll stick it out."

"That's it, Ann." Denise patted her on the back. "Tits out, two fingers up. Anyway, we'd best get on with it. Something tells me it's going to be a busy day. I'll double your tips if you keep shouting 'Where's my baby?' from the back kitchen."

The two were in such hysterics that they didn't hear the door open, nor see who was standing there watching them buckled over the counter holding their stomachs. It was Denise who turned first, instantly straightening and smiling broadly. Denise nudged Ann in the ribs and Ann looked up at Denise, who was gesticulating wildly towards the door with her head.

"Ann, I came as soon as I heard."

CHAPTER TWENTY-THREE

Ann could scream! The downright cheek of him, standing there with a great big stupid grin on his face, staring at her.

"I came as soon as I heard." What the hell did that mean? Heard what? Ann propelled herself towards home.

"What?" she spat, brushing past two women standing outside the newsagents, who'd paused mid conversation to watch her agitated approach.

They'd probably heard all about her, too. Then again, perhaps they were simply staring at an unhinged woman, storming along the path, muttering away to herself.

Ann rounded the bend into the Estates, reaching into her pocket, when she heard her phone buzz. It was Denise. Ann waited for it to stop before stuffing it back in her pocket. Shit! She paused on the path as it dawned on her that she'd just stormed out of work and slapped a practical stranger and potential customer across the face. The reaction had come from nowhere. What was she thinking? Maybe she did need to take the day off, after all. She was clearly losing her marbles.

"I wanted to see if you were all right?" He reached out.

Ann looked down at his hand on her arm and then back at him, her insides quivering with rage.

"How could you? You promised." She stared at him

and then before she could stop herself, she reached up and slapped him hard across the face.

"Jesus," he gasped, his hand flying to his face.

"Don't," she said through gritted teeth. "Just don't."

Ann tugged at her apron awkwardly, wrestling with the ties before throwing it at the counter, grabbing her bag from the back of the chair and rushing out of the door, leaving both Denise and Mark staring after her.

"You must be Mark?" Denise raised her eyebrows.

"That's me." He rubbed his face.

"I tell you, Mark, there's only one sentiment that can spark a reaction like that. You know what they say?" Denise disappeared behind the counter for a moment before handing Mark a packet of peas from the freezer.

"What's that?" He rested the peas against his cheek.

"There's a fine line between love and hate."

Mark grinned back at her. "So what you're saying is, I have a chance?"

The fragmented episode churned around in Ann's mind as she continued up the road. What was it Denise said again? The residents of Knockmore House had called the local paper to see if they could find out more. Well, that made no sense. If Mark had told her story to anyone, surely it would be his parents? He didn't even live in Knockmore as far as she knew and the story wouldn't be of much interest to anyone outside town. Perhaps he'd told what he considered to be an intriguing story to a total stranger and it had somehow filtered back to Knockmore. Unlikely, Ann thought. Maybe she should have just asked him, instead of assaulting him in the middle of Tea and Sympathy.

Ann could still picture his shocked face. He'd looked

well, too – clean-shaven, smiling warmly at her. Well . . . until she'd hit him. Ann put her hand to her face, still able to smell his aftershave on her skin. How did she continually manage to attract awkward, weird situations, no matter how hard she tried not to?

"Do you know what you are?" Sophie told her last year after another discussion of the strange string of incidents that so far made up the life of Ann. "You're a calamity. No. Scrap that – you're a cal-Ann-ity. See what I did there?"

At that moment, Ann couldn't agree more. She was nothing more than a giant magnet for catastrophic situations.

Walking with her head down, she pushed open the little iron gate to her house, desperate to get inside and gather her thoughts.

"Oh, for fuck's sake," she muttered to herself upon seeing Tracy standing in her usual position under the little hooded porch, arms crossed smugly.

All Tracy was short of was a scarf knotted under her chin and a beige overcoat to complete the stereotypical vision of nosy neighbour. Instead, Tracy was wearing a pair of old grey tracksuit bottoms, a horrible old T-shirt that at one time must have been white, flip-flops and a thunderous expression. It confirmed Ann's theory that Tracy's mood was reflected by her appearance and today, it was *not* looking good.

Ann closed the gate, pretending not to notice her.

"Morning, Ann. Day off?"

"Yeah. Something like that."

Ann rooted in her pocket for her keys, to no avail. She must have put her keys down on the counter in work. Ann dropped her bag to the ground, bending over it to scrounge around, fiercely praying that the missing keys were hiding behind her purse, or tucked into her headphones, and she could escape inside.

"Lose something?" Tracy tilted her head to the side, her chewing gum making a clicking sound as she watched.

"My keys, it seems."

Ann stood and slung her bag over her shoulder, ready to slink back up the road, crawl in through the door of Tea and Sympathy, then tumble and roll under the counter to retrieve them unnoticed. She desperately hoped Mark had left by now, but knowing Denise, he was probably sitting at a table, eating a full Irish breakfast and taking advantage of the name of the cosy country café.

"Funny," Tracy smirked. "There's a lot that seems to go missing around here. Keys . . . reverends . . . babies . . ." Tracy paused as Ann looked up sharply.

"What did you just say?"

"You heard me."

Tracy came closer and rested both of her hands on the iron railing separating the two terraced houses. At that moment, Ann wished there was a twenty-foot wall made of barbed wire between her and her neighbour. It still wouldn't have been enough. Perhaps they could add a high-voltage electric fence.

"What *is* your problem?" Ann spat.

"I think you might be the one with all the problems." Tracy looked at her. "You have more issues than a magazine, by the sounds of it, Ann. Or is that even your real name? I think I have a right to know who I'm living beside. Don't you?"

"Whatever you heard, from wherever you heard it, you're mistaken. It's a stupid rumour and some nasty little lowlife made it all up."

"Is that right?" Tracy leaned closer. "It didn't sound made up to me."

"What the hell does that mean?"

"Well, I heard it straight from the horse's mouth, so to speak." Tracy grinned smugly.

"Oh? And who was that?"

"You, Ann. I heard it straight from your mouth. Stolen babies. Teenage pregnancies. You sent away at seventeen. It sounds like you'd quite the start in life."

Tracy looked so satisfied that Ann wanted to reach up and grab her by the throat.

"See, you caused quite the racket on Saturday night with your little garden party. Woke all the kids up – all four. But that seems to be you all over – selfish. Out for yourself."

Ann watched Tracy mount her soapbox.

"Anyway, I came out to tell you to shut the hell up, but instead, I happened upon quite the story. Didn't I?"

Ann stood frozen to the spot as it dawned on her who'd actually let the cat out of the bag. If she thought she'd been angry with Mark, it was nothing compared to this.

"It was you! You listened in and then you told everyone. How could you?"

"Well, nowadays you just don't know who you're living next door to, do you? And like I always say, there's no smoke without fire. A dodgy past leads to a dodgy future. I was scared for my children." Tracy pouted her lips, self-satisfied.

"Are you having a laugh? What does my mother's childhood have to do with the safety of your children?"

"I'll thank you for lowering your voice," Tracy said innocently. "You're troubled, Ann. At first, I thought you were just a snob. We all saw it that night we were out. I told the girls not to be so quick to judge you. I even convinced them to let you come to the next night out. I'd have invited you, too, if you'd opened the door to me, but no. No, Ann's hiding indoors.

"You were quick enough to judge me that night, weren't you? I did try to make you feel welcome, Ann, but you were having none of it. I mean, it's understandable, isn't it, with a past like that. A broken marriage. What else are you hiding? People around here have a right to know. I don't like secretive people and my children come first. You have to see that. I was concerned."

Ann guffawed sarcastically. "Concerned for your children? Really? You're not the only one who overhears things, Tracy."

Tracy took a step back and narrowed her eyes.

"Yes. I've heard plenty of your little chit-chats outside my window telling anyone who'll listen what a curse the four boys are – four boys, four kids. Oh, the four are terrible . . . Well, I have the four. If I had my time again . . . Four, four, four," Ann mimicked Tracy. "And cursing at them like a banshee, all day, every day. Maybe people would like to hear that, too."

"How dare you!" You could almost see the steam coming from Tracy's ears.

"No. How dare you!" Ann pointed at her. "For your information, I had the worst year of my life last year. My whole world tumbled apart. And you know what, Tracy? All you wanted was the gossip from me.

"I clocked you straightaway. That's why I backed away from you. You had no real interest in me. Thank you for the kind invitation to girls' night, where you dumped me as soon as we got in the door, tried to make a fool of me and then called me a drip as I left. I could have plenty to say about you, Tracy, but do you think I went around gossiping about my next-door neighbour? Do you think I spread all over Knockmore what I overheard you saying? No. I kept myself to myself."

"You stupid bitch. You've no idea what it's like, how hard I work. How dare you judge me. I do *everything* for them. Sacrifice every piece of myself. And you, swanning about in your designer shoes and a house to yourself . . . Well, you wouldn't know how hard it is to be a mother." Tracy's hands were flying everywhere. "They just kept coming. After the two, I swore . . . and then the third came, and then the fourth and . . . how dare you. How *dare* you!"

"I can judge you as much as I like, just like you can judge me, Tracy. But the difference between us is I keep my opinions to myself. If you wanted to find out the truth of what you overheard, you could have just knocked on my door. And if you wanted to stop having kids, you should have walked around dressed as a giant human condom," Ann shouted, stopping when she saw a little pair of eyes materialise from behind Tracy's legs.

"Oh, shit. Tracy, I'm sorry. I didn't mean . . ."

Tracy bent down and scooped him up, tears freely flowing down her face. She turned on her heel and slammed the door, leaving Ann standing there, looking up at the sky, silently cursing before sinking onto the front doorstep, curling her knees up and resting her head down. What was happening to her? She'd never have spoken to anyone like that before. How could everything go from being so amazing to utterly terrible in the space of a few days?

"Ann?"

She was almost afraid to look up.

"Ann?"

Ann raised her head to peer over her arms like a frightened child. He was outside the gate, standing with his hands tucked into the pockets of his jeans, his shoulders hunched over unsurely. There was no smile this time, just a look of concern. Ann lifted her head a little more as her face crumpled like paper and she started to sob.

Mark was with her in seconds.

She wondered afterwards if he'd jumped the gate. He put out his hand and she reached up to take it, allowing him to pull her to standing. Searching his eyes, she allowed herself to fold into his arms, feeling them circle her.

"I . . . I'm . . . I don't . . . I . . ." The words wouldn't form.

"Are you okay?" he whispered, resting his cheek on her head. "I didn't tell anyone. I'd never do that."

It felt so natural to be in his arms, as if she'd always known him.

"I know. I'm sorry. I thought it was you. I hit you. I'm so sorry," Ann said into his chest, enjoying being held, realising it was what she'd been craving for so long.

"It's okay. I brought your keys," he told her. "Denise gave them to me, told me where to come. She also gave me a bag of frozen peas for my face and an extraordinarily terrible coffee," he mused.

"It's bad, isn't it?" Ann looked up at him. "Hi, again. It's been a while."

"A year? But who's counting." Mark was smiling down at her, one side of his mouth lifted a little higher than the other. "I didn't think I'd see you again."

"Here I am. In all my glory."

"So you're back here, in Knockmore?" He wiped the tears from her face.

"Yeah. A fat lot of good it's done me." She rolled her eyes. "Still lost."

"If I'd known . . ."

Ann took the keys from his hand. Releasing herself from his arms, she turned and unlocked the door before looking back at him behind moist eyes.

"Do you want to come in?"

CHAPTER TWENTY-FOUR

Mark

The evening sun poured through the slatted blinds, casting little shadows along her skin. Mark ran his fingers along them, tracing them up and down Ann's back. She shivered, yawned and turned her head to look at him. He was leaning up on one elbow, the sheet wrapped around his waist. Ann rolled onto her side to face him.

"Hi," she whispered, her arm discreetly covering her breasts. "What time is it?" she asked, looking confused.

Her hair had tumbled over her face and he reached over to brush it away gently before looking at his watch.

"It's four thirty."

"What?" She shot up quickly. "How did that happen? I have to call Denise. She'll be worried sick."

Ann tugged at the sheet, pulling it away from him and wrapping it around herself, leaving Mark naked, feeling exposed in more way than one. He reached down and grabbed his boxer shorts off the floor, quickly pulled them on. Ann left the room and he lay back, feeling awkward, putting his hands behind his head, unsure what to do next. Maybe this is what all those girls from his past always complained about.

"I never know where I stand with you. It's like I'm the one waiting on instructions of what to do next," they'd reveal after Mark finally called it a day with them, unable to hide his disinterest any longer.

Now, for the first time, it was Mark not knowing what to do next.

He moved his hand from his neck down his chest and tucked it into the top of his shorts. Maybe he should get dressed – although, he was still hoping she might return, climb back into bed and wrap herself around him as she had earlier.

Mark closed his eyes. It felt different being with Ann, at last. There were none of the usual feelings as though he were being strangled by a boa constrictor, attempting to squeeze him to death and consume him. Instead, it was he who couldn't get close enough to her, wanting his skin to mesh with hers, securing them together, making it impossible for them to separate. It was incredible. *She* was incredible.

Mark never imagined for a moment, when he received the frantic phone call from his mother on Monday afternoon, that by the next day, he'd be in the bed of the woman who'd monopolised his thoughts for the last year. He almost hadn't answered the call, pressing "decline" on the screen, resulting in his mother calling back three times before he excused himself from his meeting.

"Mother, this really isn't a good time," he said brusquely into the phone, stepping into the foyer. He'd been trying to secure a meeting for months with Wicklow County Council regarding an upcoming project. "Is everything okay? Is Dad okay?"

"Yes. Fine. Fine. You won't believe it," Olive began.

Mark listened, expecting some new idea for the refurbishment that required him to drop everything and leap into the car. Instead, his eyes widened as his mother revealed what she'd overheard while lurking near a bucket of rare blue hydrangeas in the local florist.

"Are you there, Mark? Did you hear me?"

"Yes. Fascinating, Mother." Mark feigned disinterest.

"Well, obviously I called the local papers immediately to—"

"You did *what*?" Mark interrupted Olive's steady flow.

His mother's voice often reminded him of one continuous droning sound. He rarely interrupted, having discovered that the quickest way was to allow her to run out of breath and slowly wind down.

"Well, apparently, she lives right here in the town – the girl. Ann, I think they said her name is. Is that not the plainest, god-awful name you've ever heard? Shouldn't she be called something far more interesting like Gwendovere? Anyway, the *Knockmore Times* said they were going to investigate. Said this might be the biggest story to break in Knockmore since they found the dead cow in the reservoir. How a cow could climb a reservoir wall is beyond me."

"I think Ann's a nice name," Mark said without thinking.

"Don't be ridiculous, Mark. There are hardly enough letters in it to make it an actual word. It's more an article."

"Mother, why are you talking about grammar? Where did you say she lived?"

"Here, in Knockmore. Moved back a while ago. She works in Tea and Sympathy – that terrible place on the main street, with the sticky oil cloths instead of actual tablecloths. Imagine having a food emporium connected to a funeral home! Just doesn't seem right. Unsanitary. I'd say they keep the cheese slices in the fridge, next to a corpse."

"Tea and Sympathy?"

"Yes, Mark. Why are you repeating everything I say? And what do you think of the connection to Knockmore

House? Isn't it fascinating? A historical house filled with secrets and lies. It's like that wonderful television show *Downton Abbey*."

Mark groaned. He had a feeling his mother was going to grab on tight to this snippet of information and not let go.

"I have to go, Mother." He disconnected the call and loosened his tie, which had suddenly become tighter. The Olive effect.

After the meeting, Mark drove straight back to Wicklow, not bothering to return to the site to check on the lads. Sitting in his armchair, alone at home, a six-pack of beer on the table beside him, Mark wrestled with what to do. He didn't know Ann, much as she filled his thoughts like some teenage infatuation. Mark could go for weeks pushing her out of his mind and then something would spark it again, making him wonder if there was, in fact, one second that went by when she wasn't in some way on his mind. Sometimes he'd wake thinking of her, close his eyes and think of her – dream of her. Her face. Her smile. Her story. The sadness behind those blue eyes. When he saw her last week from the window of the study, his heart had almost burst.

Mark realised, even without really knowing Ann, that she'd be devasted being the victim of gossip, which his mother had gone and thrown a bucket of fertiliser over by contacting the papers. But mostly, Mark knew, there was nothing he could do to release her from his mind until he saw her. Maybe there was a reason Ann had stumbled back into his life again, their paths destined to cross once more.

When he woke at dawn the next morning, still in the same chair as the night before, he knew wild horses weren't going to keep him away. His heart was hammering as he parked the car and walked towards Tea and Sympathy, watching her through the window: her back to him, her hair tumbling down her back. He couldn't help smiling as he saw them laughing together.

The other woman saw him first. When Ann turned, he'd held his breath. Her expression was sobering – and then the moment he'd imagined for so long stung his face . . .

"Sorry about that," Ann said now. "I just needed to call Denise."

Her phone was in one hand and she was leaning against the doorframe, still wrapped in the sheet. It was tied in a knot at the front, like a long white strapless gown. Her hair was tousled, her eye make-up slightly smudged under her eyes. Mark's stomach flipped.

"Mark . . . I . . ."

"Ann . . . I . . ."

They both spoke simultaneously and then laughed.

"You first." He swung his legs over the edge of the bed and ran his hands through his hair.

Ann sat down beside him, looking up at him unsurely.

"No. You first."

Mark wanted to put his arms around her, lie her back and kiss her. Earlier, in the heat of the moment, there had been no awkwardness, no questioning glances, no thought process. The passion between them was automatic. Ann had reached up, unexpectedly kissing him as soon as she shut the door. She did it with such fire that Mark had stumbled backwards over the little table in the hall.

Recovering fast, he'd put his arms around her waist and lifted her with ease. Instinctively, she'd wrapped her legs around his body, pressing herself against him.

"Upstairs," she'd whispered, her head falling back as he'd kissed her neck.

He'd carried her upstairs and laid her on the bed, peeling off her clothes as she grabbed at his belt. It was fast. It was passionate. And Mark knew he'd spend the rest of his life wanting more from her. It could never be enough for him.

Afterwards, she'd fallen asleep almost instantly. Mark had wanted to shake her awake, talk to her, but instead, he'd lain there, thinking about what he'd say when he had the chance.

How different it felt from all those times where he couldn't wait to pull his clothes back on and escape, using a work emergency as an excuse to bolt rather than having to make a plan with another girl he knew he'd never see again. For so long, he'd told himself that his life was complicated. For so long, he'd hidden behind his dysfunctional family, believing that he could never let someone in – until now.

Ann . . . I . . . I've thought about nothing else since I met you.

"That was incredible." It wasn't what he'd meant to say.

Ann was staring at the ground, her hair hanging down so she couldn't see his face. He'd ruined it.

"Ann, what I meant to say was . . ."

She stood and turned towards him. He waited for it. *You're so insensitive. Let me in, Mark. Show me the real you.*

Ann said nothing, her expression impossible to read, and he wanted to scream.

Slowly, she unknotted the sheet, letting it fall to the floor. Mark watched her, afraid to move, to shatter the moment. She stepped closer, straddling him, putting her hands on his chest and leaning back to look him in his eyes.

"So that you know, Mark. My life is an absolute mess. Worse than it was before." She pushed him back against the bed and kissed him.

"Mine, too," he whispered, nuzzling her neck. "Mine, too."

But she didn't hear.

CHAPTER TWENTY-FIVE

"Where the hell have you been?" Sophie's voice was frantic.

It was Friday evening and Ann was sitting on her bed with her legs crossed, cradling the phone between her ear and her shoulder. What she really wanted was to take a long shower, or indeed a bath, and not have to listen to Sophie's reprimands. Perhaps Liam, the handyman, had been right, after all, about the hasty removal of the relaxation vessel from her life. She was certainly regretting her decision to get rid of the bath. He had tried to warn her.

"I've been worried sick."

Ann let her rant, knowing deep down she'd been avoiding her all week, replying monosyllabically to Sophie's frantic messages.

"I was just about to get in the car and drive down there, only I called Ian and guess what? He said he spied you today walking through Knockmore with someone he described as a mix between Brad Pitt and Ryan Gosling. I said, 'Ian, you are *obviously* mistaken. First, this would never occur without my knowledge. Secondly, there's no way there's anyone in Knockmore, let alone Ireland, who resembles a mix between these two fine specimens.' I said if he *had* seen you, owing to your inconsiderate lack of contact, I hoped it was with a stereotypical Irish fella in full Gaelic football quick-dry kit, possibly a county jersey, complete with red fiery hair, transparent skin and more freckles than a tiffin cake."

"Well, I do love the GAA and come to think of it, he does look a little like Ryan Gosling. Brad Pitt's a stretch." Ann was trying not to laugh at Sophie's description of Hollywood actors in Knockmore, of all places.

"Then, Ian told me that Denise told him it was Mark!"

"You know, I've just discovered how small this small town is. Actually, Ireland is too bloody small. Maybe I'll use that flight and head to Australia, conveniently forget to book a return ticket home."

Ann was half enjoying torturing Sophie by being elusive after spending the last week feeling as if she'd been laid out on a glass slide under the Knockmore microscope and picked apart for everyone to examine.

"I'm going to reach down the phone and strangle you if you don't tell me what's going on," Sophie pleaded. "I was worried, but now I know you're alive and I'm not receiving text messages from your captors as you lie in a darkened cellar, tied to an old kitchen chair, I'm also ever so slightly annoyed with you. Now, spit it out."

Where to start? How could she explain that the last week had been one of the most frustrating and exhilarating weeks of her life?

"It is Mark," Ann said finally.

"The guy from Knockmore House? I knew it! I knew he was supposed to feature again somehow."

"Yes, Sophie. Right again."

"So, he lives there all along?"

"No. It's his parents' house and talking of which, I'm going to meet them there tomorrow."

"What? Meet the parents? Already? Okay. Back up the truck there. Start from the start."

"Okay."

Ann took a deep breath and told Sophie everything, from her paranoid run on Monday and her altercation with Tracy, to Mark turning up.

"So, it was that string-bean neighbour, hiding behind the fence earwigging? And she managed to broadcast it all over town quicker than a kid can spread Nutella on toast? Impressive." Sophie listened in awe. "And then Mark's mother overheard it in the florist."

"Uh-huh," Ann confirmed as Sophie worked it all out.

"And then the mother rang Mark. Mark put two and two together and turned up at Tea and Sympathy."

"Yep. You have it now, Sophie."

"You never told anyone?" Ann asked Mark after they'd made love a second time that first day and eventually got round to talking.

"No," he answered, leaning down to kiss her forehead. "I never mentioned it to anyone. I did think you'd call me, though," he told her, unable to hide his obvious disappointment.

"I'm sorry." Ann covered her eyes with her hands, pretending not to look at him. "After I found out the truth, I went back to Dublin and let's just say everything accelerated into high gear. I haven't had a moment to breathe since." She was facing him now, leaning up on one elbow.

"Did you come back to Knockmore straightaway?" he asked. "If I knew you were here all along, I'd have come sooner. It's mad to think that most weekends, we've been a few miles from each other. My mother's doing another refurbishment at the house. It'll be starting soon. I'll be here a lot."

"Really?" Ann sat up. "But it's so beautiful." She wasn't sure why the thought of Knockmore House changing was making her feel strange.

"Yeah. Not that it needs it, but—"

"I go running past the house a lot. I suppose I should have called in, but I never saw your car and . . . what?" she asked, noticing a smile creep across his face.

"Well, my mother . . . she spotted you outside the house a few times. She pointed you out to me last weekend. You were with another girl."

"Sophie," Ann said. "That was Sophie. She was down for my birthday. I wanted to show her the 'scene of the crime'. How did she notice me?" Ann asked, and then remembered the time she'd waved at the figure in the window and winced. "Oh, God, I think I waved at her one evening. I don't know what came over me. I suppose I have this odd connection to the house."

"She said you always stop and stare in as if you're trying to see what's going on inside."

Ann was embarrassed. "I didn't realise. She must think I'm crazy."

"If I'm honest, she's a bit crazy herself," he half laughed.

"Yes, but someone staring in through the windows? She must have been terrified. I don't know what it is about that house. I can't explain it. Even though it's where my mam was most unhappy, I feel this powerful link to her whenever I'm near it."

Mark watched her as she spoke, trying to find the words to tell her that he knew exactly how she felt, that every time he set foot over the threshold of Knockmore House, all he could think about was Ann.

"Maybe you *are* linked to the house in some way. Like

it's in your blood. I mean, wasn't your mother pregnant with you in that house? In a way, it was the first place you ever lived."

"I suppose." She'd never thought of it that way before. "Please tell your mam sorry from me. I didn't mean to frighten her."

Ann looked so worried that Mark almost laughed. His mum hadn't been frightened, she'd been nervous, but he could never tell Ann that.

"Don't worry about her."

He could have stayed here with her forever – inside their own little bubble, where no one could reach them. He wanted to know everything about her, couldn't ask everything quick enough, but he was also terrified of scaring her away, as he himself had been so many times before. It was almost laughable how the shoe was now on the other foot.

"Can I ask you a favour?"

"Anything," he nodded, hoping she was going to ask him to walk away from his life and join her in a bed-in like John Lennon and Yoko Ono.

"Can you please ask your mother to contact the *Knockmore Times* and call off the investigation?"

"Well, apparently, it's the biggest story since the dead cow in the reservoir," Mark laughed.

Despite herself, Ann smiled back. "I bet it is. Way bigger than that cow. The funny thing is, I remember that. I was about thirteen when it happened," she giggled.

"Are you there, Sophie?" Ann said now, stopping mid flow, sure that she hadn't heard any breathing for at least a few minutes.

"Holy shit! Like *what the actual*—"

"Wait. Let me finish." Ann went on to explain that Mark had spoken to his mother and been forced to reveal that he'd met Ann last year in Knockmore, and that he'd known the story all along.

"And what did she say?"

"Well, she couldn't believe it. She instantly called the paper and said that it had all been a hoax, a rumour started by a jealous neighbour."

"Well, she was right about that," Sophie tutted. "What a weapon that Tracy one is."

"I don't know, Sophie. I think I had her wrong. I'm going to call in on her and make amends. She shouldn't have gossiped, but I think it was a misdirected cry for help. Maybe she's just lonely, too."

Ann still felt terrible for the way she'd spoken to Tracy. Maybe Tracy *had* been offering Ann a lifeline all along and Ann had snubbed her.

"Now stop that, Ann. Don't you go forgetting what that wagon did."

"Yeah, maybe. Anyway, it turns out Mark's mother seems to be a little more discreet. At least I hope so. She wants to meet me. On Sunday."

"Really? And you *are* going?"

"Well, yeah."

Sophie said nothing.

"Sophie? You there?"

"Yeah. I'm here. Don't you think it's all a bit fast, Ann? This time last week we were celebrating your birthday and now, suddenly, you appear to be trapped inside a soap opera, and not even a good one. Like a cheap one they make on one of those Irish channels that no one watches except when teenagers fail their Irish exam and their parents force them to."

"Come on, Sophie. It's not that dramatic. Don't be giving out to me – it's been a rough week."

Ann closed her eyes and bit her lip. It hadn't *all* been rough. More than a few times, Ann had felt on top of the world, or at least on top of Mark, wondering how this incredibly handsome man had sauntered back into her life when she least expected it.

"Ann, in the space of one week, you're the subject of small-town gossip. You appear to have found a live-in boyfriend. You're going to meet his parents on Sunday, in the house where your mother was the victim of abuse. And you seem to have forgotten to go to work. This is *not* normal Ann-like behaviour. This is Sophie-like behaviour."

"Sophie, you're blowing it all out of proportion. He's *not* my boyfriend. I like him. But he's not my boyfriend. He's not living in. He's not even here."

Ann heard the front door close and listened as he climbed the stairs.

"Food is downstairs," Mark whispered. "Come down when you're finished." He gestured at the phone.

Ann held her hand over the receiver until he'd gone.

"Denise gave me the week off work as the place was literally full to the brim with everyone trying to get a piece of the action. I'm meeting his parents to try to stop her from talking to anyone about the story."

Ann felt terrible for lying to Sophie. Mark *had* stayed all week – leaving early for work each morning, returning as soon as he could. She knew it was insane, but she couldn't help herself. He knew all the things about her that she'd struggle to tell anyone else.

"You know, he was there that night in Lennon's with his dad. We figured it out afterwards."

"Oh, God, a stalker. Did he hear you sing?"

"No. He was in the bar, not the lounge where we were. Strange, though, isn't it? You said something was about to happen to me and it did."

Discovering that Mark had been there in Lennon's the night Ann sang on stage had surprised her, making her wish that it had been Mark she'd encountered that night, and not the stranger at the bar.

"I'm not sure I meant all this." Sophie was struggling to see the connection. "It's just not like you, Ann, to rush into something head first. It usually takes you months and months to be yourself around anyone. That's what's great about you. It just seems odd that after a few minutes, you and this Mark are wrapped around each other, in bed! Do you even *like* him? Or are you lonely?"

Ann got up and shut the door, starting to feel irritated, not wanting to answer the question that she'd already asked herself.

"Sophie, you keep telling me to live, so I am. And now it's too much? I'm sorry I didn't call you all week, but please don't give me a hard time. Yes. I do like him. I feel at ease with him. That's got to be good, right?" Ann asked, catching a glimpse of doubt in her eyes reflected in the mirror and then looking away.

Wasn't a sense of ease with another person what everyone wanted? Great sex and ease?

"Hmm. We'll see."

Ann walked downstairs into the kitchen, where Mark had a Chinese takeaway on the table, a bottle of wine, and two candles lit.

"Dinner is served."

Right now, Ann felt like she was doing exactly what she should be. What thousands of other women like her were probably doing – enjoying a cosy night in. For once, she wasn't alone.

Ann pushed the niggling feeling that she'd stumbled into a happy relationship with a man she hardly knew to the back of her mind. Mark was different, wasn't he? He was the total opposite of Dom, for a start. Happy to be in her company, dressed in slippers, drinking cheap bottles of wine instead of parading her through town like a show pony. Here, she was more like the donkey and cart from her neighbour's garden down the road and for some odd reason, that felt right.

"You know what they say – if they're perfect on paper, chances are they have a car boot full of rope and a portable shovel as a key ring," Sophie always said.

But Sophie wasn't always right. The same Sophie had encouraged her to take a leap of faith, open herself up to the universe. Ann couldn't win. She was tired of considering everything in minute detail. Just for once, Ann didn't want to ponder if this was the right thing, if Mark was exactly the person she needed in her life right now – she wanted to *feel*.

"What did you say his mother's name was again?" Sophie had asked before hanging up.

"It's Olive. Olive Dempsey."

"Well, now. That name sounds like a mouthful of trouble."

CHAPTER TWENTY-SIX

Olive paced the floor, backwards and forwards. Everything was ready. Surprising, she mused, experiencing a little fizz of excitement, how the mundanity of everyday life can be unexpectedly, and pleasantly, interrupted. She looked in the mirror one last time, admiring her outfit selection: monochrome, sombre enough to bear witness to this Ann's story without being too morbid. It was precisely what she should be wearing to make a good impression when meeting her son's love interest.

"I've never seen him like this before," she'd whispered to Eugene after her son's visit during the week.

Olive had just sat down, carefully removing her shoes, when she heard the gravel crunch in the driveway. Rolling her eyes, she reached down to put the dreaded shoes back on – the thought of it almost brought tears to her eyes. Having worn sensible shoes all her life, she was somewhat blessed to have arrived at her age without the usual curled-up toes and bunions that may have been acquired by attempting to squeeze her feet into more fashionable shoes in her youth. Still, she was in her sixties and there was only so far one could walk in pointed blush suede slingbacks.

The shoes pinched her heels as she stood up to peer round the shutters of the bay window. For a moment, she held her breath, a fleeting sensation of impending doom jolting her, before exhaling slowly when she saw Mark standing there.

Even dressed the way he was, like a ten-year-old boy, wearing a grubby old pair of shorts and a T-shirt that looked like they'd been slept in, he looked handsome. No matter how old they got, they'd always seem like children – running to her with a grazed knee, a wobbly tooth, a splinter or something far worse. When they were small, their problems had been easy to fix. It was later they became harder to solve, the blunders more significant.

"You have to let them make mistakes, learn from them," Eugene used to say.

Shame her husband hadn't heeded his own advice. No. They were her children. Their business was hers – always would be, no matter how much Jessica called her overbearing, interfering, smothering. Mark never minded his mother trying to help him out. Then again, he'd always been more manageable. If Olive had been any of those things, it was for their benefit. You do what you have to do for your children. It's just that some take it better than others.

"You've always preferred him," Jessica would say. "Always."

Even if it were true, she could never admit it. It was the number one cardinal sin of parenting, to acknowledge that you preferred one over the other – even if you did.

She hadn't heard from Mark since they spoke on Monday. He'd been abrupt, wholly disinterested in her discovery about the house. Taking matters into her own hands, she'd walked into town again yesterday, talked to a few shop owners on the main street. They, too, were dismissive when she'd quizzed them on the local gossip doing the rounds until, of course, she revealed that she was the current owner of Knockmore House. The man in the fruit and veg shop had been most accommodating after that.

"I went up toward de café meself to have a schnoop about," he'd told her, dragging out his syllables. Olive couldn't make head nor tail of what he was saying with his Knockmore drawl. "But Den-ishhe told me if I wasn't goin' ta spend de mini-mum charge and if I were only der ta gawk, to get de hell outta her schop, unless I wanted to end up in one of dem coffins out da back," he said. "De girl's not der anyways. If I were you, I wouldn't bodder."

Olive had arrived home deflated. Eugene had no interest, either. And Jessica . . . well, all Olive could expect from her was a grunt, or having something thrown at her head.

"Well, this is a surprise, darling," Olive called to him from the front steps. "To what do I owe the honour? I assume you're not going to insult my intelligence and say you were passing."

"Hi, Mum. I was sort of passing," he lied before checking himself. "Actually, no. I wanted to speak to you, if I could. Dad, too."

"Is it about the refurbishment? I've told you, Mark, it's going ahead with or without your help. I was thinking of tiling the hall. The wooden floors are so marked. What do you think about going back to the original black-and-white tiles? Far more in keeping with the era of the house and it'll contrast the modern additions."

"No, I mean, yes. Tiles sound perfect. It's not about the house. Where's Jessica?" he asked, looking over his mother's shoulder. "I suppose she should be here, too."

"Really?" Olive looked confused. "Whatever for?"

"She *is* a part of this family, Mother. Perhaps if we include her and treat her normally, she might start acting a bit more normal." He wasn't in the mood for secrecy and games, keen to get this over with and straight back to Ann.

Mark sat opposite them in the living room.

"Get on with it, will you? Are you gay or something?" It was Jessica who broke the silence.

"No, Jessica. I'm not gay. I have met someone, though."

They stared at him blankly.

"Well, only very recently. And I wouldn't even be telling you, except Mum rang me on Monday with some news about the supposed history of Knockmore House and well, how can I put it? The two are linked."

"What *are* you on about, Mark?" His mother sat forwards on the sofa. "What do you mean, linked? Are you talking about this Ann person?"

"Who's Ann?" his father asked.

"Oh, for God's sake." Olive turned to look at him sharply. "I told you what I'd heard in the florist."

"Who the hell is Ann?" Jessica looked bored.

"Okay. Let me start at the beginning. You remember last year when you were in France and, Jessica, you were back in Wicklow, and I ended up staying here for a few nights?"

"Yes," his mother nodded.

"No." His Father shook his head.

"Did you?" Jessica asked.

"Oh, Christ, just listen, will you? So I met this girl . . ."

He began the story, watching their confused faces as he relayed it.

"The stolen baby!" his mother interrupted halfway through.

"Well, yes. It was Ann's mother."

"Who's the mother? Do we know the mother?" Eugene looked even more perplexed.

"Oh, keep up, Eugene," Olive tutted. "Go on, Mark. Continue."

It took Mark several attempts to relay the story before they finally started to comprehend.

"Didn't I tell you, Eugene? Didn't I say there was something about this house? It's like a novel."

"Yes, Mother. It *is* like a novel, but here's the thing. It's not. It's Ann's life. So I'm asking you, can you please contact the papers and put a halt to this whole thing. Please?"

Olive watched him for a moment before replying. Her son was positively glowing.

"Of course. Of course," his mother agreed, registering the look of relief sweep his face. "On one condition. We must meet the girl. She must be a part of Knockmore House. Don't you think, Eugene?" Olive issued Eugene a jab in the ribs.

"Why?" Eugene looked back at Olive. "Yes, I suppose," he corrected when he saw her face.

"Well, it's settled. Bring the girl on Sunday. Is Ann short for anything? I wonder. Maybe Annabelle, Annemarie?"

"No. It's just Ann."

"Disappointing. Well, Anna will have to do."

"Just Ann, Mother, just Ann. And it was her – the girl you saw outside. That was Ann. She said to say sorry if she frightened you. She was just looking at the house, I suppose. It's a big part of her past."

Olive looked out of the window again, awaiting their arrival. It felt good to be anticipating something positive for a change, something that she could assist in, give a gentle push in the right direction if needed. The way Mark spoke about this Ann was thrilling, absolutely thrilling. And it was a huge relief to learn that the girl who'd been peering in at her was Ann and not another surprise guest from her husband's past. From what Olive had already seen from the window, the girl looked remarkably pleasing to the eye. Olive hoped that up close, Ann wouldn't have any significant facial anomalies, at least not ones that couldn't be corrected.

She wondered if the orangery would be ready for next spring. She'd be sure to tell Ann about it all, suddenly positive she could hear wedding bells chiming – and what better location for a wedding? Olive had been right to insist on the large conservatory. It was as if the house was guiding her, whispering instructions to Olive, somehow, and beckoning Ann home. It was magical. It was an opportunity to rectify mistakes.

"Stop the car!"

"You okay?" Mark glanced at Ann nervously before doing as instructed and pulling over to the side of the road, jamming on the brakes.

"I just need a minute."

Ann rolled down the window and stuck her arm out, attempting to scoop air into her hand and waft it towards her face, the dead heat of the July day offering no respite from the feeling of panic. Mark watched as she fanned her face.

"I think I'm going to be sick," she whispered beneath anxious eyes.

"Stop that." He put his hand on her knee reassuringly and gave it a gentle squeeze. "It'll be fine. It's just a casual dinner. They're looking forward to meeting you."

"Just a casual dinner," Ann repeated, nodding like a child. "Anything I need to know? Anything at all? Any topics of conversation out of bounds?" she quizzed.

"No, not much out of bounds."

Mark wondered if he should warn her that she was about to set foot into one of the most complicated families on Earth. Perhaps she wouldn't notice. Maybe they were more reasonable than he imagined.

"Give me a visual," Ann pressed. "What does she look like? Your mother?"

"Well," he began, trying to muster an appropriate description of someone whose face hardly moved, whose hair was so fixed with hairspray that a naked flame next to her could wipe out an entire village and who was so uptight that she made a poker look relaxed.

"She's tiny. Blonde. Neat."

"Okay. Tiny is good. Tiny I can manage." Ann nodded along. "And your sister?"

Oh, Christ. There wasn't enough time to explain.

"There are some mental health issues," Mark admitted. "Mum and Dad are taking her to Spain in a few weeks while the house is being done up. Maybe a change of scene will do her good."

This time, it was Ann's turn to place her hand on his leg.

"There's still so much we don't know about each other, isn't there? It's been a bit of a whirlwind."

"You can say that again. But a good one," he reassured.

Ann suddenly sat up straighter. "Actually, Mark. There's something I need to tell you." It wasn't that she'd decided not to tell him, it just somehow hadn't come up. "I think maybe you should know before . . ." She paused when he reached over to stroke her face gently.

"Whatever it is, it can wait. Let's just get this over with so I can have you to myself again later."

Despite her nerves, Ann's stomach fluttered deliciously as Mark started the car and pulled back out onto the road, up the hill towards the gates of what was once her mother's childhood home.

As they drove through the granite gateposts, Ann suddenly felt as if she'd been transported into her mother's body. It was impossible not to picture Felicity coming through this same gate as a girl, many moons ago, where unspeakable heartache awaited her.

"It's just a house. It's just a house," Ann repeated to herself, closing her eyes briefly before opening them and trying to picture it with fresh eyes.

It *was* stunning. There was no denying it. Almost perfect. The house had retained many of the original features, making it practically impossible to tell what era they were in. The sash windows were pulled down to allow the afternoon breeze to filter through. The trellis either side of the front door was in full bloom, supporting substantial pink flowers. If Ann didn't know better, they could have been sweeping up the driveway in the 1800s.

Ann smiled at Mark, delighted, at last, to be able to appreciate the beauty of Knockmore House rather than fear it. Glancing back at the front door, Ann watched it slowly open, half expecting a woman in full skirts and a bonnet to emerge, waving a white satin glove at them. Instead, Ann caught her first glimpse of Olive.

The spell was broken.

CHAPTER TWENTY-SEVEN

Perched on the top of the three steps was the tiniest person Ann had ever seen, with an immense presence. She was standing motionless, freeze-framed except for the sway of her skirt – white pleated chiffon that fell to the ground, decorated with black polka dots and cinched at the waist by a thick elastic waistband. Underneath the sheer material, Olive wore fitted black trousers to her ankles, complete with silver strappy sandals. In contrast, on top, she wore the plainest black scoop-neck fitted top, her full chest decorated with the most delicate gold chains. The outfit was surprisingly fashion-forward for a woman of her age, reminding Ann of something Sophie might wear. Olive's hair was neat, bobbed, very blonde, unmoving – like her face.

Mark, too, had seen his mother materialise and knew they were about to witness the performance of the year.

"I think I may be underdressed." Ann looked down at her simple blue wrap sundress and flat shoes, feeling dowdy in comparison to the apparition on the steps.

Mark turned to look at her. "You look beautiful."

He'd watched her earlier, coming down the stairs: her hair loose, her face clean, very little make-up needed to enhance what was already there, wearing a blue dress that made him feel like he was floating on a cloud, in the bluest sky.

Mark squeezed her hand briefly, jumped out of the car and ran round to open the door for her.

"This is *not* a trial." He kissed her lightly on the lips and led her towards the steps.

On this occasion, Olive chose not to descend the steps. Instead, she stood with her hands clasped together, observing their advance. What a handsome pair. They reminded Olive of a couple in Saint-Tropez, in the south of France – expensively dressed. Not that she'd ever been to St Tropez, but they were precisely who Olive might expect to see there. They looked understated. Yes, that was the word – demonstrating an air of confidence that comes from breeding, money, wealth. Such was the visual compatibility that Olive felt sure her son and this girl were born to be together.

A frisson of excitement ran up her spine and if her face had allowed, she might have beamed at them, sure she was witnessing the beginning of a fairy tale. Instead, she smiled stiffly, the corners of her mouth barely lifting, concealing the euphoria that bubbled under the surface.

"Darlings," she sang, offering them each a hand.

Mark moved forwards first, kissing her on the cheek, while Ann stood back a little, trying to take it all in.

It was enough that Ann was about to be back in Knockmore House, without the added pressure of meeting her lover's family. Is that what they were? Lovers? It was a word usually reserved for dalliances outside marriage or French people. Partners? No. Ann hated that word. That was for older people. Boyfriend? Surely not. She wasn't ready for that label.

"You must be Mark's girlfriend." Olive smiled sweetly, but it looked as if she'd just got a taste of something intensely bitter. "Let me look at you." Olive held Ann's hands at arm's length. Her eyes travelled unashamedly over Ann. "Max Mara? Am I right?" Olive raised her thinly pencilled brows, nodding at the blue dress with a forced tinkly laugh.

"Eh, yes I think so," Ann answered unsurely, having no idea where the dress was from or who Max Mara was. "Mrs Dempsey. It's lovely to meet you."

Olive folded Ann into her thin arms, forcing Ann to bend down. Their height difference left a gaping expanse between them, making it look like they were forming a human bridge rather than sharing a first embrace.

"Please, call me Olive. Mrs Dempsey was my mother-in-law and that's not something I care to repeat," she chimed, pushing the front door open and leading them inside. "Well, here it is." Olive splayed her arms outwards as if revealing the top prize on a game show. "But a little birdy tells me you've already been here. Naughty, naughty. Isn't that right, Mark?"

Ann's gaze followed Olive's hands. Once again, she tried to picture it through her mother's eyes – the winding staircase leading to the gallery above, the chandelier, the parlour door to her right, the kitchen to the left, the dining room. Ann looked at the parquet wooden floors and then back at the front door, which was still open, revealing the granite steps.

"Ann? Are you all right?" Mark was at her side.

"Yes. Yes. I'm so sorry. I just . . . I'm . . . it's beautiful," Ann stammered, trying to block out the stories Lucie had told her about her mother's life here.

"Isn't it just? Mind you," Olive said, not noticing Ann's face, "we've barely scratched the surface. We're about to do a *huge* job on the house. Bring it bang into the future, if you please, erase the past."

Ann glanced at Mark, who shrugged.

"Yes, Mark told me. I think it's lovely how it is. Sometimes I think certain things should be left as they are."

Olive looked puzzled. "Now now, Ann. Everything can be improved. And that's not the talk of a developer's girlfriend. Developers develop, I always say."

Ann ignored the girlfriend label again, which was beginning to make her feel uncomfortable.

"It all looks brand-new to me," Ann answered. "I love the doors." Ann touched the porcelain handle of the study door, noticing the floral design and the small cracks in the creamy ceramic.

"All that will be gone soon," Olive continued. "We're going open-plan at the back of the house and underfloor heating, of course. And they say these old houses can't be heated. We'll show them. Isn't that right, Mark?"

"Sorry," Mark mouthed to her, shrugging again at what Ann anticipated would be the second of approximately eighty shrugs by the end of the day.

"Now, I imagine this might all be a little overwhelming for you, dear, being back here. Mark told me the history of the house – your mother's history, might I add. We can't wait to hear it straight from a direct source. Come, let's have a drink and I can show you where the orangery will go."

Ann didn't bother looking at Mark, whose shoulders were probably in overdrive. Instead, she followed Olive through the drawing room and out onto the soon-to-be-demolished patio, where Eugene and Jessica were sitting on rattan furniture, puffed up with cream cushions under a vast umbrella.

Ann warmed to Eugene instantly, who immediately got up and hobbled towards her.

"A friend of Mark's is a friend of mine." He shook her hand firmly. "Mark tells me you've had a right old trot of it, girl. I'm truly sorry for your loss and I hope it's not too hard to be here. You know, my old man used to say that houses are just bricks and mortar. It's the people who make a home," he smiled broadly.

"I couldn't agree more," Ann smiled back, suddenly relaxing.

"This is Jessica . . ." Eugene gestured towards her.

"Hi," Jessica mouthed quietly.

"It's nice to meet you, Jessica. You have the prettiest hair," Ann said.

Jessica touched her hair and ran her fingers down the length of it, dragging it down over her features, moving over to allow Ann to sit down.

"Isn't Mark's girlfriend's dress lovely, Jessica?" Olive said, not looking at Jessica and turning to Ann. "I did tell her to change but, seemingly, shorts and a vest with no bra is acceptable for guests."

Ann turned to Jessica, who was crossing her arms self-consciously.

"I hate bras, too," Ann whispered. "If I could, I wouldn't bother."

Jessica's eyes glinted briefly as Ann accepted a glass of prosecco from Mark.

"We've so much to ask you. Isn't that right, Eugene?" Olive smirked, crossing her legs, twisting them behind her.

"Do we?" Eugene asked.

Olive erupted with explosive laughter and hit his leg playfully. Eugene flinched.

"Of course we do. What a story! Have you reported your findings to the authorities? Have you tried to locate those involved? Perhaps you have family out there you don't even know about."

Ann took a breath. She'd been expecting curiosity, but this felt like a formal inquisition.

"Well," she began. "To answer everything. No. I haven't reported it. It was forty-seven years ago now and most of the people – in fact, all of the people involved – are no longer alive. As for family out there, I have an aunt in Australia and that's it."

"Yes. Leah, isn't it?" Olive waved her hand like the teacher's pet.

"No. It's Lucie. Lucie is my family and as for my mother's 'real' family . . ." Ann made air quotes. "Well, apparently, it was just them and all three are dead. My 'real' great-grandparents and my 'real' grandmother." Ann paused, satisfied she'd answered everything.

"What about the reverend? I have an amount of sympathy for him," Olive persisted, leaning forwards so her breasts were squeezed together, swallowing all of her gold chains and reminding Ann of someone's backside. "After Mark told me the story, I jotted it down so I wouldn't forget anything. But there was minimal mention of what happened to the reverend, aside from the letter he left." Olive's face was fixed in concentration.

"Well, I did think about him," Ann started again, trying to remain poised. "If, and it's a big if, he's still alive, he'll be around eighty-three now and maybe he's happy to leave the past in the past. Besides—"

"But don't you think he has a right to know that Felicity's dead and you're here in Knockmore? Don't you think—"

Olive was so far forward in the chair, Ann wasn't sure how she was still sitting.

"Olive," Eugene coughed. "That's enough."

"And the Catholic Church, should they not be held accountable in some way? I mean, you read about—"

"Olive!"

Olive held up her hands in defeat, sticking out her lower lip, taken aback by Eugene's sharpness.

"It's okay, Olive," Ann said, feeling braver, thinking of Lucie and how she'd probably be on top of Olive by now, wrestling her to the ground. "We haven't fully decided what to do. The truth is, nothing will bring back my parents. Nothing will change what happened to my mother in *this* house and nothing will ever make this anyone else's business but my own.

"I'm a private person and I like it that way. I came here today to ask you to respect that. I understand that Knockmore House is now yours, but the story that took place in it is solely mine and I'd very much like to keep it that way," Ann finished, her face puce from exertion.

There was a moment's silence, during which all four faces stared at her, before Eugene started applauding and Jessica let out a hysterical laugh.

"Well, then." Olive clapped her hands together, nonplussed. "Then I suppose we are linked, oddly. All a part of this wonderful house – soon to be even better. Come, let me show you what I intend to do with the kitchen. Now, I know that most people would want to have stuffy old wooden cupboards but, surprisingly, I'm thinking high-gloss . . ."

It was everything Ann hated: shiny, glossy, falseness. It was everything she'd left behind in Dublin.

CHAPTER TWENTY-EIGHT

It was too hot to sleep, even if he could have. Mark pushed back the covers and looked at his phone. It was after three and yet, he was sure his eyes still hadn't closed, not even for a moment, his thoughts incessant. He got up, threw on his shirt and opened the door to the bedroom. Standing in the hallway, he listened for a moment to the creaks and motions of the house, then made his way downstairs to the kitchen.

He opened the fridge and took out a carton of milk, drinking straight from it before setting it down on the marble worktop. A thin stream of liquid ran down the side of the cardboard, pooling on the worktop below. What did it matter? It was all going to be pulled out soon, to make way for a new kitchen – probably not that different from this one. What a waste!

Ann was right. There was nothing about the house that needed amending – a shame to disrupt what was already beautiful. It was the residents who required improvement – especially his mother. He ran his fingers through his hair and exhaled loudly.

"She's nice."

He jumped, turning to see her sitting there in the half-light, her back to him, facing the window.

"You frightened me." He walked towards her. "Can't sleep, either?"

Jessica shook her head. "Never can." She continued to stare out of the window at the oak tree, its branches now moving in the breeze that had, at last, arrived, too late to banish the heat from the earlier dense air. "I hate it here," she muttered. "There's something weird about this house. Like there's something trapped in it. Or maybe that's me," she half-smiled.

"Jessica . . . I . . . I'm sorry you're where you are." It was all he could manage. "Maybe you should go and talk to someone," he suggested, sitting down in the chair opposite hers. "Or talk to me," he offered suddenly. "We used to be close. What happened?"

Jessica laughed – more a sharp exhalation. "Yeah. I used to be a lot of things." She got up. "You really don't know, do you?" She stood over him, waiting for a reaction.

Mark didn't answer. She shook her head and headed for the door.

How could he tell her that he did know something but had done nothing? The moment of taking action now long gone. Revisiting it, dragging it all up, would be harder, more painful than ignoring it.

"Jessica?"

"Don't, Mark. Please don't. I can't bear another lecture about pulling myself together. I know what you all think of me. I know you all think I'm a mess. I know it's painful to watch, but what no one realises is that I'm not stupid. I can see it myself." She shrugged. "It can't last forever. Sooner or later, I'll snap out of it, right? Whatever it is."

The pain in her eyes was hard to take. It was visible – tortured, punished. Mark looked away. He felt it, too. Not all of it, but a little – enough to know she was sinking. He experienced it whenever his mind drifted to the secret he knew but didn't know how to articulate. He wanted to help her, but he didn't know how.

"Jessica?"

She turned. "You know, today got me thinking," she said from the doorway. She looked young, standing there in her bare feet, her hair thrown up in a ponytail, wearing a T-shirt. "All that happened to her, to Ann. It's hard to believe. It's hard to picture it all here, in this house. All those secrets. All those lies. And that man, the reverend, he knew and he said nothing." Jessica widened her eyes, openly handing him the opportunity.

"He was trying to protect Felicity by keeping the secret, I suppose," Mark said finally.

"What's the opposite of protecting someone?" Jessica asked, gripping the doorframe. "I think that's what he did. But in the end, it always comes out, the lies. They grow and grow until they erupt and then all that's left is a great mess to clean up. Do you ever feel like you're standing on a ticking time bomb?"

Mark shook his head.

"I do," Jessica said quietly. "But she's nice – Ann, I mean. A lot happened to her and yet here she is. She's nice. Strong. I like her."

Jessica left the room and then came back.

"Mark?"

"Yeah."

"It's to destroy. That's the word. It's when you destroy someone. Don't let Mother screw this up for you, big brother. If you like this girl, get her the hell away from here. Away from *her*."

After Jessica left, Mark walked outside. He sat down on the rattan couch, resting his legs on the glass top of the box-shaped coffee table, thinking of Jessica's words. It was the most Mark had heard her say in a long time. He was more astounded by the sense she made than by the bitterness that saturated her words.

He took a deep breath, experiencing the sudden and familiar sensation of suffocation coiling itself around his body. He didn't want to be here tonight, in this house. He'd thought they'd leave after dinner, Ann and him. Drive back down the hill towards the Estates and reimmerse into the bubble they'd left earlier that day. Except, now the bubble had burst.

Mark had watched Ann throughout the evening, knowing at times she was uncomfortable. Once or twice he'd caught her staring up at the house, her expression void as if in a trance, looking from window to window, glancing over her shoulder towards the oak – remembering. At other times, Ann had chatted happily to Eugene, enthusiastically asking him about his business. She was patient with him – undiscouraged by his slower speech.

During those moments, Mark found himself contentedly watching the interactions, but his mother kept sticking her oar in. He had to hand it to Ann – nothing Mother launched at her made her recoil too much. Ann had fielded the non-stop questions expertly – well, except for one or two – and some of her answers had surprised him.

"I did try to tell you in the car," she told him after dinner.

Eugene was snoring gently in a chair and Jessica had retreated to her room, as usual, even the prospect of a guest not enough to keep her in her mother's company for long.

"I know that now."

They were standing beside the oak tree. Ann was leaning against it, looking down, her hair hanging over one shoulder, her face hard to read, plucking at a dandelion.

"Does it bother you?"

"No," Mark replied. "It doesn't bother me. It was just unexpected." Finding out she was married and in the throes of separation didn't concern him – it was more the idea that whatever had been going on for the last few days, this idyllic existence wouldn't or couldn't last. Sooner or later, reality always hits. "I guessed there was someone. I just didn't realise you were married. Did you love him?"

He was trying not to envision her with someone else, winding her arms around another man, burying her head in his chest, running her fingers down his body. Was he jealous?

"I thought I did," she answered honestly. "Looking back now, I think I loved the idea of not being alone more. I was naïve."

"He sounds like an arsehole."

Ann smiled. "He was . . . *is*. But I've no regrets. Everything that happened brought me here. Reunited me with Lucie. It brought me home."

"I'm glad it did." He took her hand. "It changes nothing for me, anyway."

He leaned in to kiss her and she kissed him back chastely, then continued picking at the weed.

"Ann?"

She looked up again.

"I'm sorry."

"For what?"

"Everything. I feel like being here has opened up lots of wounds for you. We shouldn't have come."

"It's okay. In a way, I like being here." She dropped the dandelion to the ground, every little seed now plucked away, every wish already delivered outwards. "Is she, Olive, I mean, is she really going to do this big job on the house?"

"Yes," he nodded, casting his eyes upwards. "She wasn't always this way, you know," he admitted. "She was different, up until, well . . ."

"Your dad had an affair?"

"How did you know?"

"Well, when she managed to get it out of me that I was married and it broke down because Dom was unfaithful, I saw her glance at your dad. Her face changed. I just knew. And then the way she went on about me staying strong, making sure I take him to the cleaners, never to stand for that treatment. To make sure I get what I'm entitled to and that she could recommend someone for me to speak to, well, it seemed obvious," Ann grinned. "Must have been hard for her, though. It makes me appreciate her a little more. The same thing happened to me. It changed me. It changes you."

"It transformed her! She used to be this tiny mum who was all about us. Then she found out he had this other family and when Dad got sick, well, she became someone new. I hardly recognise her. Her face doesn't move," Mark grimaced.

"Yes, I noticed that. Maybe that was how she dealt with it. That was a lot for her. Do you feel differently about your dad? Did they stay together because he was sick?"

"For a while I was angry with him, but life is complicated. People are complex. Mum would never have let him go. Sick or otherwise. I suppose you do what you think is best."

Ann nodded. Mark was going to say more, but they saw Olive signal from the patio, pointing at a tray of coffee in front of her.

"So, you don't hate her?"

"No," Ann replied. "She's not the most straightforward,

but I get her – and she's not the first transformation this house has seen."

That had been the best part of the evening. Mark alone with Ann, relieved he hadn't lost her altogether. Then came Olive's next line of questioning.

"How did your mother die, Ann?" Olive asked matter-of-fact, taking a sip from her coffee.

"Cancer," Ann answered woodenly. "She was thirty-four."

Mark observed Ann's knuckles turn white, where she was holding the edge of the table.

"Tragic. And your father?" Olive persisted.

Ann said it so robotically, as if telling them what day it was, but Mark could feel her body beside his begin to tense.

"He was killed in a car accident coming home from a gig. The other driver was drunk."

Everyone was silent, not knowing what to say. Ann shifted in her seat and then tucked her hands under her legs.

Olive brushed some crumbs off her skirt, her jaw tightening. "Oh, dear. Now, I must clear the rest of the plates." She stood up and walked back inside.

Eugene coughed awkwardly and started to say something, but Ann spoke first.

"Can we go?" She turned to Mark. "Would you mind? I need to go."

They'd left almost immediately. Ann was polite, but the evening had come to an end, a heaviness now hanging in the air that no one had any inclination to try to disperse.

"Would you mind if I stayed by myself tonight?" she asked when he pulled up outside her house and opened the door to get out.

Mark shut the door again.

"I'm exhausted," she smiled apologetically.

"Do you want to talk?"

She shook her head. "It was all a lot to take in." She couldn't meet his gaze. "Maybe we're moving too fast."

There it was. The excuse Mark had uttered so often. How it stung to be on the receiving end. Ann leaned over and kissed him on the cheek, resting her forehead there for a moment before hopping out.

He'd driven away, the whole time wanting to put the car into reverse and go back. Mark didn't want to let Ann slip away, to be frightened off by realism – by his mother, by his family, by the house. Mark reached for his phone again. It was too late to call. Instead, he tapped out a message, not caring that she'd see the time and know he was wide awake in the middle of the night, grappling to make amends.

CHAPTER TWENTY-NINE

"Bit late for that now, don't you think?" Denise muttered, plopping down on a stool opposite Ann and pouring tea from a floral teapot into two mugs.

Aside from an elderly couple down the back, the café was now empty. It was Monday morning – one of the slower days in Tea and Sympathy.

"Bit late for what?"

"You've already embarked on a relationship with Mark. Jumped forwards twenty paces, if you don't mind me saying. So it's a bit late to be saying you're not sure if you want to start a relationship with the poor fella."

Ann rolled her eyes, recognising that Denise was already firmly in the Mark camp, having met him twice and been unable to stop gushing about his strong shoulders and film star hair.

"Are you having doubts?"

"I don't know. Maybe. It's all been a bit fast. It was all fine until I met the mother. Ugh, I can't describe it. First, she kept calling me his girlfriend and then she successfully gleaned more information from me in the first five minutes of meeting than you did in a month. After a while, I just gave up, told her everything she needed to know, which resulted in me telling the boyfriend who I didn't even know I had that I'm still married. His face!" Ann put her head in her hands and pretended to cry. "I'm just not programmed to be that open."

"Well, tell me something I don't already know. It's not a bad thing being open, you know, Ann. It's liberating."

Ann ignored her and continued. "And being there, Denise, in that house . . . I don't know. It was so strange. And you should see what she's going to do it – remove all the nice parts and replace the entire inside of the house with some form of space-age shiny kitchen."

"Oh, I like those shiny kitchens." Denise tilted her head to the side and leaned forwards, placing her hand on Ann's. "But it's not your house, Ann. What do you care what the woman does to it? So, Olive is overbearing. Most mothers are. None of that is Mark's fault." She sank back again, crossing her arms. "Looking for problems, so you are."

"I'm not," Ann smiled. She adored Denise's blunt ways. "Mark's great. He is," she paused, suddenly feeling as if she was trying to convince herself. "I mean, he's kind. I'm attracted to him. I'm incredibly relaxed around him. He knows my struggles . . . well, he does now, anyway. The sex is—"

"Ah, Jaysus." Denise waved her hands in front of her face. "I'm almost old enough to be your mother, don't be talking to me about the sex. Besides, I haven't had it in so long. I wouldn't know what to do with it," Denise said matter-of-fact while Ann giggled.

"Christ, Ann, you don't know how lucky you are. Really! You've had the shite marriage and now you have a chance to have a second go at finding someone half decent. You could end up with someone who you still have the sex with," Denise whispered out of the side of her mouth. "And right up until you're decrepitly old. That could be Mark. Who knows?"

Denise got up to go to the till, where the elderly couple were waiting to pay. She leaned into Ann's ear. "You deserve to find someone fabulous at the click of a finger, to have wrinkly sex with. And, you know," Denise called across the counter as she rang up the couple's bill. "There's a reason you met him and he's wound his way back into your life, twisting himself up in the sheets of your bed."

Ann recoiled as the couple looked over at her.

"Isn't that right?" Denise beamed at the woman, who was adjusting her lilac mohair cardigan.

The old woman raised her head and nodded at Ann knowingly. "A lot to be said for *the sex*," she acknowledged before taking her husband's arm and leading him outside like the bewildered.

"See! *She* knows what I'm talking about."

"But shouldn't there be more than great sex?"

"Isn't there?"

"There is. Yes, there is, I'm sure, but isn't it all a bit fast?" Ann asked seriously. "Shouldn't I still be on my own and getting on with things? See about singing at a few more weddings. Continue working here. All nice and easy."

Denise came over to her and put her arms around her, hugging her tightly.

"Ann, love. We can't help when or where we meet someone, just as much as they can't help the family they were born into. Give him a chance. Maybe this is one of those moments in life that presents itself, where you have to decide to go for it and throw caution to the wind, like your singing.

"Besides, I told you, working here is just a stopgap for you. You're too young and too intelligent to be pouring tea for pensioners all day. You'll die from boredom and end up in one of those coffins out the back. Mind you, I'd make sure it was a nice one, with all the extras – plush velvet lining, a nice squishy cushion, a gold knocker in case you wake up and need to get out – but still, I don't want your imminent demise on my hands," Denise continued, barely drawing breath. "So things are moving fast? Slow them down a little."

"You're right. I can't help being wary after Dom, but Mark's different."

"Speak of the devil." Denise looked over Ann's shoulder before walking briskly around the counter, going into the office and shutting the door.

Ann had seen the text from Mark blink up on her phone in the middle of the night. *We need to talk*. She, too, had been awake, thinking of it all. It had been such a strange day, from beginning to end. At various points throughout the evening, being in Knockmore House, Ann had experienced great peace. Being so close to the past, having the ability to visualise it and touch it, was somehow therapeutic. At other times, she'd ached to stop the mindless chit-chat, point up to a window and say, "Right there, that's where my mother was locked in a room."

"Over there, that's where Margot shoved her against the tree."

"Up there, that's the room she attempted to kill herself in."

There. There. There.

And then there was his mother . . . It was as though Olive felt she had the right to Ann's story, with no regard for her suffering. Olive was more interested in knowing everything for the sake of knowing it. There had been no compassion whatsoever in her drilling interrogations.

Tracy sprang to Ann's mind. What was it about certain women needing to know everything there was to know about the other? Was there something wrong with Ann that she didn't feel the need to benchmark herself against others' shortcomings? Twice now, Ann had encountered the type who Aunt Lucie had warned her off. Twice was enough. Olive was just another version of Tracy – nosy and insecure. Perhaps that was what all the surgery was about and the need to improve the house, dressing like a woman half her age. Bored, more like it. The woman clearly had far too much time on her hands.

His father was charming and his sister seemed nice. Ann felt sorry for her. Jessica was strange, somewhat detached, a little odd, and even though she was the same age as Ann, it felt as if Jessica was decades younger. She was almost childlike in her mannerisms. Ann couldn't help thinking there was more to her than met the eye. From what Mark had told her, at one time, Jessica had been quite the live wire. Something must have happened, but it was none of Ann's business. She had enough on her plate without worrying about other people or taking on their dilemmas.

She hadn't planned on asking Mark not to come in after he dropped her home. As soon as Olive began to ask about her parents, Ann had felt the need to extract herself, fast. And then, "Maybe we're moving too fast." It had rushed from her brain to her mouth before she could stop it. Mark's face had filled with disappointment and a sudden clumsiness had descended over them – the parallel universe they'd been living in for the last week instantly shifting back into line.

Perhaps Sophie was right. They'd grown too intimate,

too fast, dashing ahead months already from where they should be, and now it had caught up with them.

Ann turned to look over her shoulder at Mark, standing there holding a bunch of flowers. His blue shirt was hanging out over a pair of shorts, one tanned leg crossed over the other. He hadn't shaved, the light stubble indicating that he wasn't having the best morning, either.

"Hey," she smiled weakly. Seeing him in the flesh, it was easier to push away her fears.

"Hey yourself."

"Are you going to come in?"

"I'm just waiting to see if you're going to smack me or ignore me," Mark grinned sheepishly.

"Do I have to come to you?"

"Safer that way. There's been a few incidents of vicious attacks by attractive blondes in the area," he said as she walked towards him and rested her head against his shirt. He patted her head and pulled her face towards him.

"I'm sorry about last night. I panicked."

"I'm sorry, too. It was all a bit much. I should have stopped Mum *and* I should have warned you. She was excited about the story of the house. I suppose she forgot how distressing it was for you." He looked down at her, his eyes full of concern.

"Can we start over? Just us this time. I'm not ready to be part of someone else's family. Your mother, she was . . . well . . . it was hard. I'd like to see where this goes without all the pressure."

Denise was right. He couldn't help who his family were.

"I'd like that and yes, just us. Except, I wanted to talk to you about something," he said, leaning away from her and putting his hands up. "Before you say anything, it does involve my family but, more importantly, Knockmore House. It was actually my dad's idea. I spoke with him this morning and I think it makes sense. For everyone."

If Ann had known who was really behind it, she might not have agreed so fast. All the coaching from Denise about finding a proper job and the tether Ann felt to Knockmore House seemed to be pushing Ann in the right direction – a direction carefully orchestrated by the lady of the house.

"Going to bed already, Olive?" Eugene asked on Monday evening.

"Yes. I've a lot to get ready for our trip this week. I wasn't expecting to be going earlier than planned," she called from the stairs, making her way to the sanctuary of her room.

Sitting at her dressing table, she smoothed on some face cream, ensuring to massage it into her neck and shoulders in small circular motions, just like the lady in the department store showed her. That would do.

Olive folded down the covers of the bed before sliding beneath the sheets. It was warm out, too warm even for a sheet, but Olive liked to have something over her, for protection. She lay back against the pillow, extending her chin forwards ever so slightly, remembering what her dermatologist told her. Sleeping on her side would give her another line where the skin squished up between the pillow and her face, and "prevention is better than cure". Wasn't that true? Prevention.

There was so much Olive could have prevented over the years. Her mind drifted to the girl. There was no disputing how stunning she was: fresh, line-free, yet to be tainted by the struggles of middle-age. And confident –

surer of herself than Olive had ever been. Had the girl's life honestly been all that bad? Indeed, she'd been dealt a few blows, but nothing compared to what Olive had been through, but everything could be fixed. It had taken all of her resolve not to remove one of her diamond rings from her finger at dinner on Sunday, thrust it at her son and force him down on one knee in front of the girl.

It had come as a bit of a shock that the girl was already married – what a shame. "Spoiled goods," her mother would have said, but to Olive, it was a minor setback. Anyway, in this day and age, you had to be open-minded. Olive applauded the girl for leaving that lying, cheating husband, even all of his money. It showed strength of character. It demonstrated the guts that had eluded Olive when it came to her own situation.

Olive knew of the ex-husband's family – the Fitzgeralds. Who didn't? Well, their loss was Olive's gain. They were wealthy – enormously so – but Olive was willing to bet that the Dempseys had that bit more to offer.

Olive closed her eyes. Yes, the girl was beautiful. Ann and Mark looked perfect together, and not just a pretty face, either – an accountant. What on earth was she doing working in that terrible coffee shop with the cheap pine tables? No. That wouldn't do. It was gallant, though, taking a job beneath her in an attempt to stand on her own two feet. And this singing business? Well, it was nice to have an interest, Olive supposed, but that wasn't what Ann should be doing, either. The girl was far too majestic to be entertaining unsavoury people at weddings, not when Mark could take care of her – give her the charmed life. What girl didn't want that?

Olive had played the overbearing "mother-in-law" seamlessly on Sunday, firing question after question at her.

The girl had answered them all. Olive hadn't expected that. Had hoped she might lose her temper and storm off. But the girl had kept her cool. Olive admired that, too – calm under pressure. They were more alike than she was sure Ann would ever care to admit. Of course, had the girl stormed off, as she'd expected her to, Olive would have prompted Mark to follow her. That would have been easier. After all, a man who stands up to his mother would cement the relationship all the quicker.

"Not staying out, darling?" Olive had asked sweetly when Mark had arrived home after dropping Ann back, tail between his legs.

He'd looked at her like he wanted to strangle her. Maybe questioning the girl about how her parents died was a step too far. How Ann's father died almost took the wind from Olive's sails. Almost. Olive had excused herself quickly, rushing into the kitchen and standing with her back to the door, breathing heavily until she'd been able to still her thoughts in time to bid Ann a stiff farewell. Of course, that made it look all the better, she supposed, as if Olive was utterly insensitive.

Olive hated Mark being upset with her, but it would be worth it. It would only make Ann realise sooner that she'd met a man to cherish. There was nothing dreamier than feeling as if it was the two of you against the world and that Mother dearest was secure in second place. Another success.

After Sunday evening, Olive was sure that she'd just accelerated the darling couple's first argument, which would undoubtedly force a reconciliation – and Olive knew just how to make that happen. With the trip to Spain looming, she was sure she could push it forwards by a week or two. The plans for the house had already gone out to tender. All they needed now was someone to supervise the job – a presence in the house to oversee things. Coupled with the fact that Mark needed someone to help him with payroll since Kate was going on maternity leave . . . well, it couldn't be more ideal. Praise be to Kate's ovaries and their impeccable timing. Now, who could they possibly choose?

It had been far too easy to make Eugene assume it was all his idea. All she did was plant the seed and her husband took the bait.

"Oh, I don't think so, Eugene," Olive had tossed in for good measure. "We don't know her, do we?"

"Actually, Dad, I think it makes sense." Mark cast Olive a glare. "I think Ann would be delighted to be helping with payroll and the accounts, and what better place to do it than here in the house. Kill two birds with one stone. She can work and oversee the building job. Especially since you'll all be away."

"Could we go a week or two earlier, Olive?" Eugene asked. "What are we waiting for? And aren't you keen to start the work in the house? Believe me, you don't want to be here when they start to demolish walls."

"I'm not sure. Having a stranger in the house? I'm just not sure."

"You don't like her, do you, Mother?"

"Don't be silly, darling. I think she's very . . . agreeable. Do you think we can trust her?"

Olive had left the room, smirking to herself. Men! So naïve.

With them all off in Spain, the scene would be set for a blossoming romance between Mark and Ann. The girl's connections to the house only made it all the more impressive. It was almost as if it was all meant to be. Olive couldn't help but notice how the girl was so obviously mesmerised with the house, unable to hide her draw towards it. It was where she belonged. She'd come to realise it in time.

It finally felt as if everything was heading in the right direction. Olive had steered the ship off course, but that was the thing with life – there was always the chance to steer it back in the right direction. All they needed now was a builder, but with their connections, that shouldn't be hard.

CHAPTER THIRTY

Nathan

He'd thought about nothing else for weeks, determination burning behind his eyes, sharpening his mind. As soon as he'd seen Olive coming out of Knockmore House, that smug little face, looking like the cat that got the cream, Nathan had known he couldn't let things lie. Whatever fleeting moment had made him believe that he could move on, forget it, had flittered away, resignation taking hold once more.

After he'd left Knockmore, he threw himself into a building project. After that, Nathan told himself he'd sort it, decide what to do. The job – a garage conversion, kitchen and utility – should have taken a couple of months, but he finished in record time, working the lads harder than he should have, on a mission to reach the end. Once the bill was settled, he was back in the truck, back to Knockmore.

It was time.

He'd done a little digging in the meantime, just to be sure – it was amazing what ex-neighbours were willing to divulge to a total stranger with a charming smile. Apparently, the brother still lived in the house in Wicklow.

"Mind you, he's rarely here. Must be like father, like son. Olive, Eugene and Jessica all moved to . . . Oh, what was the name of it again? Knock-something."

"Knockmore?" he asked, already knowing the answer.

"That's it, Knockmore. By all accounts, the house is massive. Mind you, Eugene had a bit of making up to do. I'm not one to gossip, but from what I heard, he'd been dipping his wick into everything that walked for years. Never made a pass at me, mind, and for that I was minorly insulted." Her head bobbed as she spoke.

"He must be blind," Nathan grinned at her, his eyes twinkling.

"Oh. Now. Aren't you a rogue! Still, I wouldn't do that to a neighbour. Would have been nice to be asked, though. I think they came into a bit of money. There were little changes here and there. Olive was never one to splash the cash unnecessarily."

For someone who didn't like to gossip, she'd kept Nathan almost forty minutes.

"Can I say who was asking?" the woman called down the driveway as he inched away from her, bored from feigning interest.

"Bit late for that," he muttered to himself before walking away.

He'd called his brother, too, instantly regretting it.

"It's been a while. Are you okay?"

Nathan could hear the concern in his brother's voice.

"Getting by."

"Can I see you?"

"Have you heard anything?"

"Nathan. Leave it. What are you doing? Mum's worried. Will you go and visit her? Please. Tell her the truth. Tell her what you told me."

"Worried? Really? She told me she wanted nothing more to do with me. I think the words she used were, 'You're no son of mine,'" Nathan replied sadly.

He missed her. Nathan missed them all, but he had to set things right first, then he'd try again. He knew he couldn't stay away forever. It was too hard and far too lonely.

"It's been too long. The dust has settled. Can we see you? Please."

"I have to go." Nathan shouldn't have called. His brother's voice was too easy to listen to, too familiar.

"Nathan. Please. You've got to stop this. It was a mistake. What's done is done. You can come back to work, here, where you belong. I need you. Remember the plans we had?"

"Soon."

"Nathan, wait. I did hear something," his brother blurted, trying to keep him on the line. "They moved, bought a big house in some town. I can't remember the name. I ran into a friend of hers. No one has seen her in ages. Nathan? Are you there?"

"Yeah. I'm here. Mind yourself, little brother. I'll be in touch soon, I promise."

He'd hung up before saying, "I miss you."

Pulling up outside, Nathan parked the truck away from the gate, turning it round so he was ready to leave straightaway in case things turned nasty. He'd planned the conversation in his mind so many times that now he couldn't remember how it started.

"Remember me?"

"Hello there. Remember? You ruined my life."

He took a breath and walked up the driveway, climbing the three steps and finding the doorbell hidden among the flowers growing up the side of the house. Pressing it quickly, he stepped back. He could hear music coming from inside, sounds of laughter drifting from the back of the house.

The door opened.

"Hey. You're early. I wasn't expecting you until later. Great start. I'm Mark." He extended his hand.

Nathan took it, lost for words.

"Come in." Mark stood back to let him pass. "Listen, thanks for coming on a Saturday. That your truck outside? You want to bring it in? The road is narrow enough."

Nathan shook his head.

"Anyway, this is it . . ." Mark gestured at the house. "The other builder was all set to start then let me down at the last minute and to be honest, I'm a bit under pressure to get this job under way. You want to glance at the plans?"

Mark rolled them out and placed them on the large circular table in the middle of the hall. He pushed back the vase of flowers, now wilting, petals dropping onto the glass top.

"Sorry." Mark picked the petals off the plans and threw them back into the vase. "Parents are away. Mum usually changes these every few days. Not my thing," Mark laughed and then pointed at the plans again. "It's fairly straightforward. A few interior walls, new kitchen, extension out the back and this monstrosity . . ." Mark pointed at the glass structure at the back of the house. "You did O'Reilly's job, right? They're friends of my parents. You come highly recommended. Anyway, my folks are away for the next three months and I want to get this done before they come back. Sorry. Jason, isn't it?"

Nathan nodded, removing his cap. "Yeah, Jason. That's right, pal. Sorry. It was a long drive." Nathan found his voice in time. "This looks good. Can I see the kitchen?"

"Sure."

They walked through the door, Nathan looking around cautiously, glancing at the group of people sitting out back. He walked towards the window and stopped suddenly, edging back and pulling his cap back on. It was her – Ann. He could hardly believe his eyes. He almost smiled seeing her and then remembered himself. What was she doing here?

"Do you want me to come back? Looks like you have people over."

"Nah. Not at all. That's just my girlfriend and her friends. She's a singer – just done her first wedding," Mark said proudly. "We're celebrating. Sorry. Would you like a beer? I'll show you the back of the house."

"No, thanks. I don't have long. Anyway, I can see from here."

Nathan noticed them getting up from the chairs outside and watched them walk towards the end of the garden. The sight of Ann took him by surprise. Nathan asked the question and held his breath.

"The blonde one, is it?"

"Yeah, that's right."

It wasn't the answer he'd hoped for. Nathan looked around again, knocking a few walls with his knuckles for good measure and running his hand over a few of the surfaces.

"I can get a price done up over the weekend, if you like. Can I take the plans?" he asked.

"Sure. We're in construction ourselves, but our own guys are maxed out with work and I don't like to mix work into our personal lives. I told you that, right?"

"Yep. Copy that," Nathan agreed.

"So, it's just labour. We supply all the materials. I can have them here by Wednesday if you can do up that quote.

Here's my email." Mark handed him his card. "It was great to meet you, Jason. I guess that's it. Any other questions?"

"Will there be someone here for the duration of the job? You said the folks are away."

"Yes. With my sister. But my girlfriend, Ann, works from here. Actually, she'll be the one paying your bill. She's an accountant, helping me out with the books for the business for a few months," Mark told him. "Ann will open up for you and lock everything behind you. I hope you don't mind. My folks are older, a bit nervous, you understand?"

"She sounds like a real all-rounder," Nathan smiled warmly. "No problem. Oh, and listen, I'll give you my new mobile number. I had to change providers today, so I just got a new one. Apparently, the same number was given to some fifteen-year-old on a pay-as-you-go phone."

"Nightmare," Mark laughed. "Shout it out to me there and I'll save it straight to my phone."

"Great. I'll just have a walk round the side before I head off. I'll see myself out. You get back to your celebration." Nathan shook his hand.

"Hopefully see you next week. And thanks, Jason," Mark said, shutting the door and leaving Nathan in the driveway alone.

Nathan stood for a few moments, his hands on his head, staring towards the road, trying to make sense of what just happened. Why had he gone along with it? He'd been caught off guard. Nathan lowered his hands, went to walk towards the gate, let out a grunt, then turned, stalking back to the house. What the hell was he doing? He stopped again, trying to think.

So, that was Mark. Nathan had never met him – heard all about him, of course. He seemed like a nice enough guy, but he wasn't part of the plan. Then again, maybe Mark knew the whole story. Perhaps he was in on it, too. He kicked the stones by his feet. Think, Nathan, think.

And her, Ann – Nathan had almost bolted when he saw her sitting there. To think she'd almost made him want to disregard these people when she was one of them, too. Nathan suddenly felt paranoid. Of course, Ann was too good to be true, making eyes at him in the bar, when all along she was with this Mark. It made sense for someone like her to be perched in the garden of a house like this. It was a shame, but whatever he felt that night when he'd heard her sing, he ignored now – wishful thinking. She wasn't what he was here to do.

Although . . .

Nathan stared down to where his boots were now covered with dust and then back at the house, a fit of unexpected rage gripping him. Standing here like a clown, while they were living their lives, carrying on as if nothing had happened! They'd taken everything from him. Left him with no future, no hope – a shattered past and a constant sense of dread every time he closed his eyes. These people deserved everything they got. The original plan had been to get in, get what he was owed and leave. In and out, then move on – for good, this time.

Perhaps this was better. There was more than one way to skin a cat. This was his opportunity for lasting revenge. No . . . He stopped himself. The anger was morphing his train of thought. That wasn't what this was about. But Olive deserved it. They all did, he reasoned – three months and it would all be over. They'd come back, he'd spring it on them and that would be the end.

Nathan saw the van pull up outside and he walked

towards it without hesitating. The plan had already formed. All he had to do was get rid of the actual Jason, fast.

"Jason, is it?" Nathan asked as the window rolled down.

"Yeah. Are you Mark?"

"That's right." Nathan looked over his shoulder towards the house to make sure no one was looking. "Listen, I'm sorry for wasting your time. I've been trying to call you all morning."

The real Jason picked up his phone and looked at the screen, confused. "Really?"

"Yeah, mate. It was saying out of coverage. Anyway, the job's off. Something came up. A family tragedy, very sudden." Nathan was speaking fast and edging away.

"Oh, right."

"I really am sorry. I have to go back in. You understand? If anything changes in the coming weeks, I'll give you a shout, but things aren't looking good." Nathan shook his head slowly and looked at the ground in dismay.

"Right. Okay. I'm sorry to hear that."

"Me too, mate. Me too."

Nathan waited for Jason to reverse back out of the gate and drive up the road before getting back into his truck. He started the engine and pulled up to the gate, glancing at Knockmore House one more time before driving off.

He had the weekend to decide for sure, but he already knew what he was going to do. Nathan could easily be "Jason" for a few months. He wasn't sure how he'd explain it to the lads, but they knew enough now at this stage not to ask questions.

There were a few things Nathan had gleaned over the years, working with a few lads who had what you might describe as questionable morals. He'd do the perfect external job on Knockmore House, with a few added extras, all free of charge, which would come to light over time: an open sewer pipe under the floors – that one was an easy fix, if you knew what you were trying to fix. Perhaps some incorrect measurements – something the planning authorities would like to hear about once Nathan had disappeared for good. Maybe an open vent to channel cold air through the house – the same cold air that had been directed right through Nathan's life.

It was a beautiful house. Once, Nathan had dreamed of living in a house just like this one, with a brood of kids, a few chocolate Labradors sleeping on the steps, someone inside, waiting on him to come home. The sudden memory of it fuelled him.

It was a shame to mess with such beauty, but so was ruining people, so was destroying others to protect yourself. If Ann happened to get caught in the crossfire, that wasn't his responsibility, either. No, that was on them. It was all on them.

He drove away from Knockmore knowing he was driving straight towards destruction, but he didn't care. He had nothing more to lose and for the first time in years, Nathan felt alive.

CHAPTER THIRTY-ONE

"Wow. This is nice." Sophie leaned towards Ann. They were sitting in the garden of Knockmore House, sipping prosecco in the afternoon sun. "What time will Denise and Ian be here?"

"After work."

Ann kicked her shoes off and curled her feet under her on the outdoor sofa. The kitchen door was open, the music drifting towards them as they sat there chatting.

"Where's Mark?"

"He's just gone inside. There was some builder calling today to see about the renovations. Looks like he was early. Good start. He said it won't take long to show him the plans."

Sophie was sitting on the other side of the sofa, her legs stretched out, eyes closed, letting the sun warm her face.

"The lads seem to be getting on well. At least Jack has someone to talk balls with now," Ann giggled.

"At last, someone who speaks my language," Jack added from where he was sitting opposite them.

Mark and Jack, Sophie's boyfriend, had already had a full-scale conversation about golf.

"How's the new accounts job going? What's it like having Mark for a boss?" Sophie asked.

"It's great, easy," Ann smirked. "When the renovations start next week, I'm going to be doing the books out of here. There's a lovely office inside and I can be a set of eyes while the builders are here."

"Really? How do you feel about that?" Sophie knew Ann had a strange love–hate relationship with Knockmore House.

"Good. You know, we've spent a little time here since Mark's parents absconded to Spain. It was easier when I wasn't being drilled by Olive," Ann laughed. "I'll show you around when Mark gets back."

"Yeah. I'd love to see it. Have you spent the night here yet?" Sophie reached over and nudged her leg.

"No, I haven't, and I don't intend to. I like my little house better."

"Maybe tonight," Sophie cooed. "I wouldn't mind a go in one of those four-poster beds you described. How do you always get rich ones? Although Mark seems lovely, Ann, seriously." Sophie pushed her sunglasses down over her eyes and sat forwards. "I mean, I really wanted to give him the whole 'hurt her and you'll have me to answer to' speech, but I can't bring myself to be mean to him. He's too nice and no offence, Jack," she said, looking over at her fiancé and grinning, "but he is *fine*. I want to press his face to see if he's real."

"None taken." Jack held his hands up and grinned back. "I mean, I want to do the same thing," he mimicked.

"Be my guest," Ann giggled. "Press away."

She was on cloud nine. Everything had gone so well that morning in the church, singing at her first ever wedding.

"What are you doing here?" Ann had squealed earlier that day when she saw Sophie and Jack drive into the church car park.

"You didn't think I'd miss it, did you? Ian called ahead to make sure it was okay if a few of your friends crashed the church part of the wedding to support you. He promised we'd sit on our hands and not scream while you sing," Sophie explained.

"Jack!" Ann hugged her friend's fiancé as he appeared out of the passenger seat of Sophie's car. "This is the best surprise ever and congratulations on your engagement. You've chosen wisely. I can vouch for her."

"Well, considering you'll be singing at our wedding, I wanted to see what all the fuss was about," Jack grinned.

Ann stuck out her tongue. They were such a great couple. Sophie looked beautifully weird, as always, wearing a full net skirt, waistcoat and boots. Jack was ideally suited to her, dressed in jeans, a white shirt and a plaid jacket that would make any other man look like Rupert the Bear but made him look like he should be sipping a coffee on the streets of New York.

"No pressure, so. A singing, dancing, speech-making bridesmaid you've got me down for? What *have* I let myself in for?" Ann giggled, reaching out to take Mark's hand and pull him into the circle. "Sophie, Jack. This is Mark." She smiled nervously, making a face at Sophie and mouthing, "Be nice."

"It's terrific to meet you both." Mark took Sophie's hand first and then shook Jack's.

"Likewise, buddy," Jack smiled.

"All right, Mark?" Sophie pursed her lips and looked him up and down as Mark turned towards her. "Nice to see you, finally. Not on social media, eh? I always question a person without an online presence." Sophie raised her eyebrows. "Odd in this day and age. No? Like, what are you hiding?" She jerked her head to the side inquisitively.

"Oh, well. It was just never really my thing," Mark stammered, taken aback. "But maybe you're right. I never thought it might seem strange," he considered.

"Very," Sophie said bluntly, staring at him intently for a few moments before bursting out laughing. "I'm messing. You should see your face." She put her arm around him. "But it is bizarre, Mark. Sort that shit out."

Mark grinned back at Ann, who was shaking her head and rolling her eyes.

"Maybe you could set me up this weekend?" Mark asked Sophie.

"I'd be delighted to assist. Much easier to stalk you that way," she told him, smiling. Sophie linked his arm, moving out of the way to let a car pull into the car park just past them. "Hey, have you heard her sing yet, Mark?"

"Not yet."

"You think you like her now," Sophie winked. "I estimate in approximately one hour, you ain't ever gonna want to let her go. Mind you . . ." She leaned over. "I think by the looks of it, you may already be in that mindset."

"That obvious?" Mark winced.

"Yeah. You may want to cool your jets there, pal."

"I like you, Sophie. I was terrified to meet you, but I think we'll get on."

"Much as I hate to admit it, I think I like you, too."

Sophie had been impressed by Mark. She'd been concerned all month, listening as Ann told her of all the developments in her life. It wasn't that Sophie wasn't happy for her – it all sounded fantastic, if not a little whirlwindy. Then again, wasn't it Sophie encouraging Ann to seize life and go for it in the first place? Of course, she hadn't really expected Ann to turn herself into a human dandelion clock and offer herself out to the universe. Things seemed to have settled somewhat, though, after an initial series of speed bumps, which Sophie had listened to over the phone, cringing. Sophie suspected there was a strong possibility this was a rebound relationship – a springboard for Ann, back into the world of men. But hey, what did it matter? The main thing was that she was putting herself out there again after that lying, cheating wretch, Dom.

Sophie glimpsed Ann reaching up and kissing Mark a little too passionately for a church setting before taking her place in front of the microphone.

Or maybe this was the real thing . . . Even Sophie had to admit that if it all worked out, it would almost be too good to be true.

Ann had sat at the top of the church, watching the guests filter in, fixing her sheets of music, admiring the mish-mash of style that had slowly begun to seep into the church and take their seats.

The groom, Colm, who looked as though he might faint at any moment, was much the same colour as his grey suit. Colm nodded at Ann, who smiled broadly and gave him the thumbs up. He returned the smile with a watery grimace – terrified. Ann knew how he felt.

Ann was glad she'd enlisted the help of Ian to draw up a list for the nervous couple to choose from.

"You have to have something religious, something uplifting and something to pluck at the heart-strings," Ian had informed her confidently. "We want laughter. We want tears. We want . . . Jesus," he'd finished with dramatic jazz hands.

In the end, Colm and Martha had picked a range of classic and modern songs – and, of course, the version of the A-ha song, 'Take On Me', they'd heard Ann sing in Lennon's. So far, only Ian had heard her perform them all as he lay stretched out on her sofa in the evenings like musical royalty, and she the jester.

"Again."

"More emotion."

"I'm not feeling it, Ann."

"Own it," he'd shouted as he sipped a G&T, sporadically spitting olive pips into a bowl, tapping his hand on his leg until gradually his shouts turned to, "Now you're sucking diesel, girl."

"That's it – take her home."

Painstakingly, Ann had played until every error was ironed out, every note seamless, and Ian was reduced to silence, moved to tears by her voice.

"I believe you when you sing, Ann," Ian had told her the night before. "You have the voice, but it's more than that – you have the story, you have the pain and, lately, my little songstress, I can hear joy."

"Sometimes, I can't believe I'm doing it – that it's me singing."

"But you weren't ready before," he'd assured. "All along you've been harnessing all these emotions life has thrown your way. That's what makes you special, Ann. Now, it's your time to shine." He'd kissed her forehead before leaving. "And remember, if it all goes tits up, just close your eyes. Pretend you're singing to me. And one more thing . . ." Ian had poked his head back round the door. "Wear something plain. Something that when people look at you, they can't see you, but by God, they'll hear you."

"At last, something I can relate to," she'd called after him, closing the door.

Ann barely noticed the bride approach while she sang. Shivers ran up her back when she finally glanced over to see Martha standing there looking up at Colm. All tiny and innocent, more like a girl making her communion.

By then, Colm had regained some colour in his face as he stared down at his bride. Ann had noticed the slight tremor as Colm shook his father-in-law's hand and the older man whispered some jovial warning into his ear. A smile. A nod. A story.

As the ceremony drew to a close, Colm and Martha made their way to the top to sign the register and Ann took a deep breath. Here it was. *The* song.

She picked up her guitar and began, her mind instantly catapulting back to the first night she'd sung it in Lennon's, staring into the eyes of a complete stranger. Ann hadn't thought of that night much since, nor the man who'd captured her attention so vividly – the experience slipping away from her when she'd started seeing Mark. But she thought of it now – how she'd somehow, even though impossible, glimpsed her future in his gaze.

Ann sang the entire song now thinking of him, picturing him watching her as he had done in the dimmed atmosphere of the pub, speaking to her without words.

When she finished, she'd opened her eyes, half expecting to see *him* standing there. Instead, it was Mark's eyes she met. He'd moved to the side of the aisle, pushed out by Sophie, to watch Ann perform the one song she was born to sing.

The audience slowly began to clap, quietly at first, unsure as to whether or not it was the "done thing" to applaud the wedding singer. Egged on by Colm and Martha, who were smiling broadly, the guests clapped enthusiastically and Ann nodded her head graciously. Glancing down the church again, Ann could see Mark watching her, his smile so pure it almost hurt.

"Wow," he mouthed.

At that moment, Ann was sure of two things. She was confident she'd found what she wanted to do with the rest of her life – to sing, to share these happy celebrations with delirious people. And secondly, Ann knew she may never again feel the way she had when she'd first sung that song in the packed bar, to an audience of one. Intensity. A feeling so powerful that it was difficult to breathe. But was that what she really needed?

What she had with Mark was steady, sure, relaxed. She'd had so much upheaval in her life already, been so hurt before. Surely, Mark was the one to give her the security she craved, so she could stop feeling as if she were constantly searching and instead feel found. No. Ann knew she may never feel again how she had when she'd sung to an unknown – but maybe, just maybe, that wasn't a bad thing.

"I have to say, Ann," Jack said now. "That song, the A-ha one, it was pretty special. I almost cried."

Sophie looked at him over her sunglasses. "You were blubbing like a baby."

"I have allergies. The pollen count is particularly high today."

"You seem okay here in the garden," she smirked. "But it was beautiful, Ann. I cried. Were you thinking of Mark?" Sophie raised an eyebrow.

"Thanks, guys," Ann smiled but didn't answer, not wanting to admit the truth as to whom she'd been imagining.

Mark *is* perfect. Everyone who met him told her the same. She shook the doubts away, reminding herself that she was with a gorgeous man, in a magnificent house, with her favourite people. Ann closed her eyes and smiled.

"Look at you." Sophie threw a cushion at her. "I haven't seen you like that in a long time. You totally killed it today, pal."

"I did, didn't I?" Ann agreed smugly. "And more bookings out of it, as well. Not a bad morning's work."

Ann could hardly believe it when two separate couples came up to her after the ceremony to get her details and ask if she would sing at their weddings.

"And don't forget. Denise has an in with all the funerals," Sophie reminded her. "You could be singing away at them, too. And sure, you could nearly sing the same songs. No one'll notice. You have this sad quality to your voice. 'You Raise Me Up' could refer to love, or jacking someone up into heaven."

"True. Not sure 'Signed, Sealed, Delivered' would work for both. But you never know!" Ann laughed.

Ann could see Mark talking to the builder in the kitchen. He had his back to the window, while Mark pointed towards the patio.

"Come on. Let me show you the famous tree. Jack, this is where I discovered the letter about Mam. The tree of secrets, I call it. Our Olive wants to chop it down," Ann told them, getting up and padding across the grass, followed by Sophie and Jack.

"I'll chain myself to it. We won't allow it." Sophie was outraged.

Jack went to look over the garden wall at the back, while Ann bent to show Sophie the opening in the oak tree, where all those years the letter had been waiting to be found. Ann looked up as she saw Mark walking towards them.

"All done? Already?"

"Yep. I was eager to get back to you." He put his arms around her and kissed her. "He seems good. A decent guy."

Ann smiled up at him.

"You were fantastic today, my little singer. Are you sure you don't mind working from here and keeping an eye on things?"

"I'm sure. And it might be nice to see the renovations happen. I might pick up a few tips. I've become quite handy in my own house! Did I mention I put up a shelf in the kitchen at home last week? All by myself," she said proudly. "I do have one problem, though . . ."

"What's that, my little handy-woman?" he asked, brushing her hair to the side.

"Can you ask Olive if we can keep the tree?" She was trying to keep it light, but her voice cracked ever so slightly.

"I'll chain myself to it," he promised.

"Looks like we're all chaining ourselves to the tree, then," Sophie said, joining them. "Now, I don't know about you two, but I'm thirsty and hungry, but mostly thirsty." She squashed herself between Ann and Mark and linked their arms. "Shall we?" she asked, dragging them back towards the house.

CHAPTER THIRTY-TWO

The moon hung so low, suspended in the cloudless sky, that it looked as though it might plummet at any moment and glide across the grass. The stars were dotted visibly, making the black sky appear even darker against the contrast. Ann reached out, placing her hand on the pane of glass, pressing her palm against it. The cold was sobering. She settled herself in the window seat, resting her back against the shutters, tucking her feet up under her on the now cushioned softness of the wood.

She could see where the expansive branches of the oak tree shaded the ground beneath it, stretching well beyond the trunk, to where the orchard had once been, preventing the grass there from becoming the same lush green as the lawn. She wondered if Olive knew there had once been an orchard there, a stash of bitter apples piled on the ground ready to bite into. Or that from the gallery upstairs, you could see into the Estates. Or that the door from the dining room to the patio rattled in the wind.

"Makes sense," Tracy had said after their heart-to-heart earlier that week. "A big house like that suits you more than here. Now, I'm not complaining, I promise. I've turned over a new leaf. I'm going to be content with my lot, but there's just something about you, Ann – like you're destined for more. I noticed it straightaway. Maybe that's why I was so interested in you. Here, in the Estates, is not where you'll end up. Mark my words."

Tracy's words had echoed what Sophie had said to her recently when they spoke about her singing. "I always thought it – you're special, Ann. While Ann, the accountant, is a marvellous example of alliteration, it's not your calling. There's something bigger out there for you. I'm sure."

Ann wondered if the "something", or her calling, was the inexplicable draw she felt towards this house. It irked her that she couldn't work out how it made her feel, or how she somehow knew more about Knockmore House – implanted in her, revived from stories told – than anyone else, as if she were the keeper of its reality. Perhaps Olive was right and the garden would do better without the immense tree – the giver of shade, the symbol of wisdom, the guardian of secrets. Some people were more sentimental about those kinds of things than others. Ann knew which type she was. When you've already lost so much, you cling to whatever remains – the reminders, the symbols.

Not like Olive, so prepared to throw out the old, make way for the new, continually trying to improve, advance. It must be exhausting. Then again, trying to hold on to the past was just as disheartening.

Or was Mark her calling? Would he become the family she so craved?

"It was a great night. I don't know, seeing the house this way, with music blaring and everyone laughing . . . well, it's so different from how it is when my family's here. Or maybe that's what you do to the place, Ann. Light it up," Mark had told her before closing his eyes and starting to snore gently.

Afterwards, Ann hadn't been able to sleep, thinking of it.

"Up the stairs, second door on the left." She remembered Lucie's words, directing her straight to Felicity's old room. It must have been quite different in her mother's day. No four-poster bed, or plush cushion in the window seat to soften Felicity's reality. No shocking pink chair in the corner.

Ann had to hand it to Olive, it was the perfect mix of old styles with a peppering of eclectic pieces. The bright pink chair shouldn't have worked beside the four-poster mahogany bed frame, but it did. Maybe Olive did know what she was talking about, after all, and what she had planned for the house would take it to the next level.

Ann still didn't understand why she cared so much, or why Olive's splashes of modernity, and wondering if they would work, was filling her mind. Ann supposed there were lots of things in life that shouldn't have worked together but did. She rested her head back and smiled, thinking of the ideal evening she'd just spent here, with her friends.

"Talk about the odd bunch," Ann said to Denise earlier.

"Oh, yes, let's see, what do we have?" Denise glanced around the table. "Okay, I have it. Me – disgruntled mother and café owner. Ian – gay hardware store owner. Marvellous Mark – CEO of a construction company. Sophie – bubbly marketeer. Jack – trendy electrician and—"

"A lost, separated, lonely, orphaned wedding singer," Ann finished.

Denise smacked her arm and frowned. "Stop that, now. Things are going far too well for you. I have no further sympathy to offer. From now on, it's just tea or wine." Denise took a slurp from her glass of white and turned back to Mark. "Mark, tell me all about your hair, I mean, your business?"

On paper, the six people gathered together should have been a recipe for disaster, but everyone was getting on like a house on fire. They'd lasted outside for hours, failing to give in, gradually wrapping themselves in blankets, cuddling into each other before Denise could take no more.

"Guys, can we sit inside this legendary house before I freeze to death. I'm older than most of you. My circulation isn't what it used to be."

Inside, huddled round the kitchen table, Ann observed them all. Sophie was resting her head on Jack's shoulder, one hand on Ian's arm. Ian's head was thrown back with delight at Sophie's stories. Denise was gazing a little too intently into Mark's eyes, telling him all about her kids and Steve's habit of leaving his jocks on the bathroom floor for the last twenty-two years.

Denise was right – everything was going well lately. So, she was separated – there was nothing she could do to change that. She was orphaned – yes, her parents were no longer with her. But was she still lost?

Technically, no.

Ann had unearthed her own little modern family. She had a good job, using her qualifications as Denise had insisted and being paid well above average to do so. And, most importantly, Ann had found her singing voice and couldn't put into words how much satisfaction it brought her to use it. Was she still lonely? Well, she had Mark.

"Ann, you're a saint!" Ian interrupted her thoughts, waving his hands about as he spoke. "I can't believe you did that!" he exclaimed, still unable to believe what Sophie had just told him. "I know what I would have done. I would have told Tracy to go and shite."

Ann looked up. "Is this about Tracy? It just felt like the

right thing to do," she shrugged. "You never know what's going on in someone else's life, do you?"

"But offering to babysit? And the shoes? I'm most upset about the shoes. After everything she did . . ." Sophie shook her head.

"Tell me about the shoes?" Denise piped in. "What did I miss?"

"Only that Ann is some sort of walking saint. I'd be ordering a tonne of manure and having it delivered into her driveway, or sending a band of Bible-bashers her way – the ones who won't give up, ever, or throwing eggs over the wall at her, or—"

"Okay. Okay. I get the idea, Soph, and I did think about the manure," Ann giggled. "I'm not that saintly."

"Tracy, can we talk?"

Tracy had been fumbling with keys at her door as Ann came up the path on Monday after work. Tracy paused when she heard Ann's voice and turned in slow motion to face her. Ann was sure the delay was caused by Tracy silently cursing under her breath.

It was Tracy this time who'd been avoiding Ann since their confrontation, mortified by what she'd done. Even her husband wasn't talking to her after Tracy told him the story, looking for sympathy, only to be met by disapproval.

"Ah, Jesus, Tracy. What the hell have you done now?"

"I . . . I'm . . ."

"Do you want to come in for a cup of tea, Tracy? Just a quick one. I won't keep you. I have muffins . . ."

"Oh, well. All right. Thanks." Tracy put her leg over the metal fence and crossed the threshold onto Ann's turf. "Wow. You've done wonders with the place."

Tracy looked around as Ann opened the door and finally let Tracy inside. She followed Ann into the kitchen.

"Thanks. It really was a mess."

"I'm not surprised. Those nurses were always throwing parties. Noisy bunch. That's why they were always offering to babysit, so I didn't call the guards." Tracy smiled coyly.

Ann boiled the kettle and set a muffin on a plate in front of Tracy.

"Ann, what I did, I'm so sorry. I don't know what came over me. Well, I do. It's just not terribly easy to admit."

Ann waited.

"Ah, I suppose I've been having a hard time lately. I can't work with the kids – the cost of childcare is too much. God, I miss it so much. Money is permanently tight. I never do anything, except that one night with the girls, and truth be told, I have nothing in common with them, really. I'm not like them, baking and making and doing all the homely things. And sometimes, even though I have all of these little people around me, I'm just so lonely.

"I don't look like I used to. I don't feel like I used to. I'm always knackered . . . and there you are, on your own, with peace and space, and . . . I was jealous, Ann. God, I'm so ashamed to admit it, but that's what it was. A case of the green-eyed monster.

"I could spin you some story, try to make you believe there was something else, but I'd be lying. What you have here, it's everything I'd love."

Ann smiled sadly. "And what you have, Tracy, is everything I'd love: a family, kids, someone to love."

Tracy grimaced. "The grass is always greener . . ."

They'd chatted for a while then. Tracy telling her all

about when she was a hairdresser and make-up artist, and how much she'd loved it.

"Now, that makes sense. Your hair that night we went out was gorgeous. And your make-up."

"Thanks. I wish I had time to do it more often. I'd love to go back to work, but finding something that fits around the kids is tough. Anyway, I'd better go. I've killed off all the rumours, Ann, just so you know, and I'm sorry, truly."

Tracy stuck out her hand to Ann on the doorstep and Ann took it.

"Let's start again. I'm Tracy. Welcome to Knockmore."

Ann giggled.

"Can I ask you something? The jeep I've seen outside . . . is that your new man?"

"Yeah. That's Mark."

"Not the guy they were talking about on that night out in the Italian? The one who nearly knocked the child off the scooter!" Tracy held up her hand. "I won't say anything, Ann, I swear."

In the spirit of the day, Ann quickly filled Tracy in on how she and Mark had met again. It was then that Tracy said what she'd said about Knockmore House, taking Ann by surprise.

"And thanks, Ann. You've made me remember how lucky I am to have what I have and what an arsehole I can be. I'm here, if you need me, and hang in there. Things will get better for you. I know it. Maybe we can do this again sometime. Just the two of us."

"I'd like that, and listen. What size shoe are you?"

When Tracy woke the next morning, there was a coveted pink box on her doorstep containing a pair of hardly worn black patent Christian Louboutin sky-high heels – Ann had never been able to wear them anyway, they made her far too tall – and a note. Perhaps she and her neighbour had more in common than their shoe size.

I'll be in at seven to babysit! I think you deserve it. Go out for a bite to eat, the pair of you, with your new shoes. Ann.

"The house was utterly spotless," Ann told them earlier. "For some reason, I expected it to be a mess. Poor Tracy. She's run ragged with the Frantic Four. And they are frantic – two hours with them and I considered tying them together and gagging them. Imagine four kids, and she's still so young," Ann giggled. "It's like she's trapped in a dense fog of tiny Y-fronts and smelly socks! And she did apologise. And maybe I should have been more open with Tracy from the start."

"Well, she'd want to have apologised, after what she did. The cheek of her. My little empathetic Annie." Ian patted her hand.

"She came back a different person after her night out. She was dying to get rid of me, practically wrapped around her husband when they came back! There might be a fifth along soon. Let's hope it's a girl."

"Racy-Tracy!" Ian exclaimed, and they all laughed.

"Besides, I have her by the balls, now." Ann clenched her fist and pursed her lips. "She can't go saying anything to anyone now if she ever wants to get out again."

"Maybe not so saintly, after all." Mark feigned shock. "A ball-breaker."

"Hey, everyone deserves a second chance. And like I said before, I was far too quick to judge Tracy. We wiped the slate clean. I'm not sure we'll ever be best buddies, but we understand each other."

"A saint!" Ian laughed again.

"Come to think of it . . ." Mark took Ann's hand. "I should be thanking Tracy. If it wasn't for her, Mother dear would never have heard about Ann and I may never have known you were tucked away here in Knockmore all along. I might offer to babysit for the Frantic Four myself."

"Now who's the saint," Ann grinned.

"Oh, he is a saint, Ann. I'm not sure about you, but Mark is." Denise batted her eyelashes at Mark, who blew her a kiss.

"To Saint Mark and Saint Ann." Ian raised his glass.

"Hear hear," everyone laughed.

Mark was right. This evening, Knockmore House had been filled with warmth. Ann had felt it all day, wrapping itself around her. She wondered, was it the first time that the house had been brimming with joy? In a way, she wished Mam could have seen it like this. They'd all undoubtedly been joyous by the time they were going to bed. Denise and Ian had slunk off in a taxi, Denise wobbling down the driveway and tumbling backwards into a bush before Ian righted her and pushed her, head first, into the car.

"Shh," Mark whispered when Ann walked back into the room after seeing them off, gesturing towards the other pair wrapped around each other and snoring gently on the sofa.

"Should I wake them?"

The plan was to get a taxi home with Sophie and Jack.

"No. Let them sleep. We had a lot to drink," Mark hiccuped.

Ann looked over at the kitchen counters, covered in wine and beer bottles.

"Oh, gosh." Ann gritted her teeth. "The empty bottles strike again."

"Stay," Mark said, nuzzling her ear. "Stay here with me."

Ann exhaled, suddenly feeling flat after all the excitement as she peered out at the stars, hoping they might blend somehow, to deliver her a message. Had the stars led her back here to this house? It felt so right being here, as if she belonged. Did she belong with Mark?

"There you are."

She heard him behind her.

"What are you doing in here? Come back to bed." Mark reached out, and she got up and walked towards him. "Hey, you okay?"

"I'm fine. Just couldn't sleep."

"Come on."

Ann followed him, hoping with every fibre of her soul that she was on the right path, that Mark was the missing piece to her future. There was no point looking out at the stars hoping for direction, trusting they'd deliver her a sign. Deep down, Ann knew that the only person who could answer that question was herself.

CHAPTER THIRTY-THREE

"Peaks and troughs, little Annie, that's what it's all about."

Ian was balancing on a ladder in his shop, trying to remove a bucket from a high shelf, using a mop to grab the handle. He flipped the broom towards Ann, who unhooked the bucket and set it on the counter as he clambered down.

"See, a lot's happened you in the past few months and even though not all of it was good – like being in the Knockmore rumour mill, *par exemple* . . ." He shook his head at his little bit of French. "Well, it was all keeping your mind busy – occupied.

"There was getting to know Macho Mark, changing jobs, launching your fledgling career as a blossoming songbird. And now, my dear, you're in a S-L-U-M-P." He spelled it out, emphasising each letter, finishing with a little clap to accompany the P.

Ann sighed. "Thanks for that, Ian. That's made me feel marvellous." She leaned forwards, resting her arms on the counter. "So I'm in a trough stage?"

"Yes, indeed you are." Ian pushed up the sleeves of his shop coat, wiping the sweat from his upper lip. "Talking of which, *I* could climb into a water trough. It's so bloody warm."

"Why do you wear that thing?" Ann pointed to the donkey-coloured canvas overcoat.

Ian opened the first three poppers of the coat to reveal a loud Hawaiian-print shirt.

"To hide this," he giggled. "Dear Lorenzo, my Italian man, sent it. Three more weeks and he shall descend upon Knockmore for his yearly stay. Watch as the rumour mill transfers to *moi*."

Ann watched Ian do a little dance of joy, kicking out his tanned ankles as he went, wearing loafers *sans* socks.

"I see you haven't given the socks a go?" Ann laughed, remembering the story Ian told her about the woman from the dry cleaners arriving at the hardware shop to present Ian with a bumper pack of fluffy white socks that she'd picked up in the euro-saver store.

"But I'm gay," he'd told her.

"I know you are, love, but this is Knockmore. You can't be going around with your trousers flying half-mast up your leg and not a shred of cotton between your shin and your shoes. You'll get blisters – and then you won't be gay, you'll be in feckin' agony."

Ian finished his dance and sat down opposite Ann. "As you can see, as soon as Lorenzo arrives, I'm about to peak." He shot his hand in the air and then pushed his tortoiseshell glasses up on his nose.

"That you are. Ian?"

"Yes, my little songbird."

"Do you ever get lonely, living alone?"

"Never."

"Oh."

Ann was still reeling over her conversation with Sophie earlier in the week, where she'd hinted that Mark may be about to ask her something.

"It's like this, Annie. When you live alone you make

sure you spend as much time out of the house as possible, so any time you are there, it's a gift rather than a hindrance. Are you lonely, Annie?"

Ann looked up from where she'd been arranging paint sample bottles into a pyramid.

"Not really. Not so much during the day – not at the moment, anyhow," she smiled, thinking of the recent comings and goings in Knockmore House and her new work companions. "Sometimes in the evenings. Mark's been so busy the past few weeks. I've hardly seen him. But he's coming tonight. I don't know. I just feel a bit bleugh." She made a face.

"Well, you know what'll make you feel a little less bleugh, as you put it? Making an effort with your appearance." Ian looked her up and down, turning his nose up. "Hanging around with builders all day seems to be rubbing off on you. Get home early, get showered and prepare to get your groove on." Ian jumped off the stool and did another dance, swishing his hips from side to side, clicking his fingers. "You know what they say, Ann. It can't be sunshine, lollipops and rainbows every day. There's been lots of excitement for you lately. It will come again."

Ann picked up her bag to leave. Perhaps Ian was right and she was just in a slump. Things with Mark had settled into a nice routine and she was enjoying getting to know him. It was so wonderfully simplistic with him. Perhaps this was how it was the second time round: you reach a level of comfort far quicker when you've gone through the heartache of a broken marriage, bypassing all the silly little dating problems, wondering when to text, or when to let them see you at your worst. It wasn't exactly not caring. It was more realising that what you feared most had already happened and you knew that you'd survive if things didn't work out.

Of course, Mark had never been married, but he, too, seemed to be enjoying the fact that Ann was comfortable with him and not laden down with the usual insecurities of a new relationship.

"I love spending time with you," he'd told her the last time. "And I love that you're not needy," he'd giggled.

Mark hadn't divulged that at times, it was him who felt needy with her, but her next words had reassured him.

"I love being with you, too. It feels . . . natural."

"I wish I could be with you more. Travelling up and down from Wicklow seems like a waste of time, when I could be here with you instead."

"Stay, then," she said as he'd kissed her. "Here with me."

Yes, it was all very fast, but Ann was sure it was normal.

Almost as normal as she felt working in Knockmore House. She loved it – being here, watching the house change, having daily company, feeling part of something. It was almost four weeks now since the team of builders had descended following the weekend of festivities with Sophie and Jack. If she were honest, there was no real effort in supervising the building work. All that was required was to open up in the morning and lock up in the evening.

But she almost always stayed during the day, to fuss over the lads, supplying tea, coffee and snacks. The accounts element of her job was a breeze and she'd usually finished what she had to do by lunch, but Ann enjoyed the buzz, the banter – albeit at times so vulgar that at first, it made her blush from her toes to the roots of her hair. She was getting used to it, though, even managing to deliver a few epic one-liners in response, which saw even Tats, the plumber, who often used the most shocking of phrases, lost for words.

"And I thought you were a lady. You're not fooling me with that blondie hair and innocent voice."

"I am, but one who's been coached by all of you. What is it they say? Bad company corrupts good character."

"Hah! You'll be wolf-whistling at fellas passing you on the street next."

Ann had given a pathetic whistle as Tats walked past.

"From the heart, Ann, that was shite."

Ann was so accustomed to seeing five builders' cracks located in alternating positions throughout the house that she'd given up trying to avert her eyes. She even felt proud that she could now identify them from behind by how their jeans slipped down to reveal the top of their arses. Mind you, she still mixed up Sully and Winker. They were a hard pair to *crack*, but she was working on it, sure that if she ever got the opportunity, her specialist topic on the quiz show *Mastermind* could be "Builder's Bum".

The vans appeared through the gates at 8 a.m. sharp each day and she was almost disappointed to see them leave again, heading back out on to the Dublin Road at 5 p.m., just as sharp. Well, most of them. The blue truck was always there later than the rest. The same blue truck that had arrived on the first morning, pulling into the driveway with a tiny caravan attached to the back.

It had driven through the gateposts, reversing the trailer into place and depositing it at the side of the house. It couldn't be seen from the house, except, as Ann discovered, if you stood on your tiptoes in the upstairs guest bathroom and peered out of the open frosted-glass window.

"Great news," Mark had told her the Monday after

the weekend spent in Knockmore with Sophie and Jack. "That builder, Jason, just emailed the quote and it's perfect. A tiny bit more than the other guy's, but they can start this Thursday. Can you be there? Get Jason set up on the accounts system? He'll go through how he wants to be paid with you and I'll email you the rest."

Ann had been at the house as promised, sitting on the front step sipping her coffee, the hood of her jacket pulled over her hair, when she saw the blue truck pull in, followed by two white vans. She'd almost slept in. Having no time to shower, she'd pulled on an old tracksuit and stuffed a bag with clothes to change into later.

"All right, missus," one of them waved as the vehicle doors were thrown open, toolboxes and tools emerging, ready to be delivered round the back in preparation to start.

Ann sat watching absent-mindedly, wondering which one Jason was, none of them standing out as the boss.

Eventually, she'd gone inside, showered and changed into a pair of denim shorts and a slouchy T-shirt that made her look more seventeen than thirty. That was one advantage of working from "home" per se – there was no need to dress to impress.

Ann was sure that when he was ready, Jason would come and find her. She'd peeked through the door of the kitchen a few times and seeing them all busy at work, had left them to it. By lunchtime, feeling hungry, she'd pushed open the kitchen door, shocked to see that the back windows were already out, the furniture shoved into the kitchen area, and that she'd have to contort if she wanted to make it to the fridge.

"That was quick," she smiled as she walked outside to

see four heads sitting in a row, their backs to what they'd just demolished.

The heads turned. One stuffed the remainder of a sandwich into his mouth and chewed frantically. Another knocked over his mug of tea. The third looked at her as if she'd just walked out naked, and the man on the end almost toppled the blue crate he was sitting on.

"Hi." Ann smiled again, oblivious to their faces as they exchanged glances. "I'm Ann."

They all stood, four sets of eyes flitting over her.

"Holy shit," one of them whispered, whistling approvingly, to be delivered a sharp elbow in the ribs by another. "Oi," he responded, elbowing back.

"How are yah, Ann?" A tiny man stepped forwards and winked. "Don't mind that lot. Swear they've never seen a beautiful girl before," he winked again. "Everything all righ', love? Hope we weren't too noisy for yah. I know how youse lot like to sleep in."

Ann laughed. "There's a nice thought. I just wanted to introduce myself. I suppose we'll be seeing a lot of each other over the next few months. My office is inside, so if you need anything, just shout," Ann said.

They all stared at her.

"Your office?"

"I work here. I do the accounts and, well, I'm kind of overseeing the job, in a way, sort of," she attempted to explain.

The small man grinned. "Jeez, sorry, love." He smacked his hand off his forehead. "I thought you were the daughter or something. Too young to be an accountant, you are," he winked.

"Yeah," said the one covered in tattoos. "I thought you were a teenager. Lads, where are our manners? This is the boss lady. I'll introduce you to everyone. That's Sully . . ." He pointed at a larger bearded man in his early fifties. "He's on bricks."

Sully didn't look up.

"This here is Foxy."

A younger man with fiery-red hair and an enormous smile, minus one front tooth, stepped forwards.

"He's on roof."

Foxy saluted her.

"This young man is Winker."

Winker, the tiny man and the oldest of them all by far, winked again.

"He's on sparks."

Winker made a fireworks motion with his fingers and unsurprisingly winked once more.

"And I'm . . ." He motioned down his arms, where not an inch of original flesh was visible. "Well, I'm Tats, on taps, but we all do a little bit of everything. Masters of all trades," he finished.

They all took a little bow.

Ann smiled broadly. "And like I said. I'm Ann . . . on strings." She strummed an air guitar and they all laughed.

"We're gonna get on just fine. As long as you don't mind a bit of language now and again. We shall try to refrain," Tats said, putting on a posh accent and dropping into a curtsy.

"My dad was in a band when I was a kid," Ann said. "Luckily, I'm used to it. I no longer hear bad language. So, which one of you is Jason?" Ann asked.

"Who?" Sully looked up suddenly and Tats stood on his foot.

"Jason?" Ann repeated, looking confused.

Tats laughed. "Oh, yeah. Sorry, Ann. See, we don't call him Jason. Isn't that right, lads?"

They all nodded, shifting awkwardly from foot to foot.

"To us, he's simply De Boss."

Ann followed his hand in the direction of the caravan.

"De Boss is inside," Tats said. "Give him a knick-knock, see if he answers."

"Oh. Okay. Right, so. Thanks, lads."

Ann walked towards the caravan, where frilly peach curtains covered the windows and a sign saying "Do Not Disturb Under Any Circumstances" was nailed to the door. Ann ignored the deterrent, knocked and stood back.

There was no movement.

She reached up and knocked again louder, and this time the door was flung open. He had to slouch to stand up inside. His baseball cap was tipped down over his face and all Ann could see were beige work trousers and heavy boots.

"Didn't you read the sign?" he asked, not looking up and reaching inside to grab something off the table.

"Well, it's permanent, so I thought it couldn't apply all the time. Otherwise, you'd never be disturbed."

Ann craned her neck inside. She saw him stuff a phone into his pocket before stepping outside, across her. His back was to her as he locked the door.

"That's the idea."

"Are you Jason?" she said to his back. "I'm Ann. I wanted to introduce myself."

He turned to face her, using his index finger to push the peak of his cap up slowly until he was looking straight into her eyes, taking in her shocked face.

"It's you!"

CHAPTER THIRTY-FOUR

Ann left Ian's, jumped into her little car and sped off down the road. She stopped at Tea and Sympathy to pick up a few scones for "the boys", as she'd affectionately come to call them.

"Can't stop, Denise," she called over her shoulder. "I've a hot date tonight. Just going feed up the boys and head off to spruce myself up. According to Ian, I'm a mess."

Denise popped her head out of the door of the back kitchen, looked at Ann's messy hair, grubby shorts and T-shirt, and nodded.

"Agreed. They must all be in love with you, feeding them up all the time. You're like Snow White and the Seven Dwarfs. Make sure none of them gives you a rotten old apple to eat. Steve has no time to be making glass coffins. More people are cranking it these days than he can keep up with. Must be the warmer weather. We're not used to it." Denise came to the door of the kitchen from where she was making rounds of sandwiches on big silver platters for yet another funeral party and leaned against the frame for a rest. "Come to think of it, I might die myself from the heat. It's roasting out, isn't it? Or maybe I'm having a hot flush." She mopped her brow and screwed her face up. "Are you sure you don't want me to put you on the books as a singer for the stiffs? You'd make a killing, pardon the pun."

"Thanks, Denise. Not yet. Starting out, I think I'd like this to be a little more joyous and I'm busy up at Knockmore House until the building is complete."

"Are you sure? Honest, I can't keep up. They're dropping like flies. It'll be just us left around here soon. Someone needs to have more babies. We need repopulation, fast. Give Tracy a shout, see if she has another bun in the oven yet. Or maybe Mark and you could oblige," Denise winked.

"Now now. None of that," Ann giggled and waved before rushing out of the door and back to her car – her little hunk of junk.

Ann had been out chatting to Tracy on the road, when Mark drove towards them a few weeks ago, wedged into a tiny metallic blue car, beeping the horn.

"What in the name of Jesus is that?" Tracy nudged Ann. "Where's the big tank? Mind you, he still looks bleedin' gorgeous, even in that. I'll leave you to it." Tracy waved at Mark and disappeared inside.

"Times must be tough," Ann laughed as Mark rolled down the window of the 2001 Nissan Micra. "Where's the Range Rover, or the Big Tank as Tracy's cronies call it?"

"This is for you." He dangled the keys as he emerged backwards from the tiny car. "That was like a rebirth, trying to get out of that." Mark bent to kiss her. "And before you say anything, it cost nothing. It has bog all miles on the clock and it's safe as houses – belonged to some little old lady who drove it to Mass every day, possibly to ask for forgiveness for never taking it out of first gear."

Ann looked at the car. "Really? For me? I'll have to pay you for it."

Mark ruffled her hair. "Take it as a bonus. I would have bought you something nicer, but I knew you wouldn't have accepted, so it's this." He handed her the keys and she jumped up and down. "This will enable you to get more bookings for weddings and *get you to the church on time*," he sang.

"I love it," she laughed. "It's perfect. Thank you." She put her arms around him and hugged him tightly.

"Happy?" he asked and she nodded, nuzzling her face against his chest.

"You smell good." She pressed herself against him. "Want to come inside?"

"Oh, absolutely." His hand snaked around her waist. "But first," he grinned. "Hop in. Let's see what she can do on the open road. I think if you press the accelerator really hard, you may be able to get her to seventy."

Ann wasn't sure now how she'd coped not having a car, even though she never would have admitted that when Dom took back her car. She hadn't thought of Dom in a while – at least not until she received a letter from the solicitor saying that they had a date for the hearing for their legal separation. Sophie was going to come with her. Of course, Mark had offered, but it hardly seemed appropriate bringing her new boyfriend to her separation hearing – although she was sure Sabrina would make an appearance.

Ann drove through the gates of Knockmore House now and parked the car beside the steps at the front. In just four weeks, the internal part of the house was really taking shape. The once medium-sized kitchen was now simply *huge*. The wall between the dining room and the sitting room had gone, and the archways were now in place that would eventually lead to the conservatory, or orangery, as Olive was describing it.

"Hi, boys," Ann sang as she rounded the corner laden with treats.

They all looked up – everyone except *him*.

"It's you!"

Ann stared up at him after he'd slammed the door of the caravan and turned to face her, pushing his cap up slowly until he was looking her directly in the eyes. Her entire demeanour had changed that first morning as recognition crept over her features and her jaw fell open. Ann stood frozen for a moment, forgetting to breathe as her heart fluttered unexpectedly and her hands went numb. Nathan watched her, his face almost breaking into a smile, but he stopped himself.

Ann searched his eyes. Nathan stared back blankly.

"Who's that, now?" he'd asked, tilting his head to the side and dropping one eyebrow quizzically.

Ann straightened, grabbing her ponytail, bringing it over her shoulder and twisting it round her hand.

"I saw you before. You were there, that night," she uttered, urging him to remember.

"Oh, really?" He dropped the keys he was holding into his pocket and started to walk away.

"Yes, in Lennon's. You were there." She caught up beside him.

"Was I?"

He turned to look at her again just before he reached the patio. The lads had stopped their chatter to watch the exchange with interest. Ann stuffed her hands in her pockets to stop her hands from trembling.

"Weren't you?"

"Never heard of the place." He took off his cap and brushed his dark hair back then put it back on.

"Are you sure? It was a while back, a couple of months ago. I was . . . well, I was singing and I could have sworn . . ."

It *was* him. Ann would have recognised those eyes anywhere – when she allowed herself to travel back to that night, they were all she could see.

Nathan took a step back and held his hands up. "So, you sing in a bar? Good for you." He clapped sarcastically. "But that's not my thing, sweetheart. Sorry. Wrong guy," Nathan grimaced and walked off, leaving Ann staring after him.

"Hey," she shouted after him.

"What? Look, I'm busy, sweetheart. What can I do for you?"

Ann walked towards him. "My mistake." She gathered herself. "I'm Ann. I take it you're Jason."

"Yeah. That's me."

"Well, I would say nice to meet you, Jason, but you seem to be a little disgruntled. Is that an everyday thing or just a today thing?" she snapped. "Just so I know, for future reference. I need to set you up on the system to pay you and your band of merry men." She gestured towards the lads, who were still watching the interaction, nudging each other and laughing.

"Can we do it later? I need to get back to work," he said gruffly.

"I'll be inside. Door beside the kitchen, that's my office. And I'll be here every day. So if you have any questions, please direct them to me and I'll contact Mark. How does that sound, *Jason*?" Ann spat his name and thrust her shoulders back.

"Great." He was nearly impressed by her gutsiness. It wasn't what he'd been expecting. "Here's a question. Why was all the furniture not moved out of the rooms?"

"Did you ask for it to be moved?" Ann challenged.

"Well, no. But it's common sense."

"Well, that's why it hasn't been moved, also common sense." Ann looked behind her. "There's a garage over there. It should be dry enough to store everything in." She pointed at the building. "I'm sure the lads won't mind giving you a hand to move everything."

Sully, Winker, Tats and Foxy, who were still watching, all nodded vigorously.

Nathan shook his head. "Fine," he muttered. "One more thing. Around here, they call me Boss, not Jason. It's what I answer to."

"Is that right, Boss?" She leaned forwards, so she was inches from his face. "And you can kiss my arse."

Ann strode off, passing the lads, whose shoulders were now shaking. Winker was winking as if something had flown into his eye and was now lodged behind it.

Foxy let out an almighty "Whoopla," as she walked back towards the kitchen, climbing over the furniture as best she could in an effort at making a dramatic exit.

Back at her desk, Ann sat down and stared blankly at the laptop screen, trying to catch her breath. She hadn't meant to be so bolshie, unsure if she was furious for being slighted, or perturbed that he didn't remember her. It *was* him, or at least someone who looked remarkably like him.

Ann leaned back in the chair and put her feet up on the desk, resting her arms behind her head, and closed her eyes. Was she wrong? She'd had quite a bit to drink that night, the nerves of singing for the first time in public getting the better of her. Ann knew one thing for sure: if it was him, she couldn't have got him more wrong. What she'd been staring at that night was a figment of her imagination and not that obnoxious man outside. Perhaps this was a good thing. She'd spent weeks fantasising over an imaginary man, when she should have been thinking of Mark. Clearly, she'd slapped the wrong face.

"Yes?" Ann called, hearing a light knock on the door and sitting up.

"Can I come in?" he asked, sticking his head round the door.

He'd removed his work boots and was standing in his socks. His work trousers were covered in dust and his black T-shirt was speckled with white.

Ann sat up straighter. "What can I do for you?"

He thrust a piece of paper at her.

"It's all there. The bank account details and the payment instructions," he paused. "It's Sully's account. He pays the lads weekly and well . . . I agreed with Mark that I get a cash payment at the end of the job." He was looking at the ground. "Don't suppose accountants like that sort of thing."

Ann took the paper. "I'm just filling in for a few months. I do what I'm told."

She glanced up at him. His arms were toned, tanned, and his face so sun-kissed that she wasn't sure if it was an actual tan or dirt. His hair was dark, greying at the sides a little, or was that dust? She could see the same lighter colours in the hairs on his face – not quite a beard, but more than stubble. And his eyes . . .

"Listen." He put his hands back in his pockets. "I think we got off on the wrong foot," he said awkwardly, finally meeting her eyes briefly before looking away again.

His eyes were chocolate brown – piercing, haunted. Kind? Ann wasn't sure, but there was something there now that she hadn't seen earlier.

"I wanted to apologise. I get a bit antsy at the start of a job. Especially with an old house like this. I'm keen to do the best job and, well, I'm a bit of perfectionist. My tragic flaw."

Ann watched him speak. It was a different person to the one she'd met earlier. He was almost fragile, hesitant. His eyes met hers and she felt it again. The electricity jolted her and she looked away.

"It's okay," she replied, shuffling some papers on the desk. "We all have bad days. Glad to see you're passionate about what you do."

"Anyway, I'd better get back." And then: "So, you're a singer?"

"Well. Trying to be. Sorry, that makes me sound like I'm a wannabe pop star. I want to sing at weddings, events, that kind of thing. I've only done a few. I play the guitar." Ann pointed at the guitar in the corner.

"So, soppy stuff."

Ann laughed. "Yeah. I guess so. In my spare time, I like some real stuff too, though."

"Real stuff?"

"Not the soppy ones. You play?"

"Used to. Not any more. Not a fan of soppy, though." He almost smiled again.

"What do you like, then? I bet it's The Eagles or something. Neil Young?" She was grinning.

Nathan looked up once more and this time, the corners of his mouth lifted and his eyes crinkled. Ann's stomach somersaulted.

"Now that would be telling," was all he said, gently closing the door behind him and leaving Ann more confused than she'd ever been in her life. Confused and intrigued.

CHAPTER THIRTY-FIVE

"You've been busy." Ann shielded her eyes from the sun as she walked round the back of Knockmore House to see the morning progress.

The wooden floors had been ripped up and were resting in a pile in the centre of the grass, ready to be replaced with the large flagstone tiles. The intricate wiring of the underfloor heating was in place and the back wall of the house was now almost entirely glass. Ann was enjoying watching the house evolve, despite her reservations about the plans to change it. She'd been afraid that it would erase her mother even more, but she'd been wrong, she could see that now. The process was fascinating to watch.

"I brought some treats from Tea and Sympathy, Denise's finest."

The builders all gathered on the patio as she tore the bag open, placing it, along with five cans of icy Coke, on the makeshift dining table: planks of wood resting on scaffolding.

"You're a doll, Ann," Foxy exclaimed, dropping his tools and rubbing his hands together. "I was getting a bit hypoglycaemic here. I could do with a bit of sugar."

"Hypoglycaemic! You're full of shit, Foxy." Tats walked past and knocked the hard hat off Foxy's head as he went. "He'd a rake of pints last night, Ann. Left me sitting outside this morning while he was barfing, you wuss!" Tats whacked him on the back just as Foxy was taking a sip from the can.

"I did not. I've a sensitive constitution." Foxy wiped his mouth.

"Sensitive constitution! You weren't saying that when you were stuffing a breakfast roll in your mouth on the way here."

"Grab the guitar, Annie. Give us a tune while those feckers argue like women." Winker grabbed a can and opened it.

It had become a little routine – Ann playing whatever song she was working on during their afternoon break. At first, she'd been mortified, but it was an opportunity to get used to playing to a crowd, instead of sitting as she usually did, in her mam's old bedroom in the window seat, playing to herself. It was Sully who'd spotted her up there one day, beckoning her down and asking her to play.

"If you can play for a group of rowdy builders, you can play for anyone," he'd reassured.

They loved hearing her play. Except for Jason – he rarely sat down for a break and even if he did, he sat alone. In a way, Ann was glad, still unable to figure him out, or put her finger on why she always felt on edge in his presence. In the last four weeks, he'd annoyingly become the focal point of much of her inner thoughts, summoning more emotions than she cared to admit – mainly frustration, sometimes disdain and the odd time, sheer hatred.

Ann sat on the grass, her legs crossed, looking up at the four expectant faces. She glanced towards the caravan, to where Jason was sitting on a deckchair, cap down over his face, arms crossed, fast asleep. So far, it was Sully who'd given her the most insight into their mysterious boss.

"Ah, he's decent," Sully admitted one afternoon. "Truth is, none of us knows much about him. There's no wife. No kids. No family. He's really private, but he's kind. Looks out for us all. There's not many left like him."

Ann listened, intrigued. It was so far from how she'd have described him.

Sully, so-called for his sullen nature and not because his name was Sullivan, as she'd first assumed, was the sensitive soul of the group. A big bear of a man, hopelessly dedicated to his wife and two daughters, never really up for the banter and a little standoffish.

"He's the most like me, I suppose," Sully continued. "Deep like the ocean, my missus always says about me. Grumpy, the girls say."

"Ah, you're not grumpy, Sully, you're a pussy-cat," Ann smiled at him. "Whereas him . . ." She gestured with her head towards Jason, who was standing on the roof of the extension. "He's just plain rude."

"I'm telling you, Ann. The boss is a gentleman. He'd do anything for any of us if we needed. Maybe he comes across a little . . . gruff." He tried to find the right word. "But like I always say, there's a reason folks are the way they are, but he's a good guy. You can see it if he'll let you. Maybe there's a great big lump of sadness to him also."

Sully looked up at the roof and Ann followed his eyes, settling on Jason again, who was shouting instructions at the lads.

"If you knew what I did, maybe you wouldn't judge." Sully went to walk away.

"What do you know?"

"It's not for me to say, but everyone has a story, Ann.

They might tell it someday and then again, maybe they'll just get by on their own."

Ann stared up curiously at Jason, wondering if Sully was right. It sounded a bit like her, she supposed – a story, a history, one she, too, found challenging to share. Perhaps it was how Tracy had first felt about Ann – that she was rude and mysterious, when all along, Ann had been trying to prevent herself from going under. Maybe Jason had a story, too. Was that it? But what? What was his story? Had he been married? Did he lose someone he loved?

Once or twice over the weeks, she'd glimpsed a somewhat lighter side, preventing her from totally giving in to her initial impression when she met him on-site that morning. Ann had seen him outside the gates of Knockmore House one day, changing the tyre of a car for an older lady. And then there was the time she'd spied him in town outside the newsagents, talking to a young woman with a buggy and a toddler. Jason had got down on his hunkers to show the young boy his tool belt, and then he'd taken off his hard hat and popped it on the young lad's head, much to the boy's delight.

It just didn't add up. At times he seemed intensely surly and then, a few times, he'd flash a smile so immense that it was difficult not to smile back. Is that what she was trying to do, make him smile? Break through? Then some days he wouldn't even glance in her direction – totally avoid her, act as though she were invisible.

It was on these days, for some reason, that Ann found herself being more jovial than usual around the other men. And then later, she'd silently reprimand herself for acting like a teenager – a teenager he snubbed. Ann had even taken to trying to discover what kind of music he liked as a way to crack beneath the surface – for what reason, she wasn't sure – and would often walk past him, barely lifting her head before tossing out a suggestion.

"Bruce Springsteen? Bryan Adams?"

To which he'd shake his head, continue past as if a fly had landed on him and he was shooing it away.

"Adam Ant?"

There had been a smile that day – very slight.

"Right? What's it going to be, lads?" Ann asked them now as they munched into their scones.

"Give us something movin'," Tats called. "Something to make Sully cry again." He reached over and smacked Sully's leg, who batted him away.

"Piss off, Tats. Let the lady sing."

"Okay, I have it . . ." She thought for a moment. "Tissues at the ready, boys. It's called 'Never Change' by Picture This. They're an Irish band," Ann told them.

"Know them well. Love that one, Ann," Foxy exclaimed.

It was a song that the groom wanted to be played at her next wedding and she'd loved it as soon as she heard it. Ann took a deep breath and started to play.

Ann closed her eyes, singing the lyrics of a man with a thousand things to say, who'd never been brave enough. There was something about the words that moved her. They were honest, authentic, raw – and they touched something in her every time she sang them.

They all stopped what they were doing to watch her. Denise was right about one thing – every one of them had fallen in love with Ann in some little way: her kindness, her strength, her fragility.

"She's a lady. Sent from the heavens. Otherworldly," Winker told them philosophically one day when Ann was safely out of earshot. He was bent over, screwing a plug socket into the wall.

"Don't be telling me you wouldn't give her one if you had the chance, Winker. She'd send your lazy eye into overdrive. It would never wink again." Foxy pushed Winker over as he walked past.

"That's enough, lads," The Boss shouted at them. "Have some respect."

They all glanced at each other, raising their eyebrows.

"I wouldn't." Winker righted himself, standing proud. "She's serene. A lady – not like the ones you might find in one of your magazines, Foxy. The ones you keep hidden in the glove compartment, the ones you think we don't know about, you dirty bugger." Winker stuck his fingers up at Foxy in retaliation.

Ann got ready for the chorus, taking a big breath. When she'd finished, she glanced up shyly. They were all on their feet applauding in seconds. Sully dabbing his moist eyes and Winker doing what he did best.

"Jesus, it's like the Eurovision. Knockmore. *Dix points*," Tats yelped.

"Dunno about ten, but I'd give her one. Boom boom," Foxy added.

They all stared at his excited outburst. Ann turned her nose up as Foxy stumbled away, tripping over a crate as he went.

"The head on yer, man!" Tats stifled a laugh. "Ah, Ann, will you come to de next job with us? It's like musical t-erapy."

"I'd love to," Ann giggled. "I could do worse than being part of this team."

"Come on, lads, we'd better get back to work." Sully was still attempting to compose himself.

"Same time tomorrow, Ann?" Winker winked.

Ann watched them disperse. After putting down the guitar, she plucked at a daisy on the grass beside her, turning her head just in time to catch Jason's eye. He was sitting up, his cap now pushed up, watching her. There was no movement to his features, but his eyes met hers and rested there. Ann wanted to look away, hide from the heat of his gaze, but she stopped herself. He got up and walked towards her, his eyes still on hers as he approached.

"The house is coming on great," Ann smiled. "Are you happy with it?"

He looked over at the house. "Yeah. It looks good. Few things I'd have done differently, but no one ever wants the builder's opinion."

"Like what?"

"Well," he started, glancing back at the house. "I like the glass at the back. Inside, there's too much glass, though. It's too much of a contrast and it's a shame to remove the Tyrolean rendering. I'd also have kept the oriel bay window over there . . ." He pointed at where the dining room window was no more. "It disturbs the original window grid now it's been removed. And I suppose what's great about Georgian houses is the reception rooms . . ." He paused when he saw Ann's face.

"You know your stuff. I'll have to go and google all that. Were you always a builder?"

"Were you always a singer?" He sounded snippy.

"Well, no, sorry. I don't mean to pry. It just sounds like—"

"What? That a builder can't know anything more than how to lay bricks?"

"That's not what I meant. I just wondered." Ann wasn't in the mood for this today. She went to pick up her guitar.

"I wanted to say . . ." He stood over her. "The guest-house I'm staying in is booked up for the next few weeks. I cleared it with your fella. From Monday, I'm going to sleep in the caravan."

Ann coughed. "Oh. Okay. Right, so," she stammered. "You can use the downstairs shower in the house before I lock up in the evenings, if you want," she offered, picking at the now crumpled daisy.

"Cheers."

"I thought you went back to Dublin every evening?"

"Who said I was from Dublin?"

"I just . . . I assumed."

"Assumptions can be deadly." He didn't smile. "Anyway, it'll give me a chance to do a few extra bits in the evenings. Make up for all the coffee breaks and music time. It's like builders' day care around here."

"Whatever." Ann stood up, ignoring the dig. "I'll leave you my mobile number in case you need anything – like the poker removed from your arse, or help to get a band of wolves off your severed leg if you're attacked in the night," she drawled. "I have to go." She turned to leave.

He was laughing. At her? With her?

"It's a pack of wolves," he shouted after her.

"Dickhead," she muttered under her breath.

"Hey, Ann?"

She twisted round.

"That song . . . it's . . . I think . . ."

Ann looked at him expectantly.

"The lyrics . . . it's meant to be sung by a man," he smirked as she stomped away, determined not to let him bother her and get in the way of her date with Mark.

Nathan stared after her until she was gone, the cynical

smile fading from his face, his hands dropping to his sides. He tilted his head to the side and then glanced over at the house, where Sully was standing watching him. He nodded at Sully, who shook his head and gave him a disapproving look. Nathan ignored it and stomped back towards the caravan, went inside and slammed the door. In the silence, and out of sight, he put his head back and exhaled, replaying the episode in his mind, altering it to how he'd have liked it to play out.

The truth was, there were a thousand things he wanted to say to Ann, but he wasn't sure he'd ever find the words, or be brave enough – and watching her walk away had become the least favourite part of his day.

CHAPTER THIRTY-SIX

"Hey. What's come over you?" Mark grinned.

Ann barely gave him a chance to get in the door before catapulting towards him and enveloping him. Dressed in little more than a white sleeveless T-shirt, Mark looked at her approvingly.

"You're a little underdressed for dinner," he laughed, closing the front door and putting his hands under her T-shirt.

"And you're overdressed." Ann put his tie between her teeth and then spat it out. The action had seemed more seductive in her mind. "Let's skip dinner. I want you all to myself. I've missed you."

"Really? I wanted to talk to you about something," he attempted.

It had been on his mind for a few weeks now. It was something his father had said to him before they'd left for Spain.

"Don't let her get away, son. If I had my time over, I wouldn't wait a moment to jump right in."

Mark hadn't been able to stop thinking about it. In just a few months, he felt like he could conquer the world and was ready to grasp the future. He had no doubt that it was Ann making him feel this way. It was as though he'd wished for her and now, here she was. All that time spent focusing on her when she was nothing more than a stranger must have led him to her.

Mark had attended enough work seminars in the past on the powers of positive thinking, the idea of asking the universe for what you want and attracting it to you, to know that he'd been gifted an opportunity. Mark was still terrified of frightening Ann away, but he'd decided, especially after talking to Sophie and Jack last week, that he was willing to take a chance. After all, what's for you won't pass you and all that. All Mark was doing was hurrying things along.

Besides, they weren't teenagers. They were in their thirties – it was natural to reach each phase faster. Would Ann respond how he wanted her to? Mark hoped she would, even though sometimes he wasn't entirely sure if her feelings were as strong as his. It niggled at him at times, but he was too afraid to question it.

"Totally normal," Jack assured him knowingly. "It's what women do. It's a defence mechanism. She's keeping a little back in case she gets hurt again."

Perhaps Jack was right. And Sophie hadn't seemed shocked by Mark's line of questioning either, even though he hadn't entirely divulged what he was thinking of asking Ann.

Lately, seeing Ann working at Knockmore House, and looking so comfortable and happy there, had Mark picturing a future with her that had never before crossed his mind until now. Mark wasn't going to rush it, but he was going to start the ball rolling in the right direction. He'd do anything to make Ann happy, anything at all . . .

"So, can we?"

"What?"

"Talk."

"Later." Ann turned to walk up the stairs.

Mark followed her eagerly as she removed her T-shirt

and threw it at him. She lay back on the bed, her hair splayed around her, watching him pull his shirt over his head and remove his trousers. Ann pulled him towards her, kissing him.

"Did you really miss me?" he asked before he threw her arms over her head and buried his face in her breasts, smiling when she moaned, losing herself in the moment.

Afterwards, they lay together on the bed, Mark snoring gently. Ann rolled on to her back and looked at the clock. It was still early. Maybe they should have gone out, after all.

Ann found her T-shirt on the landing and tiptoed downstairs. Mark had been working so hard lately and was obviously tired. Ann sat down at the kitchen table, resting her hands under her chin, and exhaled, looking around at her tiny kitchen. She'd become so used to being up at Knockmore House, listening to the thumping sounds of the renovations, walking from room to room upstairs, appreciating the cornices and finer details of the old house. Even Ann had to admit, much as she hated to agree with Olive, that the renovations would take Knockmore House up a notch.

Over the weeks, it had stolen her heart, so much so that she felt almost odd being here, in her own home. Or perhaps, being in this house alone felt strange when she'd become so used to having people around her constantly in Knockmore House. Ann couldn't wait to get up each morning and leave to get there. Driving through the gates of Knockmore House had become her favourite part of each day. Her mind drifted back to the conversation she'd had with Sophie, when she and Jack had met Mark for an early dinner one night in Dublin.

"Just to warn you," Sophie told her the last time they spoke. "He kept asking all about when Jack and I moved in together. After how long. What it was like. I think he has it on the cards for you guys next. I think he was sussing me out to see how you'd react."

"Don't be ridiculous. I barely know him."

Sophie laughed. "You keep saying that and yet you spend practically every night together anyway."

"Well, not lately. By the time Mark finishes work, he's often too tired to drive down. I do miss him, though. Why do I always get the workaholics?" Ann groaned.

"Well, you'd better prepare an answer. Just in case."

Of course, Ann hadn't thought of it again, putting it out of her mind – until today. Talking with Ian about living alone had her thinking about what it might be like to share a life with someone again.

Ann was rummaging in the fridge, when Mark came into the room an hour later. In the meantime, Ann had sat staring at the wall, her head tilted to the side, half thinking about what she'd say if Mark asked her to move in together and half thinking of . . . Jason. He'd made her so angry earlier, gawking at her as if she were a freak show, and all that chat about coffee breaks! How dare he! He was just plain odd and she didn't need any more strange in her life.

Then again, there was something about him that she still couldn't quite understand, some draw to him, some mystery that she wanted to solve. But why bother? Jason would be gone in a few months and then he was out of her life for good. She'd never see him again. Why was she even wasting her time thinking of him? Good riddance.

Ann would miss her boys, though. But there was a time for everything and now she had her car, she was going to start plugging her singing. She should probably let Denise recommend her for funerals, too. Ann had done the maths, sure she could make a healthy living from her singing alone. She had her house, she didn't need much to get by and she knew that once her separation hearing was over, well, hopefully, she'd have a small amount to put away for a rainy day.

Ann would miss Knockmore House, but as Denise kept reminding her, it wasn't hers, nor would it ever be. Once the renovations were finished, she'd move on to another phase – spend more time in her own little house, fall in love with it again. Knockmore House was part of her soul. It always would be. But this house was her home. It was where she was meant to be.

Ann closed the fridge door and looked up at Mark. He was so handsome, his face filled with warmth, and she couldn't help smiling.

"You look happy," he asked. "Are you?"

Ann nodded. Was she? Mark lifted her up, sat her on the kitchen counter and stood in between her legs.

"Me too. For the first time in maybe, forever," Mark said before turning serious. "I wanted to ask you something." He leaned back slightly. "I know it's sudden. I know we've only known each other for a short time, but I feel like I've known you forever. I feel like every moment in my life has been leading me to this moment, to you."

Ann watched him.

"So, I wanted to ask you . . ."

"Yes."

"Yes?"

"Yes."

"You'll marry me?"

Ann's eyes widened and she swallowed hard.

"I . . . I . . . I thought . . . I . . ."

Mark burst out laughing. "I'm joking. Your face!" He stood back and looked at her.

"Jesus, Mark. You frightened me. Sophie said you were going to ask me . . ."

"To move in?" he asked, grinning broadly. "Did I get that right? Will you?"

"Yes!" She threw her head back in relief.

His gaze met hers. "Would the other question have been so bad?"

If her face hadn't dropped, Mark knew he'd have fallen to one knee in an instant.

Ann looked at her hands as she spoke. "Yes. I mean, I don't know. Not yet. Not until . . ."

"I know." He hugged her. "Not yet. We could get our own place. Or, I was thinking, someday it could be Knockmore House. Not now, but someday. My parents won't be able to manage it forever and I thought, if anyone is meant to be there, it's you. Would you like that?"

Ann didn't know what to say. The idea of one day living in Knockmore House had never crossed her mind for a moment. It almost terrified her. Much as she loved the house, it could never be home, not in a million years.

Mark watched her face fall.

"I'm sorry, Ann, that was too much. Ignore that bit, please."

"Oh, Mark. I never thought . . . it seems too big an idea."

It was Mark's face that fell this time. Ann grabbed his hand.

"Could we try here for a little while? I know it's not exactly fancy, but could it be here?"

Mark nodded. "As long as I'm with you. I love you, Ann."

"I . . ."

Mark's phone ringing interrupted her. He reached behind to grab it off the kitchen table, ready to decline the call so he could hear the words he longed for her to say, when it stopped and then rang again almost immediately.

"Leave it," Ann whispered.

Mark looked at the screen.

"Sorry. Two minutes," he mouthed and left the room, heading into the living room and shutting the door.

Ann jumped down off the counter and went to find her own phone. She wanted to text Sophie, knowing how happy her friend would be that Ann had decided that uncomplicated bliss was the route to everlasting happiness and that she was finally ready to embrace the rollercoaster of life, when she looked up.

"Mark? What is it?"

Ann watched the colour draining from his face.

"Mark?"

He stared blankly ahead.

"Mark?" she repeated.

The phone fell from his hand, hitting the floor with a crash. Ann bent to pick it up.

"Mark?" She took his hands. "Look at me."

"Jessica," he repeated, his hands trembling. "I have to go."

CHAPTER THIRTY-SEVEN

Nathan

Something was different. It was as if a bleak breeze had swept through the air. A sullen cloud had descended and was now lingering ominously over Knockmore House. Nathan noticed it immediately, his quiet exterior often allowing him to see more than those who were continuously glancing around. It took the others longer, but eventually, Ann's sudden lack of presence caused a stir among them, too.

"Maybe she's not well."

"I'd say a fight with her boyfriend."

"Someone cancelled her for a gig."

"Maybe she's sick of all of us annoying her."

Ann came to open up that next morning before vanishing into the confines of her office and shutting the door firmly behind her. None of them saw her all morning, aside from once, when she materialised briefly, her eyes sunken, her face drawn. Nathan regarded her from under his cap. Ann's head was down, her hair concealing her face, her shoulders slumped. She paused for a moment beside him as if about to say something. He waited, trying to hide his smile, wondering what musician she'd suggest this time, but she turned and floated away silently.

He put his hands at the back his neck, interlocking his fingers, and stretched his back. Nathan was willing to bet Foxy's theory of a fight with the boyfriend was correct. Or perhaps Sully was right and Ann was sick of them all. Sully had stared straight at Nathan when he'd said it, the accusation clear in his words – that it was Nathan who'd got to Ann, maybe more than he'd intended, the evening before.

It wasn't his fault. Ann was so easy to wind up. It had surprised Nathan at first, her usual unflappable calm suddenly disintegrating when he was around. He irritated her, Nathan could tell. Ann would become agitated, curt – a far cry from how she was around the other lads. Of course, that had been his intention at first and it amused him, knowing that his sheer presence was getting to her. Recognising that he could fuel her emotions was somehow gratifying, for a few minutes, at least, until Nathan realised it was Ann who was getting to him more.

By mid-morning each day, Ann would usually appear, emerging from the Bat Cave, as she called it, to sit on the wall outside, or on the crate Sully always chivalrously volunteered, to sip tea with them, her warm smile infecting them all. Not that day. The change in routine had Winker glancing questioningly towards her door several times before continuing his task.

"Should we check on her?" Foxy asked when they sat down for their lunch and there was still no sign.

"I saw her going to the bathroom a while ago," Winker told them. "I tried a couple of classics. 'Turn the frown upside down,' and 'Smile, sweetheart, it may never happen.' Usually works, but I never even got a wink, so I left it."

"Must be, ye know, problems in the down below." Tats swirled his hand in front of his abdomen with a new theory.

"Women's stuff," Sully explained to Winker, whose twitch was reaching dangerous levels.

Nathan smiled to himself, listening to the learned speculation among the group of seemingly *hard* men.

"She'll be fine by tomorrow," Sully issued knowingly. "My missus always says about my girls to let them have their little mood, they'll snap out of it. It's all the hori-mones."

But the little mood lasted longer than the day. By day three, Ann was still nowhere to be seen.

"My missus says it can last a week. I asked her last night. I had no idea. I says to her, 'The moods and all?' 'Yeah,' she says to me, 'there's really only one week in the month where women are okay.' Sure, apparently there's pre-menstru-iliation, menstru-iliation, there's ovu-iliation. I think that's it. There might have been another. To be honest, I was feeling a bit weak at that point," Sully explained to the other three open mouths.

"Shocking stuff! Should we go and get her a great big bar of chocolate?" Tats suggested.

Nathan crept away, to walk round the side of the house. He, too, was growing concerned as to her absence. Ann's car was parked in the usual spot, beside the front door. She was obviously in her office, inside, working away, oblivious to the intrigue she was creating around the building site.

Nathan turned to walk back and stopped, his eyes moving towards the bay window to the right of the front door. An armchair was visible, at an angle almost facing away from the driveway. He could see Ann's hair falling over the arm, her head resting against the side of the chair. Nathan inched forwards. He'd never before seen her in any room of the house other than the kitchen and her office. Ann suited it here – it suited her.

At first, he'd thought Ann was like *them*, but it had quickly become apparent that Ann was no snob, or taken by money, or the house. Ann appreciated the house, Nathan could tell by the way she spoke about it, the way he saw her looking at it, but it was in a way that he didn't quite understand – it was almost wistful.

Perhaps Dr Sully was correct in his diagnosis and everything would go back to normal in a few days, but Nathan couldn't help thinking there was something more. Ann didn't seem the type for irrational mood swings or wallowing without reason.

Nathan watched her for a moment, sleeping peacefully. Was she at peace? He thought he could see a difference to her features. Something troubled, some pain – even in sleep.

By now, he knew her face perhaps better than he knew his own. Nathan had memorised every crease, able to read Ann by her expression alone. She would try and fail miserably to hide it, but Nathan could tell what she was feeling by how her features morphed into various positions – not always pretty ones, either. The exaggerated disgust face – the one that made her nose crinkle at the sides and her eyelids fall down, concealing her eyes. That was his favourite. Or the one when she was singing, so earnest, so intense – free. The one she made when he was intentionally annoying her – the one he was sure meant that he'd successfully crawled under her skin, in the same way she'd inched her way under his. Nathan had studied every inch of Ann's face without her realising – when you learn to be invisible, it's easier to see.

From the moment Nathan had set eyes on Ann again, that first morning when she'd knocked on the door of the caravan, he'd been able to think of nothing else. Of course, he'd known she'd turn up that first morning, that he'd have to face her, eventually. Hiding in the van, he'd made himself scarce, trying to avoid her. But then, Nathan had been positive she wouldn't remember him from that night in Lennon's. There was no way some "society princess" would have really noticed the likes of him in a crowded bar. It had all been part of her routine. Ann was undoubtedly the type to look down on people like them, or through them, to tiptoe around the lowlife builders. How wrong he'd been! Instead, she'd immersed herself, becoming one of them and making them all fall in love with her – him more than the rest.

It was a million miles from the original plan. After he'd taken the job at Knockmore House and decided to become Jason, he'd had something entirely different on his mind. He'd agreed before he arrived that he was going to toy with Ann a little. Nathan could turn on the charm when he wanted to. He'd be able to make her fall for him, no problem. It never took much. A little treat 'em mean, keep 'em keen. A few intense stares, flex the muscles. They were all the same – all they wanted was a bit of excitement, a brush with *a bit of rough*, some attention, a sad story, "heal my pain".

Wouldn't that be a great result? The girlfriend getting caught with the builder – that would add insult to injury when this was all done. As soon as Mark told him that Blondie would be supervising the job – what a joke – Nathan had factored Ann into the equation. The anger he'd felt that day had almost justified it all in his mind. The gloves were off. This was his round now. After all, Nathan may as well enjoy himself a little in the process – there could be worse things than having someone who looked the way she did wrapped around you, making the caravan shake.

That was until he came face to face with her – looked into her eyes, became trapped under her spell. When he'd turned to look at her that morning, he'd challenged her with his eyes.

Remember me? It wasn't just me, was it? You felt it, too?

He'd waited for her to stare back blankly and then . . . "It's you!"

He'd seen the questions in her eyes. One side of his heart had soared, the other had plummeted. What now? He did, then, what he did best – preservation mode. Acted like a shit. Played it cool, feigned ignorance, made her feel stupid. She was feisty enough back. He'd liked that. He bothered her and *everyone* knew that was better than indifference.

Once Nathan had convinced her it wasn't him in the pub that night, he still thought he might mess with her a little. He'd gone to apologise – to try to make her interested again, intending to flash a smile, ignite a spark. He'd hardly been able to meet her eyes. Christ! she was beautiful. But it wasn't just that. There was something more, something he couldn't quite understand. Something that if he let it, had the power to take over his soul. That couldn't happen. Not now. If he allowed her into his life, even for a few months, he'd never be able to let her go. There and then, he decided to leave her out of it all as best he could – avoid her.

Ann hadn't made it easy.

Nathan could feel her presence everywhere. He was able to sense when she was close by. His breathing would grow ragged as she approached. She'd walk by, not look at him and throw out the name of a singer, a band. "Stevie Wonder?" He'd shake his head, wait until she was past and then break into an automatic smile, one he couldn't stop.

He just couldn't let her see. It was easier to be dismissive.

"Nathan, whatever this gig is to you, whatever reason you've suddenly become Jason, whoever the hell he is, don't involve the girl. I see the way you look at her. Jesus, I can see the way she's looking at you," Sully implored after that first week.

"Me and the lads, we respect you. We'd do anything for you, we've never asked any questions of you," he continued. "But leave her out of this. She's a good girl. Don't do what I think you're doing. That's all I want to say."

"She's a privileged know-it-all," Nathan retorted, childlike.

"You know what I always say – everyone has a story, Nathan. Everyone. And something tells me she has a story just as big as any of ours stood here."

Nathan stared after him.

Sully was the only one who knew Nathan's real story – well, most of it, anyway. Nathan would trust him with his life, so he did what Sully asked, knowing he was rude to her. But in the long run, it was for the best: cruel to be kind.

It was going fine, too. Well, he'd convinced himself it was – until she'd sung that song, sitting on the grass. He'd heard her sing before, of course, had learned to tune out while the other lads made goo-goo eyes at her. But this time, he couldn't bring himself to look away. The lyrics of the song walloped him in the chest. Was she trying to tell him something? Was this for him? He wanted it to be, so much so that when she'd finished, he let her see him watching her. In his mind, he'd walked over, pulled her to her feet and kissed her, absorbed her, been brave, told her the truth, let her see.

In reality, he'd acted like a fool.

Nathan had stayed in the caravan that night, even though he'd told her it wouldn't be until next week. He'd wanted to be near her, although she wasn't even there. Staying on-site was all part of the plan, giving him a chance to do the "extra" bits of work in the evenings after the lads left. That way, if something ever came back to bite them, they wouldn't have known.

Nathan had altered the plans. He was an architect, after all, and it had felt good to use his skills again, albeit in the wrong way. At one time, he won more awards for innovative design than he cared to remember, he and his little brother. They were good days. This wasn't exactly what you could call an innovative design, but it was enough.

The extension out back was marginally bigger than it should be, only by about seven feet. Nathan had seen extensions knocked down and houses demolished for less – rules were rules. The other bits Nathan had planned would be quick enough. The Dempseys would be none the wiser, at least not until a godawful smell and a Baltic breeze filtered through the house, one that would make it impossible for them to ignore.

Then he'd hit them for the money – a hundred and fifty thousand euros. That would be enough. The right amount to make amends. Nathan hadn't forgotten that they were *their* amends to make, he was just acting as the go-between. Maybe there could have been a more peaceful way. If it wasn't for Olive, there might have been, but he couldn't risk her destroying him again. He couldn't take the chance.

Would he go back to his old life? Nathan wanted to, more than anything, but since meeting Ann, all he now wanted was her. Was it strange that he could picture himself here, in this house with her? Every time the thought came to him, he pushed it away, not knowing why Knockmore House had infiltrated his soul with its beauty, its enigma, but it was more than that. Nathan had come to associate this place with Ann, somehow. Seeing her standing on the steps, her hair blowing in the breeze, her face alight, was like nothing he'd ever seen before. It felt like home.

Nathan watched Ann stir in the chair now. He had to stop himself from walking towards the window and pressing his hand against the glass. Ann Maguire was the only thing that made him want to walk away from all this – free himself. Yet in another, she was what made him stay, tying him here, doing what he knew was the wrong thing, to make everything right.

Deep down, Nathan didn't want to destroy Knockmore House, knowing that it would ruin any chance he had with Ann. He'd thought so many times about telling her the truth. Every pause in the conversation that he filled with some cynical jibe was his opportunity to show her, but what would she have said?

Restraining himself was becoming increasingly demanding, when all he wanted was to be with her, to wind his hand into her hair and never let go. If only he could let her in.

Was that look he'd seen Ann give him once or twice real? Sully had said he'd seen it and he was usually right. Nathan thought he'd noticed it, too. Years ago, he'd have been confident enough to know that she was looking at him, in the same way he was looking at her. Years ago, Nathan would have told her how he felt. But now, Nathan wasn't sure enough of himself to take the chance. Besides, if he felt anything for her like Sully said, he had to leave her be. Ann was too good for him. She was better off without him. Soon, he'd be gone, leaving her behind to continue her life.

Nathan edged away from the window and walked back round the side of the house, feeling his spirits sink further into his boots than ever before. To him, she was the sea – pure and beautiful to watch, but dangerous to mess with, for Ann Maguire had the power to wound his heart even more than it already was.

If he'd turned, he'd have seen her sit up. If Nathan had looked back, he'd have seen Ann press her hand against the glass and watch him walk away.

CHAPTER THIRTY-EIGHT

Olive

If they hurt, you hurt. If they cry, you cry. But if they fall, you can't go down with them – that's the time to stand tall.

Olive stood in the bedroom of the Spanish villa, glaring at her reflection in the mirror. It wasn't Ordinary Olive who stared back, nor the modernised form, but some smashed-up, morphed version, like the broken yellow-and-blue tiles decorating the surrounds of the glass. Olive wanted to thrust her fist at the image to shatter it further, destroy the impression that peered back, have it become irreversible, so it could never be put back together in any form – and then she'd be gone, forever. Olive longed to give in, finally allow her legs to surrender, so the floor might open and consume her whole.

"Jessica," she whispered.

The name stung her lips, severed her soul, reached inside and twisted her guts.

"My little girl."

Olive uttered the words as her hands shook, her jaw trembled, and yet she continued to stare. Don't look away. Face it – face the truth.

Never, not in a million years, do you imagine it happening to you. You hear about it – you listen to whispered tales of woe, uttered out of the corner of mouths – and you feel for them. You ache for those people, but not enough to understand it fully. You might even try to put yourself in their shoes, to imagine how they're feeling, even for a moment. The thought makes you shudder. It's too painful to fathom, too real to proceed – so you stop yourself, eject it from your mind. Not us. Never us. Things like that happen to other people.

Hadn't enough already happened? Enough that could be spread across a lifetime. But to have everything happen collectively . . . that was another thing. And now this – one more deep etch of pain, more unimaginable agony.

Coming to Spain, leaving Ireland behind for a while, had been the right thing. Olive had been sure of it. After the first week here in the villa, nestled in the Spanish hills outside Malaga, Olive knew she'd made the right decision. Distance from the past was doing them all good. Even Mark sounded like a different person on the phone. Olive could hear it in his voice. Giving him the space he needed to pave a future was the right thing. Not only that, but Jessica appeared suddenly brighter, as if the sunlight had burned away the frost, afforded her some harmony and allowed a more jovial side to break through.

Jessica looked healthier than she had in a long time – and was eating again as if tasting life for the first time. Olive quietly observed Jessica's skin turning golden, where her daughter sat on the sun lounger scribbling away in a book as if her life depended on it. It was the most Olive had seen her do in so long.

"Did you know that chlorine can turn your hair green?" Olive took a break from her swim to pause at the edge of the pool.

Jessica ignored her.

"What are you writing, Jessica?"

"Stuff."

"What sort of stuff?"

"Nothing."

"My therapist says it's good to jot down your feelings. It's like talking, but not out loud. Better to write it down. Keep it private," Olive encouraged as she swam on.

In the evenings, once or twice, Olive stepped out onto the patio to witness Jessica cuddled into her father like a little girl – the same father Jessica once said she'd never forgive for his betrayal of them all. Olive had edged back inside, leaving them to it, wishing in one way she could sit on the other side of her, tickling the velvety soft skin at the back of her arm, tracing her fingers up and down it until Jessica would either giggle or fall asleep, as Olive had done when she was a child.

"Mum, tell me about when I was little. Tell me about me and Mark," Jessica asked another evening.

Olive hadn't needed any encouragement to talk about their idyllic years in Wicklow. They laughed through stories of mischief, recollections that needed little prodding to flood to the surface. Eugene had caught Olive's eye and they'd glanced at Jessica, sitting there listening, her face resting in her hands, soaking it up. She'd stood then, kissing them both before walking back inside, her white sundress drifting behind her, her hair loose, her features at ease.

"I remember. Goodnight. I . . . goodnight." Jessica had paused at the sliding door, as if going to say something else, before floating through.

Afterwards, you look for the signs. You search your mind – every word spoken, every movement, every look. You go over and over every scene. Was that it? Was that the indication? Had the clues been there? Olive supposed they had – sudden emails to friends Jessica hadn't seen in years, reminiscing of the past, an unexpected calm where there had once been a turbulent storm.

And then the book.

Olive had seen it when she returned from the hospital, left beside the bed where Olive had found Jessica – her precious girl. Olive's legs had gone from under her that time and the screech had deafened her. It took her a few seconds to realise the scream was coming from her own mouth – the guttural sound of horror issued straight from her lungs. Thank God for Eugene. Thank God he'd known what to do, when Olive had fallen to pieces, there and then, just like she promised she never would.

Everything after that was a blur.

Is there someone we can call?

Mark.

He'd arrived the next day.

"This has to stop. You have to tell me everything. Tell me. You have to tell me what you know." His face was white as he spoke.

Olive shook her head blankly as he pleaded with her, over and over again.

No, Mark, no.

And then, "I overheard something, years ago, in Wicklow. Soon after Jessica started acting this way. It was when Dad got sick. What did I hear, Mother? What did I hear?"

"Nothing, Mark. I don't know what you're talking about."

Eventually, Mark threw his arms up in exasperation and walked away.

Olive was sure her heart had stopped beating for a moment before she pulled herself together. No. He couldn't have. Surely he'd have said something before now. He was calling her bluff. No. Jessica would get better. She had to. There was no other choice. Olive would make sure she got better and then it would all be forgotten again. They'd go back to Knockmore. They shouldn't have left. They'd all been safe there.

Then Olive had gone to clear the bottles from beside Jessica's bed – pills, alcohol, whatever she could get her hands on, Jessica had consumed them all. It had almost been enough. Olive gazed down at the scattered mess, questioning how anyone could ever manage to beat the contents of those containers and win. Jessica had – except now, she was at risk of organ failure.

How had it come to this?

No, this didn't happen to people like them. Jessica *had* to pull through. The alternative wasn't an option. Then again, neither was telling the truth. What was the point now? What was done was done. Nothing could ever change it.

Olive picked up the book she'd watched Jessica write in, praying that this time when she opened it, the words would be gone. The name that her daughter had written again and again, over and over, filling the blank space until the pen had scratched through the paper, would be erased. Olive closed her eyes and then opened them and stared at the name that she'd tried so hard to eradicate – a constant reminder that the truth was still out there.

Nathan. Nathan.

CHAPTER THIRTY-NINE

Ann placed the phone on the desk and rested her head in her arms. Mark sounded exhausted and angry – at everything. But mostly – and she couldn't understand why – at Ann. It was almost a week now since Mark had received the terrible news and dropped everything to go to Spain to be at his sister's side.

"She's still on life support. There's no change."

Ann could hear him exhaling impatiently from her questions.

"How are your parents?"

"Devastated. Mum's putting on a brave face. Dad's not doing so well. He's blaming himself."

"I'm so sorry, Mark. Let me come to you. I can jump on a plane."

"No. There's no point. There's too much going on there and not a lot going on here. It's better this way. It's family stuff. I'm handling it." His tone was bleak and she felt hurt by the exclusion.

"Mark? It must be fairly serious – her condition, I mean – to do what she did. There must be more to it. Is there? Does your mother know more?"

"What exactly are you saying, Ann?"

"I just . . . I wondered. Does your mam know anything? From what I saw, she's hard on Jessica. From the outside, looking in, it seems like—" Ann immediately regretted it.

"Really? You're going to go there?" Mark interrupted. "Point the finger of blame? You hardly know Jessica or my mother . . ." He paused. "I have to go. I'll . . . I'll . . . I have to go. I just need some space."

He'd hung up, leaving Ann baffled.

She genuinely hadn't wanted to upset Mark. The truth was, Jessica had seemed perfectly reasonable to her – depressed but sane. In Ann's mind, Olive was the one with issues. Maybe Ann *had* overstepped the mark, literally.

The phone pinged and Ann picked it up, hoping it would be Mark, looking to smooth things over.

Don't speak to anyone about this. This is private.

Ann dropped the phone with a thud, feeling frustrated. Mark had been this way all week – a barricade erected that Ann couldn't cross. She had no idea what to do or how to help him, having spent the entire week lying awake, praying for Jessica to be okay, sick with worry for Mark and wanting to be there for him. Trouble was, he didn't seem to want her.

"It's totally normal," Sophie defended Mark down the phone. "You always take it out on the one closest to you. Poor Mark. Should you just go out there anyway?"

"He told me not to. Under *any* circumstances. He was so different. I know he's under pressure, but . . ."

Perhaps Ann didn't know Mark as well as she thought. Ann was sure if the situation were reversed, she wouldn't be pushing him away as he was ousting her.

"Mark seems like a stranger, Soph. He won't talk to

me – keeps brushing me off, telling me its 'family stuff'. And, clearly, I'm not his family. I feel terrible for them all, but I'm not sure I'm meant to be part of all this. It's like I'm an intruder in someone else's story."

"Oh, Ann. I'm sorry this has happened. Everything was going so well. That poor girl. Do you want me to come down to Knockmore?"

"No. Don't be silly. I know you have Jack's friends' wedding this weekend. I'll be fine. I'll see you next week."

Ann had barely ventured out the entire week, hiding away in her office, unable to face anyone, finding it difficult to lie about what was going on. The lads were all giving her encouraging smiles whenever they saw her, tiptoeing around her. She'd even found a bar of chocolate on her desk, anonymously delivered.

"Everything all right, Ann? No songs this week?" Tats asked gently.

"All fine. Just a bit under the weather. I'll be right as rain in no time."

Thankfully, even Jason had had the grace not to bother her and had taken to smiling sensitively at her, removing himself from her path when she approached.

Ann got up from the desk and walked into the hall, where she opened the front door and looked out. It was Friday evening and everyone had already left. The blue truck was gone, too. Jason had slept there during the week, but surely even he had somewhere to be at the weekend.

Sitting down on the top step, outside the front door, Ann rested her elbows on her knees, cupped her face and sighed. It was the first weekend in a while where she had no plans. Denise was away. Ian was in full prep mode for Lorenzo's arrival and undertaking a stringent detox.

Sophie and Jack were at a wedding, Mark was gone. It was just her.

Looking out over the driveway, Ann tried to think what to do for the weekend. It was nice being here, without the racket of the builders. It felt calm. Ann had searched for peace all week, even venturing into Olive's study at the front of the house in an effort to still her mind.

Those smaller rooms, still untouched by the renovations, were her favourite. She'd sat in a chair by the window, looking up at the high ceilings and tracing the pattern on the cornices with her eyes until she'd nodded off. When she woke, Ann had glanced out of the window to see Jason, in the driveway, his back to her, walking away.

More than anything, she'd wanted to call him back, to talk to him. Ann had no idea why. Perhaps she'd wanted to cling to someone else who, at times, appeared as troubled as she felt. Ann always imagined there was something more Jason wanted to say to her, but whenever he spoke, some other terse comment escaped. Then afterwards, she'd wonder why she was so intent on discovering the truth behind his eyes.

"For someone you hate so much, you sure talk about him a lot," Ian told her when he'd dropped by at the house the week before for an eyeful of the builders.

"I do not." Ann had turned away, trying to hide her flushed face.

"Methinks the lady doth protest too much." Ian looked at her over his glasses. "Still, can't blame you for looking. Jason's the typical bad boy, isn't he? Like James Dean or Johnny Depp – the type you want to sleep with but not necessarily take home to Mammy. You know – tanned, muscular, brooding, rugged. That dark hair lightly peppered with grey, that beard . . . my God, it's perfect – and eyes like a pair of chocolate drops," Ian finished, fanning his face.

"He's an oaf."

"Except, of course, The Oaf has the most marvellous South County Dublin accent and is incredibly polite. Even you must see that. I wonder what his story is," Ian mused. "And you *are* attracted to him. An idiot could see that – as am I, Annie. Let's call a spade a spade. But I have Lorenzo and you have Mark, so we'll agree to look but not touch."

"I don't even want to look."

"Good. Maybe I'm wrong, but men are usually good at sensing these things. Besides, Mark is far superior. He's perfect for you, darling. Don't go messing that up."

Ann hadn't thought about it since the distraction of Jessica, pushing it from her mind. Was she attracted to Jason? Was Ann making it that obvious that an idiot could see it, as Ian had put it? Ann put her face in her hands, suddenly mortified. She'd almost convinced herself that she hated Jason, but she knew she didn't, not really.

Ann loved how Jason spoke about Knockmore House. She could see how passionate he was about his work and his level of knowledge *had* astounded her. It was as though he felt about the house how she did – in a way that no one else seemed to understand. And Jason *was* handsome. Unbelievably so, albeit in a totally different style to Mark. And Ian was right, he didn't sound like the other lads. What was it Mark had said before? Jason was more like them – well-spoken, a touch of class about him.

Ann was still embarrassed that she'd mistaken him for the man she sang to in Lennon's. And if that man wasn't Jason, well, that was two people who'd now disturbed her focus from Mark. It was all so confusing.

Ann shook her head. She was doing it again, overthinking. Just a week ago, she'd decided that uncomplicated was her chosen route after she'd agreed to move in with Mark, but that was before . . .

Indeed, if Ian, Denise or even Sophie had anything to do with it, Ann would be with Mark. She'd wanted them all to like Mark so much that now they did, it was with a steadfast allegiance that would be hard to break. Had Ian been trying to warn Ann off Jason? Even if Jason did ignite something more than frustration in her, Ann was never going to explore those feelings, was she? Something Aunt Lucie had said a while back, when Ann asked if she was doing the right thing leaving Dom, entered her head now, once more, before she had the chance to banish it.

"When you know, you know. And if you don't know, well, that you're searching for the answer *is* the answer."

Ann stood up. She'd wasted enough time sitting here thinking about Jason. Jason was obviously some odd test, one that she planned to ignore. Mark was her destiny. "Destiny," her mam used to say. "The one thing that you can't fight against." Well, damned destiny had led her to this house and suddenly, Ann knew precisely where she wanted to be for the weekend. She wanted to be here, in Knockmore House, alone with her thoughts and her guitar – pay a visit to the past, forget the present and the darned future, whatever it held.

Ann locked the front door behind her, grabbed her guitar and headed upstairs to sit in the window seat, to just be. If destiny had it all worked out already, well then surely all Ann had to do was let destiny roll. If Ann had waited a few seconds longer, she'd have seen the blue truck come up the hill and roll through the gateposts of Knockmore House.

CHAPTER FORTY

Mark

Mark stuffed his phone back in his pocket, took it out again and tapped out a gruff message to Ann. He was agitated – angry with her for suggesting what she had. She barely knew his family, for God's sake. To go making accusations was too familiar, even if what she'd said was the truth. Mark ran his fingers through his hair and sighed. Wasn't that what they always say?

The truth hurt most.

When Mark had arrived in Spain, he'd taken a taxi straight to the hospital. At first, he hadn't recognised her – walked right past the room and then reversed back to peer through the door. Jessica looked tiny in the bed, like a broken doll, strapped to all manner of tubes and wires, a breathing apparatus in her mouth. Mark had crumbled then. After keeping it together on the way to the airport, on the flight over, he could no longer fight back the tears of exhaustion, frustration and guilt.

How had everything got so out of hand? When did it all go wrong? It was his fault for letting it come to this by not intervening, by failing to ask the right questions to uncover the whole story. Mark still wasn't entirely sure what the full story was, exactly, but he'd heard enough that night to know it was severe and that Jessica was wrapped up in something sinister. He'd heard enough to know his sister was scared.

Mark wasn't supposed to come home that night. He was supposed to be in Dublin, staying with his then girlfriend. Things hadn't worked out as planned, they never did, and he'd come back to Wicklow late, assuming they'd all be asleep, surprised when he reached the bottom of the corridor and heard voices. He'd stood there, frozen.

"Now you listen to me. It's done, Jessica. You're off the hook. You were asleep. That's all you need to say. Look at me. *You saw nothing*!"

Mark had held his breath.

"I saw it. I saw it," Jessica whimpered over and over again.

"Shush, Jessica. You'll wake your father. Do you hear me?"

"I have to see him. I need to see him. I remember now, I think I remember."

"You're confused, Jessica. The medication."

"No. No. I can't. I won't. I—"

"Stop it. Stop it right now. Your father. Think of your father. Now, I'm warning you. By God, if you say anything, that will be the end of Daddy. He'll have a heart attack and that will be on *your* shoulders. You don't want your father to die, do you? You silly, silly girl. Look at me! I will sort this. You will never speak of this again and if you do, you'll be sorry. It's done. Forget it now. You'd never survive it. Come here. It'll be okay. It's for the best."

"She didn't move . . . she was so still." Jessica's voice grew muffled.

Mark had backed away, creeping through the house, letting himself out of the back door. They hadn't heard him arrive. Hopefully, they wouldn't notice him leave. He'd driven away, trying to reason what he'd overheard. What had happened? What did Jessica mean?

After that, Mark had stayed away for weeks, every day expecting to receive a phone call from Jessica, or one from his mother, telling him the worst. It never came. Eventually, he'd gone to see them, clocking the warning looks that passed between Olive and Jessica. Then, over the coming months, he'd watched his sister disintegrate, slowly unwind, bit by bit, distancing herself from life.

"A bad break-up," his mother would say. "Taken it hard. Then there's the shock of that business with your father and his illness. She's had a nervous breakdown. Jessica just needs normality. The best thing we can do for her is not to mention it again, move on."

"Should I talk to her?"

"No, absolutely not. Jessica asked me to tell everyone not to talk about it. She wants to forget it now."

So, Mark did nothing. Besides, it was likely he'd been mistaken. After all, almost anything you overhear can sound suspicious, unless you know the context. Then work got on top of him – taking over from his father had been busier than he'd expected. Mark was too occupied with his own life and hesitant to get caught up in another family drama, still raw after the last revelation and not wanting them all clawing at him again, expecting him to fix it.

When his parents decided to move to Knockmore, Jessica refused, leaving Mark to look after her. Jessica drank all day, every day. Didn't shower, didn't eat, didn't leave the house, wouldn't talk. A few times, he tried to press her, prompting her to tell him what was wrong, but by that time she was so unhinged that she'd cover her ears like a child, rocking backwards and forwards. Mark couldn't manage.

His mother arrived then to whisk her away. Erasing another problem in her expert fashion. And he'd been happy to see the back of Jessica, still unable to believe that his sister may be involved in one of the dreaded scenarios he'd invented.

"Did he hurt her? Did he do something?" Mark whispered to her now.

He'd heard Jessica talk about this boyfriend, but Mark knew nothing about him, except his sister was mad about him, or had been, anyway. Was he involved? Mark was struggling to piece it all together.

"I'm so sorry, Jessica. I didn't want to know, but something happened. I wish you could tell me . . ." Mark held her limp hand to his face. "I can fix it. We'll fix it – together, this time."

He'd gone straight to the villa then, to confront his mother, who wouldn't listen.

"She's always been disturbed, Mark. Even as a child. You don't remember, but she will pull through. I know she will. She has to," his mother hissed.

"Something happened, Mother," he'd yelled, losing his patience. He hadn't slept now in days, had barely eaten. "I heard you, years ago, in Wicklow. I overheard a conversation. I wasn't supposed to be there, but I heard."

His mother shook her head. "Are you losing it, too? You may have heard me discussing your father with Jessica, but nothing else. Nothing happened. You're tired, Mark. Go and lie down."

"There *is* more to this. I know it. What was his name? That boyfriend of hers. What was his name?"

"What boyfriend?" His mother narrowed her eyes. "I don't know what you're talking about, Mark, you're upsetting me." She sat down and put her hand to her heart, taking several dramatic deep breaths. "This is nothing more than a girl looking for attention. Now, we must be strong for her and *do not* upset your father. Do you hear me?"

"That sounds familiar," Mark spat, walking away, leaving his mother staring after him.

Mark promised there and then he'd find out the truth. Even if Jessica didn't pull through, he wouldn't rest until he knew the truth. Mark thought of Ann's words. "Does your mother know more?"

Mark had been avoiding it all for years. His mother *did* know what had happened to Jessica. What Mark couldn't figure out was why she was concealing it. But he'd solve it. Nothing was going to distract him now, not even Ann. He'd been short with her on the phone. But Mark didn't have the energy to focus on anyone else. The thought struck him suddenly that if he hadn't been so wrapped up with Ann, perhaps he might have seen what was coming.

"Ticking time bomb."

"You really don't know, do you?"

Jessica's words haunted him. The memory that she'd tried to tell him struck hard. All he could think of now was Jessica and rectifying how he'd let her down, knowing that if she didn't pull through, he'd never forgive himself.

CHAPTER FORTY-ONE

The warmth of the evening sun enveloped Ann as she sat with her back to the shutters in the window seat, her guitar resting on her legs, looking out at the oak tree. It was almost like a painting – the perfect view. What a shame the lives of those privileged to it over the decades hadn't been so perfect. The evening was tranquil – the still surrounds of Knockmore House in stark contrast to the bustle of the Estates. It was precisely what her soul required, to be alone here, the silence tranquillising her mind.

Ann shifted in her seat, resting the guitar down on the ground beside her, wishing she could overlook the gnawing hunger she now felt. She closed her eyes, willing it to fade so she could continue to bask in the glow.

Hearing a door slam, she sat up suddenly to peer out of the window. Unable to see, Ann stood up and walked towards the bathroom at the far end of the landing and quietly pushed open the frosted-glass window. Standing on tiptoe, craning her neck, her eyes caught a glimpse of blue reflecting in the corner of the window. The door of the caravan swung open to her right.

What the hell was *he* doing here? She hadn't expected anyone to be here until Monday morning, hugely disappointed that he was infringing on her sanctuary. Ann rolled her eyes, knowing her plan of ordering a pizza and a bottle of wine and enjoying them in the garden was now ruined. She'd walked to work that morning, hoping the air might snap her from her dark humour. He must have no idea she was still here, assuming she'd also left for the weekend.

Ann put the seat of the toilet down and sat on it with a thud. Resting her head in her hands, she exhaled loudly, irritation clawing at her, even more than the hunger, which wasn't being helped by the waft of burning coals. Whatever he was cooking smelled good.

She stood up again on the toilet seat to peer out. This time she could see his feet, sitting on that stupid striped deckchair, a portable barbeque beside him. She watched his hand reach down and place a wine glass on the ground beside his steel-capped, dusty, cement-splattered boots. Now there was a surprise – it looked like Jason appreciated a chilled glass of white. That certainly didn't match the reputation of the surly, ignorant, brooding builder.

Then the boots stood up, walked back into the caravan, emerging a few moments later, then he sat back down. Ann was just about to close the window, plan her escape route back home, when the familiar sound of strings reverberating stopped her in her tracks. She listened as he issued random notes, the sound catching her by surprise as the chords of the guitar began to mesh into a song, his voice starting to hum. Ann didn't recognise the song and feeling as though she'd happened upon a private moment, she closed the window softly.

Ann fetched her guitar from the bedroom and sneaked downstairs to the office to get her bag. Maybe it was a blessing in disguise and she should head home, instead of sitting in a big, empty house by herself. She supposed she could always drop in on Tracy, who lately, and surprisingly, had become a little more than a casual acquaintance. The pair had grown closer as Ann's life had settled down. Until now, of course. Ann felt anything but settled and was still unnerved after her phone call with Mark earlier.

Briefly, she imagined what she'd be doing now if Mark never got that call from Olive, moments after they'd agreed to move in with each other. If Jessica hadn't tried to take her life . . . But Ann still couldn't get past the thought that things between Mark and her had suddenly changed and might somehow never be the same again.

Ann opened the front door and closed it behind her, pulling it softly until she heard the click.

"Ann?"

She was almost at the gate, when she heard her name.

She had to prevent her legs from breaking into a sprint and running away, but instead, she took a deep breath and turned.

"Oh, hi." She walked back towards where he was standing at the side of the house. "I was just grabbing a few things from the office." She pointed at her guitar. "I thought you were all gone for the weekend."

"Yeah. I was meant to leave, but I thought I'd work for the weekend. There are a few bits that need to be done by Monday before the cement trucks get here to pour the floor of the conservatory."

"Oh, right. Well . . . enjoy." Ann went to leave again.

"No plans for the weekend? Where's Mark?"

Ann looked up. The usual smirk on his face was nowhere to be seen.

"Away. For a few weeks. I was going to grab some food on the way home and take it easy. Anyway," she said, beginning to feel awkward, "have a good weekend." She put her hand up to wave goodbye.

"Stay." He spoke suddenly. "Stay. Here. Please." It sounded like a plea.

"Sorry?"

"I mean, sorry. That sounded strange. What I meant was, I have food – too much for me. There are some steaks on the barbeque . . ." He gestured towards the caravan. "Some salad?" He raised an eyebrow, trying to entice her. "Glass of wine?" He raised the other eyebrow. "I might even let you sit on my chair."

"I . . . I don't . . . I . . ." Just then, Ann's stomach let out a mighty rumble. Ann clasped her hands around it and watched his eyes widen.

"Hungry?" He started to laugh.

"Oh, God, I am. I really am," she grimaced.

"Come on, then. I'll be nice." He looked coy. "I promise."

"Well, that would be a first."

She followed him to the side of the house, wondering if it was hunger or something more making her agree to stay, her usual restraint diminishing as she watched him grab a crate and set it down beside the deckchair.

Ann sat as he disappeared inside. He came out a few moments later with a glass of wine and handed it to her.

"Thanks." She took a gulp, feeling the liquid burn the back of her throat. "Wow. I needed that."

He picked up his glass and took a sip. "Tough week?" he asked, hoping she'd tell him why she'd appeared so withdrawn.

"You could say that. Didn't take you for a wine drinker." She changed the subject.

"Why not?" he laughed. "On a nice evening like this, in this setting, it seems like the right thing to drink."

"Agreed. The job looks good. Well, from my limited

knowledge, it does."

"It's all going to plan." He looked towards the house. "Great spot, isn't it? Like a little slice of heaven here. How the other half live, eh? What are they like? Your soon-to-be in-laws."

Ann spluttered as the wine caught the back of her throat. "Oh no." She shook her head. "Not my soon-to-be in-laws," she said between coughs, waving her hands. "No. No way."

"Someday, though?" He raised an eyebrow. "Things must be fairly serious with you and lover boy for you to be here all the time. No?"

He was smiling again, although Ann couldn't figure out in what way. She put her glass down and picked up his guitar.

"Thought you said you didn't play any more?" she asked, plucking at the strings, avoiding the question.

"I don't. Not really. I was just messing about." He reached over to turn the steaks on the cooking tray as she continued to pluck at the strings and twist the pegs.

"Needs a tune."

"So, is it?"

"What's that?" Ann didn't look up.

"Serious?"

"Why?" She set the guitar back down again and looked him square in the eyes.

He held her gaze, his smile relaxing. He took another drink.

"Just wondering," he said finally. "Making conversation."

"That's not a conversation. That's fishing for information."

"Hey. I'm just interested. I mean, you have the look of someone who's had a nice easy life. Someone who's going out with a nice rich boy, whose parents have plenty of dough, but I'm not sure," he paused, tilting his head. "I'm not convinced that all this . . ." He waved his arm towards the house. "Is you."

Ann looked down again. There it was, the question of the moment. She didn't know how to answer, she didn't know if she should.

"What was it you said to me before?" She looked up sharply. "Assumptions can be deadly."

"Touché." He raised his glass. "I must be right, though. Otherwise, you'd deny it." He looked smug.

"I've nothing to hide. And for your information, it *is* serious."

"But you're not sure," he pushed her again. "Are you?"

Ann sat back and took another drink but said nothing. Was she that transparent? Was he that intuitive?

"Maybe I'm wrong," he shrugged. "I wonder what he'd think of you having a drink here with the likes of me." It was out before he could stop himself.

Ann stood up suddenly.

"For someone so incredibly closed and standoffish, you sure can dish it out. Never judge a book by its cover," Ann quipped. "And you don't know me. And you know what?"

"What?" he asked seriously, his smile fading.

"You've judged me from the moment you met me. Took one look at me and presumed, like you said, that I've had some great big easy life. Well, you're wrong. You couldn't be more wrong." Ann shook her head impatiently, picked up the wine glass and downed the remainder. "Actually, it's me who's not sure what I'm doing having a drink with the likes of you. You're the ultimate Jekyll and Hyde. I'd better go."

He stood up quickly, grabbing her arm.

"Ann, wait, please. I'm sorry. Really. You're right. I know nothing about you. I guess I don't know. I see things. I made assumptions. Guilty as charged." He held his hands up. "Please stay. I'm sorry." He looked genuine.

Ann sat back down, her brow furrowed.

"Stay there," he said, pouring her another glass of wine. "The steaks are ready. Give me five and I'll have something nice for you to eat as a way of apology. And I promise I won't ask anything else."

"Okay," Ann said. "Only because I'm starving. And on one condition." Her eyes flashed at him playfully. "One more Jekyll move and I'm out of here."

Ann broke into a smile then, and it took all of his restraint not to reach down and pull her into his arms. He'd never wanted to know more about anyone in his entire life. Nathan wasn't sure what he was doing, but he knew right then, he needed to keep her here for as long as possible, despite everything. He could no longer stop himself.

CHAPTER FORTY-TWO

The evening sun had long set, the garden in darkness aside from the soft glow of light from the caravan. Her eyes adjusted and she could just make out his unmoving features. They'd eaten dinner, chatting about irrelevant things, a second and third bottle of wine opened. They spoke about the house a lot and before she knew it, his questions grew gentler, easing her to open up more than she'd originally intended.

"It sounds stupid . . ." Ann looked up at him, trying to figure out what he was thinking. "But being here has forced me to face up to the past. I'm sorry." She glanced nervously at him. "I think I've had too much wine. I didn't mean to tell you so much. Talking about it helps, but it's a dismal tale, isn't it?"

He watched her, admiring her openness. He'd had an idea that there was more to her than met the eye, but he'd no idea that her story would be this. He was shocked, totally taken aback – guilty. He'd got her so wrong.

"It's my dad's anniversary this weekend," Ann said suddenly and then gulped audibly.

He sat forwards and put his hand on her leg. "Oh, God. I'm sorry."

Ann wiped her eyes. Then he took her hand and she didn't stop him.

"I'm so sorry, Ann. I had no idea. And you're right, I judged you. I was, I've been—"

"A prick?" she laughed, removing her hand.

Nathan smiled. "Yes. Good word. A prick." He sat back again.

"It's okay." She smiled sadly.

"Are you in a relationship?" she'd asked earlier, deciding the best way to find out more about him was to be direct.

"Nah." He shook his head. "This line of work isn't exactly conducive. Have you and Mark been together long?"

Ann shook her head. "You'd laugh if I told you."

"Go on, give me a laugh."

"It's only been a few months. Things accelerated kind of fast . . . well, because of circumstances. Truth is, I hardly know him. I thought I did, but . . ."

"What about before that?"

She hadn't intended to tell him she was separated but, in a way, she'd wanted to shock him, relinquish her good-girl image, show him that she wasn't the privileged girl he thought she was.

"So, that's how I ended up back in Knockmore after all these years. I had no choice."

"That makes sense. Sometimes, you need to start over."

Ann had told him how she'd met Mark, how he'd come back into her life a year later and how kind he'd been to her when she was so very lost.

"So, that's why you love it here, isn't it?" he'd asked when she told him about her connections to the house. "I felt your draw to it. Houses do that sometimes. We learned all about it at . . ." He'd been about to say university. "What about the town? How's that?"

Ann had gone on to tell him all about Sophie and her

friends here in Knockmore, and finally, her parents. He was a good listener, but then again, she supposed those who didn't give too much away always were.

"And are you still lost?"

Ann shrugged her shoulders. "In a way, it feels like everything that's happened is pushing me in the right direction. I don't know how, but it feels like I'm on a path of no return. So, what about you?" She wanted to change the subject. "What's your story?"

"There's not much to tell. This is my life. I work."

"That's it? Surely there must be more?"

He grinned. "Are you going to ask me now have I ever been in love?"

Ann wasn't sure if it was the wine, the moonlight, the atmosphere, the house, but for the entire evening she'd been asking herself, over and over again, why am I here? What am I doing here with this man?

"Well, have you?" She twisted her hands together, waiting.

"Once," he nodded. "I thought I was, but I made the wrong choice." He put his hands behind his head.

Ann watched the muscles in his arms contract and tense.

"I made a wrong choice once, too, but it doesn't need to define your life. There's always a second chance. A chance to live again. Well, that's what everyone tells me. Someday I might believe them," Ann said.

"Some choices you can't change." He was still staring at the sky. "Some are irreversible."

Ann watched his face darken and waited for him to tell her more. He didn't.

"My dad used to say you can't change the past, but you can make a new ending."

He looked at her. "Do you believe that?"

"Then again," she grinned, "my mam used to say that life is already mapped out – you have to go through it, twists and all. Two conflicting thoughts, I suppose."

"And which one do you think is true?"

He wanted her to tell him that everything could change, that there *was* a chance for a happy ending. Ann made him want to tear up his past and walk away – write a new story, with her on the very first page. For a moment, he considered telling her the truth. It was almost on the tip of his tongue to say, "I have a story, too. Do you want to hear it?"

"I think we get two lives." She interrupted his thoughts. "I think destiny throws you choices and it's up to you to take it, or walk away. Here, let me show you something." She stood up and walked towards the end of the garden, her feet weaving as she went.

Nathan followed her, watching her long, toned legs as she padded barefoot down the grass. Ann stopped at the tree and placed her hand on the bark.

"This tree holds my past. Isn't that bizarre?" Ann slurred a little. "All those years, the answers were right here . . ." She pointed at the opening at the base of the trunk and then lay back against it. "Doesn't it seem like such a waste? My mam never knew the truth. It was in here all those years and she never knew.

"Then I found it and it turned my world even more upside down. Made me think of all the horrible secrets people keep to protect themselves, instead of just letting them out, freeing themselves." She held her arms out wide.

Ann looked down at her feet.

"The story wouldn't have changed, but maybe the ending might have." She looked up again. "I never would have been sent away. I never would have carried all that guilt. I might have been someone so different. But I was meant to find the truth, as hard as it's been."

Her words pierced his flesh like a knife – how he longed to free himself, but how could he tell her the truth now? He was too far involved. Perhaps he could disappear in the night. He'd thought about it. Immediately after he'd started this job, as soon as he spoke to her that first day, Nathan had wanted to call it all off, but he knew deep down what had made him stay. Her. Ann was the real reason he was still here.

Ann turned suddenly and kicked the tree. "Darn tree."

"Hey, careful. You'll break your toe." Nathan leaned forwards inches from her face.

"Better than a broken heart," she said, leaning back against the tree again. "So now, Jason, you know every little thing there is to know about me, just like that . . ." She clicked her fingers, brushed her hair away from her face, stared intently, a slight smile on her lips. "This is me."

Nathan stood opposite her, wondering what was happening. Was she doing what he thought she was? God, she was beautiful – even more so now that he knew every little thing about her, as she put it. If he took this plunge with her, would he be able to let go as he knew he'd have to? Walk away from her when this job was done, never to return. For an instant, Nathan wanted to run away, slam the door of the caravan, never have to see her again. Instead, he stood rooted to the spot, staring into those eyes that had hypnotised him from the first time he saw her sing on stage.

"And yet, you know nothing about me?" His voice had changed, sounding gravelly in the darkness.

"No. You're right. None of the facts, none of the small print. I've failed miserably to find out anything about the mysterious builder. Not even your favourite singer."

"You know more than you think."

He took a step closer, reaching forwards and tilting her chin with his finger until she was looking into his eyes again. Ann felt her stomach flip and she bit her lip as he moved closer still, gently leaning against her, pushing her further against the tree until he was so close that almost every part of them was touching – hip to hip, nose to nose. He moved his head to the side, his breath sending shivers up her spine as he rubbed his lips against her ear.

Ann closed her eyes and exhaled as he whispered something to her. She jerked her head in response and every nerve ending in her body came to life. Her eyes questioned his and he answered her by nodding, pressing his hand against her heart. She saw then what she'd already seen in them that very first night: a shared moment, an inexplicable familiarity, a shred of fate, a look, and she melted into his kiss. Ann heard him repeat it and she knew she'd been right. It was him.

"My favourite singer is you. Singing that song, slowly, to me."

CHAPTER FORTY-THREE

They collapsed onto the grass, no longer able to deny the weeks of pent-up desire, their bodies freeing themselves of all doubts, all the useless denial. He kissed her so tenderly that she could have stayed there forever, frozen in time, locked in his embrace. All Ann could think of was him. With Mark, she'd felt different – always trying not to think about how she was really feeling, attempting to be more in the moment, to stop her mind from drifting. Here, with Jason, she felt present.

Ann let him touch her, lost in the moment, intoxicated by him. She wanted to pull him towards her, press herself against him, but he stopped, suddenly sitting up.

"What is it?" she asked.

He let out a frustrated groan and pulled her onto his lap.

"I need to tell you something. I think I need—"

"Why didn't you say?" Ann interrupted suddenly. "Why didn't you say it was you in the pub that night?" She searched his eyes. "I knew it was. I thought I was going mad. I . . . I ran after you that night. It was before I even met Mark again. I ran out to the car park. I tried to find you . . ."

Nathan put his head back and growled loudly. "I don't know. I . . . I can't explain it."

He stared up at the sky. The realisation of the missed moment pained him. How different things might be now . . . To think he could have met Ann that night, been just Nathan. He might have asked her for a drink, kissed her goodnight, forgotten the past, let her heal him. But he'd run away, enabling her to fall into the arms of someone else. And now, it was too late.

"But why did you lie?"

He shook his head. "When I saw you here with him . . . I don't know. What was the point?"

Feeling her kiss now, her arms around him, it felt so right. Nathan knew he could never hurt her. More than ever, he wanted to make love to her right here, right now. To peel her clothes off, see her naked, feel what it was like to be part of her . . . But he couldn't do it. He'd been awarded an opportunity that night in the pub and blown it – retaken the wrong path. And then he'd spent weeks acting like a boy in a playground, trying to conceal what he could no longer hide. What a fool!

"Oh, God. You're married?"

"No. Jesus, no, not married." He shook his head, almost wishing he was. At least that would have been easier to explain.

"Maybe you're right," Ann said. "This isn't a good idea. I'm . . . well, I'm with—"

"Don't say his name. Please don't say his name."

"But I am. At least, until I'm not. I suppose this . . ." Ann gestured towards him. "Well, it proves that he and I aren't right. Otherwise this . . ." She gestured again. "Well, it wouldn't be happening. And there's stuff with his family lately and—"

"What stuff?" What did she mean?

"Complications. Recent developments. Please don't ask," she begged. "I can't talk about it. I swore I wouldn't."

That family! That blasted family. What had they done now? He wished he could tell her everything to prevent her from being sucked into it all, from potentially ruining her life. He would tell her. He had to, but not yet. Perhaps they'd been thrust together for a reason – maybe not the goal he longed for but for another reason, so he could protect her. If he couldn't be with her, at least he could prevent her from suffering the same pain he had.

He exhaled again, the force of his emotions shocking him. He wanted her so badly. Needed to taste what he'd miss for the rest of his life before it was gone, forever out of his reach.

"I'm sorry I lied to you. I'm sorry I didn't stick around that night, Ann. But I need to tell you, from that moment, from the first time I saw you on that stage, I haven't been able to see anything else. I've acted like a fool. I was trying to . . . I don't know . . . protect myself. There's something that hurt me before, badly, and I didn't want to feel what I was feeling with you. I was scared. And then there's this thing I need to tell you . . ."

Ann took his hand and kissed it. "I felt it, too. I thought I was going mad. I couldn't understand why I felt this way about you. Oh, God, what a mess."

"Spend the weekend with me, Ann?" he asked suddenly. "No questions. No past, no future, no worries, just us. Two days. You and me." He put his face in his hands for a moment and then looked back at her.

"What do you need to tell me?"

"It's . . . I . . . I . . . Just spend the weekend with me. I need to be with you, please. I *will* tell you. It's hard to explain, but I will, soon. I swear to you."

He was pleading with her and Ann could see the hurt about which he'd spoken. It was the same look Ann often had when she stared at her own reflection. One of pain – so much pain that she wanted to beg him to tell her. Instead, Ann did the one thing she could for this man, who for some reason, she knew, was even more broken than she was.

"Okay," she whispered, and he smiled so entirely that she thought her heart might shatter.

Ann had been wrong about him, too. Whatever he was carrying, whatever had happened to him, he needed her. They clung to each other then, so tightly that all of their broken pieces fused together, both wondering precisely the same thing – how they'd ever be able to let the other go . . .

Not every day is perfect. Most days are a collection of repetitive hours, easily confused with the day before. And then there are *the* days – the special ones that make life worth living, that force you to pause and inhale deeply. To absorb every last second, so you might lock it inside you forever. If you knew at the time that there was even the slightest possibility that you'd never feel again how you felt during one of those days, would you do it anyway? Would you embrace it, or would you decide not to partake, so that when the day was done, you'd never have to miss it?

"It's surprisingly comfortable," Ann smiled the next morning as she woke to the light from outside glowing against the frilly peach curtains. "Like a peach cocoon."

The smell of coffee drifted towards the bed from the tiny kitchenette just inches away.

"Coffee?" he asked. He was standing near the end of

the bed, his head slightly stooped from the low ceiling. "Shall I change the bed back into the table?"

"Not yet," she grinned.

Ann had never seen anyone assemble a bed quite so fast as he had the night before, after he'd lifted her and walked towards the door of the caravan. He'd wanted to carry her over the threshold, lay her gently on the bed, except the door kept banging closed in their faces and the bed was yet to be made.

"And you call yourself a builder? Allow me." She jumped out of his arms.

"Give me twenty seconds."

Ann had watched in fascination as he collapsed the kitchen table and threw the sofa cushions into the gap like a jigsaw, then covered it with a fitted sheet and duvet. She was pleasantly surprised by the almost instantaneous night-time mode.

"Ta-dah!" He spread out his arms and grinned, enveloping her and collapsing on the bed, where they chatted and laughed before kissing then slowly peeling each other's clothes off and making love.

Afterwards, Ann had had to turn away to hide the tears that smarted from the intensity of the moment, and the release of finally admitting her feelings. It had never been like that with Dom. All he'd ever wanted was to make sure she was satisfied, to prove he had it in him. And with Mark it was great, but there had been something absent – some emotional tether that Ann hadn't quite been able to pinpoint until now. In a way, she'd felt like she was acting with Mark, playing a role, trying to be who he wanted her to be. Ann supposed she'd been yearning companionship and it had helped, at first, to mask her pain, to dull the solitude, but she knew now why she'd been doubting herself. Mark wasn't Jason. And that inexplicable connection that her father had spoken of all his life, that nonsensical link, had been missing.

Ann reached for him now and he climbed across the bed to her. Grabbing the back of his neck and pulling his face to hers, she scratched her face against his stubble, relishing the bristly sensation.

He lay down beside her and rested his forehead against hers.

"Are you okay?" he asked earnestly, trying to read her expression.

Ann nodded.

His head moved with hers. "Me too. You hungry?"

Ann shook her head.

"Me neither."

His head mirrored hers and she kissed him, pressing her body into his, allowing herself to give in to him once more.

Afterwards, he entwined his fingers with hers, pressing his other hand against the small of her back, making her feel instantly safe. She could have stayed in the caravan forever in his arms.

"Come on." He stood up suddenly and reached down to pull her up. "Look at the weather! What we need is a swim. In the sea."

He looked like an excited boy with his hair standing on end, his chocolate brown eyes filled with life, dressed in shorts with no top. He looked even better with his clothes off than Ann could ever have imagined, aside from a noticeable farmer's tan, which made him look like he was wearing a white T-shirt, even with his shirt off.

"*Swim*? Oh, God, really? I haven't swum in the Irish Sea since I was about eight years old," Ann moaned, trying to sit back down.

He pulled her back up.

"I used to do it every single day. Well, almost," he said. "Even in winter. There was a group of us who met in Sandycove, Dublin at sunrise – they still do as far as I know. A place called The Forty Foot. One of the best swimming spots in Ireland, maybe even the world. Man, I miss it. It's the one thing that can make you feel alive in an instant, catapult you into insignificance . . ." He clicked his fingers.

"Why did you stop?"

He paused, something shadowing his face. "I suppose I got out of the habit. I'll go back someday. I'll make it my goal when I finish the job here, but for now, I want to swim with you. Where's the nearest beach?"

"Not far. A short drive."

Ann grinned. It was funny. Since they'd agreed not to ask each other any more questions, he seemed to be giving away more information than ever before. It was as though a barrier had dropped. Not entirely, but enough so Ann could see the real person inside. And try as she might, she couldn't help but love what she saw.

"Sunrise and a sea swim. Set you up for the whole day. We've missed the sunrise but we can swim."

"Sounds like hell," Ann laughed as his face dropped. "Okay. Okay. On one important condition."

"Anything."

"You try to tan the rest of your body and not just your arms and head." Ann ran her hands over his white chest.

"Hey. I'm Irish and proud." He looked down at the apparent contrast and beamed. "Deal. You go and get your gear and I'll head off and get a picnic, then we'll reconvene at 1100 hours," he ordered.

"Yes, sir." Ann stood up naked and saluted him.

"Let's make that 1130 hours." He pushed her back onto the bed and landed on top of her.

They had the perfect day.

From start to finish, both felt as if they'd taken a hiatus from ordinary life. It was just them – invisible to all those who watched the somewhat mismatched couple. Her natural, beautiful, dressed in a simple black swimsuit, her fair hair plaited down her back. Him: rugged, handsome, dark, smiling from ear-to-ear. He couldn't keep his eyes off her and nor could she, him, as they lay on the beach together, soaking up the sunshine.

A few times he picked her up, carried her down to the shore, where she attempted to run away before he grabbed her around the waist, lifted her and walked her straight into the sea. She wrapped her legs around him, clinging on, but he kept going, marching until he could no longer stand and she was forced to swim. She squealed and he laughed, the chemistry almost enough to warm the Irish Sea.

Once or twice, a mother covered her child's eyes as the couple in the sea kissed each other passionately. Once or twice, a husband looked over at a wife, wondering if they'd ever done that. And if so, when they had stopped.

They ate lunch lying on a blanket. They napped, chatted, laughed.

It wasn't a show. They weren't putting on a spectacle. It was natural and pure, and there weren't many on the beach who didn't notice them, while they saw no one but each other.

On the way home, they'd stopped off at a bar and ate seafood before returning to Knockmore House, where they showered together, washing away the sand and salt that clung to their skin, making it tingle.

"Here," Ann whispered later when she took him to show him her mother's old room. "This is where I was with her – in this room. A little stowaway secret."

They stood together staring out of the window, him behind her, his arms wrapped around her. Ann closed her eyes, relishing his closeness. It was the first time in so long that everything seemed to make sense. That nothing mattered but being with him.

"Jason." She spun round towards him, feeling a sudden panic. "What happens after this weekend?"

He felt his heart crush inside his chest. "Let's just take it one day at a time. No questions, remember?"

"You will tell me, though? You said there was something that hurt you."

"I'll try."

CHAPTER FORTY-FOUR

"Shit." Ann sat up suddenly, whacking her head on the low shelf above her. "The lads are here."

"The one day they're early. Typical," he laughed.

Ann covered her head with the pillow, listening to the vans roll into the driveway of Knockmore House. The weekend had somehow extended to Monday, after she fell asleep on Sunday evening wrapped in his arms, never wanting to wake.

"Five more minutes," Ann pleaded and then sighed, knowing the weekend was well and truly over – and Jason had yet to tell her whatever it was he needed.

Ann wasn't entirely sure she wanted or needed to know. She already felt she knew him, without knowing any of the facts. What did the details matter, anyway? Surely, what was important was here and now was how they felt about each other.

He prised the pillow from her hands and watched as her eyes welled.

"Hey," he whispered. "Come here."

"I'm sorry." She tried to hide her face. "I feel like something bad is about to happen. What now?"

He didn't answer, his tendency to clam up still present.

"I made a promise to myself once," she'd told him the night before as she lay against the velour cushions of the caravan, her bare legs stretched out over his. "When I first came back to Knockmore over a year ago, you know? Well, I swore I'd take an ounce of happiness rather than a lifetime of nothing. I made that mistake with my husband – and I almost made it with Mark."

Her face changed when she said Mark's name. The guilt was intense, but not enough to stop her, the pull of her feelings for Jason too powerful. Ann didn't want to hurt Mark, but she knew she could never love him, not like this.

Could you call what she was experiencing with Jason, love? She remembered her dad telling her so many times that he knew from the first moment he set eyes on Felicity that he'd never be without her again. That he knew against all the odds they'd be together. She wondered what her odds were with Jason.

"My point is," she told Jason. "This weekend has been amazing. You're amazing. Can you tell—"

"Soon," he'd promised, running his fingers along her face, noticing the disappointment.

Even on Sunday, when they went to visit her parents' grave, for Sammy's anniversary, she'd tried to encourage him to open up, reassure him that he could trust her.

"I often wonder if something could have changed it all, but I think it was all going to happen anyway, one way or another. My mum getting sick was unfair, but what was worse was my dad's life being taken away the way it was. It made no sense. I don't think it ever will. Nothing really matters at the end of the day. Nothing at all."

"How did he die?" Jason had asked.

"A drunk driver. He didn't stand a chance."

"Okay. I'll distract them and you sneak round the front," Jason said now, pulling a T-shirt on and climbing out of bed.

Ann didn't want this to end, for everything to go back to the way it was before. She'd switched off her phone for the entire weekend, happy to be liberated of everything but him, but she knew now it was time to emerge from the cocoon, to enter the real world again, face what needed to be faced. Mark, for one – and Dom.

Her settlement meeting with Dom was the next day. She'd have to call Mark, too, praying that Jessica would pull through. Selfishly, and she couldn't believe she was even thinking it, Ann couldn't imagine how she was going to face him ever again if his sister didn't make it.

Ann had no regrets. What had happened between Jason and herself had happened. She couldn't change it, but she couldn't continue with Mark, either – not now.

"I have to go to Dublin tonight." She picked up her clothes from the floor and threw them on the bed. "I have a meeting on Tuesday morning. I'm staying with my friend, Sophie, tonight."

"Oh, right, okay."

He looked disappointed and she knew he could feel it, too. Reality creeping through the windows, seeping up through the floor.

"And we need to talk. You know that, right? We need to talk," she said.

He nodded in agreement, closing his eyes for a second. It had been naïve to imagine that he could spend the weekend with Ann and then go back to the way things were. It was beginning to dawn on him that whatever he was up to here with this house, trying to ruin it, attempting to destroy *them* in the process, was the wrong way to go about it all. He was going to tell Ann the truth. Everything. If she chose to hate him, that was her choice.

He had to take the chance, the right path, for once, if only to protect her.

"When you get back," he promised. "I have a few things to get done here and then we'll talk. I swear to you."

He pulled her up and she stood facing him.

"I'm scared." She rested her forehead against his.

"Me too. But I want you to know, whatever happens after today, I'll only be honest with you from now on. Whatever happens, you and me, here this weekend – it was all real, every second of it, every moment. This is me."

"Jason, I . . . I think—"

"Shush," he whispered. "Let's talk on Wednesday."

For a moment, Nathan truly believed that love might conquer all and that he'd been sent a second chance. He still wasn't convinced he deserved it. He'd lied to Ann, too. Would she understand?

"Whatever it is, Jason, I don't care. You have to believe me, there's nothing you could tell me that could change the way I feel."

"We'll see," Nathan replied.

CHAPTER FORTY-FIVE

Mark

Mark picked up the phone again, pressed Call and listened as it rang out. Where the hell was Ann?

"*Señor, viene. Por favor*. Come. Now."

The stilted voice had jolted him awake in the early hours of Saturday morning. The whole way there, Mark had tried to envisage what lay ahead, imagining how he was going to break the news to his parents.

Sprinting into the hospital, his legs moving automatically, he rushed to her room.

"Oh my God. Jessica!" His legs buckled for a moment, but he righted himself.

She was propped up by pillows, tubes still sprouting from her flesh, but her eyes were open. Mark put his head in his hands, relief flooding his body, a deep, trembling sigh escaping his mouth.

"*Cinco minutos. Muy cansada.*" The nurse held up five fingers and then rested her face in the palm of her hand to demonstrate sleeping.

"Thank you."

He approached the bed. Jessica's eyes opened for a moment and then squeezed shut, freeing one solitary tear, which trickled down her face.

"Jessica." He took her hand and she pressed his so gently, he almost didn't feel it. "It's okay. I'm here now.

Don't cry. I'm here. Whatever it is, I'm going to fix it."

She nodded, exhaling raggedly.

"Can you talk? Can you tell me?"

"No talk. Sleep."

He heard the nurse behind him and he put his hand up to show he understood.

"Rest," he whispered to her. "When you're better, we can talk. I promise. Whatever it is. Okay?"

Jessica nodded once and then frowned, panic thwarting her features.

"What?"

She frowned again, looking towards the door.

"Are you looking for someone? Mum? You want her to come?"

Jessica's features twisted as she shook her head.

"Okay, Jessica. I'll keep her away."

She squeezed his hand in response.

"I'm going to go now and talk to the doctor. I'll come later – alone. Okay? Just me."

Mark left the room and stood with his back against the wall before stooping forwards to rest his hands on his knees.

"Thank you, God. Thank you," he whispered, relieved and then so angry, he could barely breathe.

He didn't care what his mother said any more. He *would* find out the truth.

"Very lucky," the doctor told him in broken English before he left. "Now rest – two weeks, maybe more. Yes?"

Mark nodded in agreement.

"Rehab. Yes?"

Mark nodded again, knowing he'd do everything he could now to make Jessica better, no matter how long it took.

* * *

"How is she?" Mark's mother rushed to the door of the villa when she saw the taxi pull up. "Mark?"

Mark paid the taxi and ambled up the steps, dragging one foot in front of the other.

"She's okay. She's awake. Barely."

"Oh, thank God, thank God . . ." His mother's body slumped forwards and Mark put his hands out to catch her.

"Come on, Mum, sit down."

His mother followed him inside, sat down and wiped her face.

"Son?" His father looked up anxiously from the sofa. He'd barely moved in the last few days.

"It's okay, Dad. She's going to be okay. They need to keep her in for at least two weeks before she can think about flying. I've called the doctor at home in Knockmore and explained what's happened—"

"What?" His mother jerked forwards. "Why did you do that?"

"*Stop*, Mum, please." Mark gritted his teeth. "Jessica has to go into a rehab unit at home. The doctor here suggested it," he said evenly, willing himself not to explode.

"Rehab? For drunks? This is ridiculous."

Mark threw his eyes to heaven. "No, Mum, it's for people who try to take their own lives. I'm taking this over, Mum. So really, there's no point in talking about it. Clearly, your system hasn't worked, so I'm stepping in. She's my sister. I turned my back on her situation – not any more."

"I think that would be best," his father agreed.

His father looked as though he'd aged ten years in the space of a few days.

"I can't help thinking this is my fault," his father said suddenly.

Mark got up, sat beside him and put his arm around him. "No, Dad. It's not your fault." Mark looked at his mother as he said it, the accusation visible in his stare.

She looked away.

"I'll just get my bag. I want to see Jessica."

"No, Mum." Mark stood again. "Jessica isn't to have any visitors for the rest of the day. They'll call me if anything changes," he told her firmly and she plopped back into the chair like a child. "It'll be okay," he assured her, wary of coming down too hard on her.

If he wanted to get to the bottom of everything, he needed to keep his mother on side.

"Well, we can't just sit here, can we?"

"Yes." Mark spoke again. "We can and we will."

"I'm going to lie down."

Mark went outside to try Ann again. He wanted to hear her voice so much, longing to tell her that everything was going to be okay. It rang out. Ann would call eventually. After all, he was the one who'd asked for space, when all he'd really wanted was someone to fill the void.

"Come and sit outside, Dad. I'll give you a hand," Mark called. He moved his father to sit in the shade outside, overlooking the pool where Jessica had swum only a few days before. "Tough few days, huh, Dad? Fancy a beer?"

"Sure, Mark. May as well drown our sorrows a little, eh?"

Mark went to fetch two beers, putting some crisps in a bowl to get his dad to eat something.

They sat quietly at first, passing the odd comment here and there, neither of them able to bring themselves to talk further about what had happened.

"Hey, I have some pictures on the iPad of the house, Dad. Would you like to see them? The work is coming on well."

"That fecking house!" his father spat unexpectedly and Mark looked up. "You know, when I first started building all those years ago," he started. "Before, you know, before it all got too big." He glanced at Mark. "Because it did, Mark. It all got too big. I didn't mean it to. I didn't intend to be working every minute God sent."

"I know, Dad." Mark put his hand on his father's shoulder, feeling it drop as he did so.

"When I first married Olive," his father smiled wistfully, "I thought I was the luckiest man alive. We built the house, you guys came along and for a while, life was perfect." He shook his head. "Christ, I made so many mistakes. I wanted to give your mother everything. I wanted to be more than the young boy who wore his brother's shoes – two sizes too big. Jaysus, my feet had more blisters than I could count. I wanted to give you all more."

"But you did, Dad. We wanted for nothing."

"Except me. You all wanted for me. The pressure of growing the business, working hard . . . I was torn. Torn, seeing your little faces looking up at me. Ah, I messed up, son. After a while, there was all this money but a great big gap between your mother and me. And it became easier not to be there. And then you know the rest." He slapped his hands on his thighs and then said, "I loved her, you know."

Mark knew who he referring to.

"I have you, and I have Jessica . . ." His voice wobbled. "And him. His name is John. He's a fine young fella. Walking image of you when you were a gangly teen, did you know that? Did I tell you that?" his father asked. "I ruined that, too."

"There's always time, Dad, to set it right, you know. I can help you. This has been a lesson to us all. It's not over till it's over."

"I walked away from my own son. He hates me. My own flesh and blood. *She* . . ." He gestured inside. "She made me do it. I'd let you all down, so badly, and then I had this blasted stroke. And sure, now I'm nothing. A cripple. A failure."

"Dad . . ." Mark could feel his eyes welling. "Don't. Please."

"Can you help me? Try to set it all right. I have to try," his father pleaded.

Mark wondered when it had all reversed, when it had changed to a child guiding a parent.

"I will, Dad."

"Anyway . . ." His father composed himself and took a sip of beer. "That wasn't what I was going to tell you. I was going to tell you and then I got sidetracked about that dreaded house.

"When I first went out on my own . . . Must have been only the fourth house I'd ever renovated . . . Anyway, I got a job doing this big old thing, not dissimilar to Knockmore but in the arsehole of Wicklow – off the beaten track. This nice young couple had bought it. Jaysus, I can hardly explain it, but as soon as I crossed the threshold, I got this feeling like I couldn't breathe. Like the air was heavy. I packed that attic full of fibreglass, but nothing could stop the chill.

"I was hard up for money then, so I took the job. It was the worst few months of my life. I couldn't wait to get out of there. Everything that could go wrong went wrong. In the end, I left with my pockets emptier than I'd arrived, but the whole time I was there, I couldn't get away from this eerie feeling. That house had a personality – and not a bloody nice one. You must think I'm cracked, but I never forgot it."

Mark listened, intrigued. "Do you think it was haunted?"

"Nah, I don't go in for that mumbo-jumbo, but I can tell you, it was like it was filled with doom.

"A few years later, I was working only twenty minutes from it and I took a drive past. The whole place was boarded up. Not a sinner for miles. Christ, I got back in the car fast," he laughed.

"What do you think happened?"

"I often thought maybe the house and the people weren't the right fit, or something mad like that. Like it rejected them. Hah! that sounds far fetched, too. I don't know. Point is, some buildings have so much history laced through them that they're not worth it – other people's history."

Mark observed him.

"You think Knockmore's the same?"

"Not quite as bad, but something's trapped there, all right. It made sense when I heard your Ann's story."

"You never said anything before."

"No. But I've been thinking about it all over the last few days – thinking that something needs to change. Olive loves that house, but nothing good has happened to us since we moved there. And look where we are now. Your mother isn't who she used to be. It's like she's become that house, all airs and graces, and the face nearly falling off her with whatever she's pumping into it. I can't understand her at all.

"And then . . . my poor Jessica . . ." He paused and turned to Mark again. "I know what I'd like to do it. Mill it down."

"Ann said her mother used to say similar."

"Maybe she had a point. Maybe it is cursed! Anyway, show us the pics while we're talking of the feckin' thing. Maybe Olive's right and the renovations will fix it."

Mark grabbed the iPad from the kitchen table, passing his mother, who was making a cup of tea.

"I'm going to show Dad the building work, try to distract him."

"Good idea." His mother followed him outside.

Mark flicked from picture to picture, showing the progress thus far.

"Ann's been keeping a photo diary for you all."

"How is the lovely Ann?" his mother asked.

"Well, maybe now isn't the time to tell you, but we've decided to move in together."

Mark couldn't help smiling. Despite not having spoken to her in a few days, he was sure when everything was sorted with his family, it would all slot back into place. Ann would understand.

"Well, that is good news, Mark. I'm thrilled for you. Oh! Look. Doesn't the kitchen look enormous," his mother cooed, peering over his shoulder. "And five builders, is it?" she asked, counting the men in the picture, some of whom were waving at Ann, who was taking the picture.

"That's right," Mark said. "That's Jason there. He's the guy the O'Reillys recommended." Mark used his fingers to zoom in on the screen. "That guy. He really knows his stuff. In fact, he loves these old buildings – said he adores digging right into the past."

His mother's hand dropped suddenly from where it had been resting on Mark's shoulder and he turned just in time to see her walking back inside.

His father shrugged his shoulders. "See, she's bats."

CHAPTER FORTY-SIX

"So, let me get this straight, because I'm ever so slightly confused." Sophie leaned her head back against the sofa and scrunched her eyes shut. "Since I last spoke to you – and let us be clear here, it was what, four days ago?"

Ann rolled her eyes and nodded.

"Well, since then, you've taken up with the builder who you despised, you're going to dump Mark, who's currently in Spain by his sister's deathbed, and you're planning to tell Dom tomorrow that you want to walk away with nothing from your divorce. Have I missed anything?"

It was Monday evening. Ann, Sophie and Jack were sitting in Sophie's apartment, drinking tea. Ann had thought about not telling her, but Sophie knew as soon as Ann walked through the door that something was up.

"Well, I wouldn't put it quite like that, but in a nutshell, yes. I mean, no. Oh, God, I don't know."

Ann exhaled loudly and looked at Sophie, who was looking at Jack, who looked more confused than any of them.

Sophie shook her head. "Ann, have you lost your mind? I go away for a few days and in that time, you've walked into a minefield. I don't know what to say. I'm officially lost for words. You're a rollercoaster and not a fun one – a 'holy shit, my eyes are going to tumble down my throat' one."

"I don't want you to say anything." Ann sounded defensive. "And yes, I know it sounds crazy, but I can't explain it . . . He's different." She stumbled over her words. "We have this connection. I feel like I've known him forever."

Ann waited.

"But you haven't known him forever, Ann. And correct me if I'm wrong, but you know absolutely nothing about him, except that he lives in a caravan on a building site and his name is . . ."

"Jason," Ann finished. "It's Jason."

"Okay. Let's start again from the beginning. You said you saw Bob the Builder the night of your birthday in Lennon's. How come you never told me that part before?"

Ann took a deep breath, attempting to explain it again.

"So what you're saying is, it was love at first sight. We all know that doesn't happen, not really," Sophie said before mouthing "Sorry" to Jack.

"It happened to my parents," Ann said quietly.

"But what are the chances of it happening to you? In the same pub? To the same song?" Sophie attempted. "Do you think maybe you're trying to recreate a moment you heard about all your life?"

This time, it was Ann who shrugged. "I know. It's crazy, but it happened, and then there he was. He turned up at Knockmore House with no idea I'd be there. That makes no sense, either. That has to mean something." Ann tried to convince Sophie. "It felt like it was meant to be and—"

"Don't say it, Ann. Don't you dare say 'everything that happened before was leading you to this moment'."

Sophie covered her ears and Ann gave up.

"You had the same feelings about Mark. He showed up too, remember? Not every person you meet is your cosmic soul mate. Like sometimes, you just have to settle." Sophie looked at Jack again, who made a face.

"Thanks," he muttered.

"You know what I mean," Sophie smiled at him. "You *are* my cosmic soul mate. Ann has two. It's greedy. Anyway, he's obviously married, or a murderer, or has done time for armed robbery or something bizarre. What could be so big that he got you to spend the weekend with him and not ask him any questions? Alarm bells, Ann. I mean, for fuck's sake, this is going to end in tears."

Sophie was losing her cool. Ann knew her well enough to know it was coming from a place of concern, but nonetheless, she was starting to get irritated.

"Come on, Soph, it's nothing like that. I'm sure of it. He was hurt before, badly was what he said, and you don't know him. He's gentle and sensitive and—"

"Sounds like a wimp," Jack piped in finally. "I liked Mark. Why can't we pick Mark? We were going to play golf," he sulked. "Couldn't we wait until after we play golf?"

"Not helpful, Jack." Sophie swiped his arm and Ann smiled.

"I'm sorry, Jack. I like Mark too, I really do, and who knows, maybe if I never met Jason, it may have worked out. But something was missing. The spark. The thing you guys have. It wasn't there. I couldn't make myself feel it," Ann explained.

"From what I could see there were plenty of sparks," Sophie said. "I warned you it was fast, but you kept convincing me that you knew what you were doing. You made us like Mark. Now, we have to unlike him. He's so perfect."

"He *is* perfect, but not for me. And yes, at first there were sparks, but if the spark was really there on my side, then

I'd never have looked at Jason, let alone end up doing what I did." Ann put her hands to her face. "Oh, God," she moaned before looking up at their bewildered faces. "I know, I really do, that Mark seems like the logical choice, but if your heart isn't in something, then really, what's the point?

"I was trying to convince myself, Soph. Even if it doesn't work out with Jason, it's made me realise that Mark and I aren't right for each other. I have to end it with him. I mean, I've spent the weekend with someone else. It's over. And maybe it's better this way before I hurt him even more."

"Well, then. No spark for Mark." Jack looked beaten. "And no golf for me."

They almost laughed.

"How's the sister?" Sophie asked.

Ann shook her head. "I don't know. He asked me not to contact him. My phone's been off for the weekend. I'm afraid to turn it on. I don't know what to tell him. I can't tell him I've shacked up in the caravan with Jason.

"I think when I go back to Knockmore House, I'll get my things and leave. I can't be a part of that any more. I'm sure Denise will give me some shifts in the café and I have plenty of weddings booked." Ann's voice started to wobble.

"Oh, Ann . . ." Sophie reached over and put her hand on her knee. "I want to tell you you've made a mess of it all, but I can't because I love you."

"I think I got swept up in everything," Ann admitted. "The house. The past. It all seemed so perfect until it wasn't. I thought I deserved it. But Jason . . . Oh, Sophie, you'd love him. When I'm with him, I don't want to be anywhere else."

"That sounds familiar. You said similar about Mark. And you do deserve it, Ann, more than anyone. It *will* happen. Who knows," Sophie shrugged. "Maybe this Jason might turn out to be the man of your dreams. Maybe he'll be the fairy tale, or maybe he'll be an axe murderer," Sophie grinned. "Just be careful.

"Now, sorry to be your reality check, but I think you'd better call Mark. If I can offer you any advice, play along until you know how his sister is and then we can work on a speech to let him down gently when he comes back. 'It's not you, it's me,' might be better than 'I slept with the builder.'

"And one more thing – I am *not* letting you walk away tomorrow with nothing. Your barrister's going to get you what you deserve. Give it to charity, for all I care, but Dom can well afford to give a decent settlement – and he is the one who screwed up. Remember that."

"Only now, I've screwed up, too."

"Yes, a little, but it's not the same. You and Dom were married."

Ann nodded and stood up, taking her phone from her bag. Sophie was right. Mark didn't deserve all this. Maybe Soph was right about Dom, too. It wasn't as if she was taking what he didn't have.

Her stomach somersaulted when she switched on the phone and saw all the missed calls. Ann sat on the bed and put her face in her hands. She couldn't face it, not until tomorrow was over and done with. If anything terrible had happened to Jessica, surely Mark would have texted or contacted Sophie if he'd been desperate to reach her.

Ann left the phone on the bed and walked back into the living room.

"Well?"

"No answer," Ann lied. "I'll try again tomorrow. It's late."

CHAPTER FORTY-SEVEN

Ann left straightaway, hugging Sophie quickly on the steps of the courthouse and rushing towards her car.

"Don't you want to celebrate?" Sophie called after her, holding her hands out in exasperation. "Do you even realise what this means?"

Ann turned and ran back, taking Sophie's hands and squeezing them.

"I do, I really do. I can't believe it, but there's something I have to do," Ann smiled, squeezing Soph tightly again.

"Are you sure about this? Are you sure about *him?*"

"I've never been so sure of anything in my entire life," Ann replied, feeling a weight lift from her shoulders, as though she'd finally been snipped loose and was now free, in more ways than one, to do exactly as she pleased.

Sophie saw the look of resignation, knew there was no point in attempting to stop her.

"Well, what are you waiting for? Go. Go and tell him how you feel. Go get your fairy-tale ending, you great big teenager. But promise you'll find out what he needs to tell you first, please. Just in case it's where he's hidden all the bodies, or he's about to divulge the location of all the money he's stolen from sweet old ladies, or . . ."

Ann ignored her, looking beyond Sophie to where Dom and Sabrina had emerged from inside, followed by her ex-father-in-law, Bernard Fitzgerald. Dom looked as though he'd just been given a terminal diagnosis, while Sabrina's face was like thunder. Bernard stopped when he saw her, nodded his head once and continued walking.

Ann nodded back, still unable to believe how everything had panned out. She'd nearly collapsed that morning when she saw the tremendous presence of Bernard Fitzgerald, walking towards her in the coffee shop beside the courthouse.

"Don't look now," Sophie muttered. "Scary father-in-law incoming."

Ann had turned immediately and almost fell off her chair. At one time, she'd have been delighted to see Bernard Fitzgerald. They'd always been close – him acting as the father figure she was missing. He was a kind man, stern but fair, and refreshingly honest for someone who sounded like a farmer dressed as a businessman.

"Don't get up."

Ann craned her neck to look up at him.

"Can I sit, Ann? Sophie, could you give us a minute?"

Ann nodded at Sophie, who made herself scarce.

"Bernard," Ann started as he sat. "I'm so sorry how it's all worked out. I know you must hate me, but I want to tell you, I'm not looking for a cent. Nothing. I just want to be free now to—"

Bernard held up his hand to stop her. "Jaysus, woman, will you stop that now. I've been trying to contact you. I wanted to talk to you before we go in here today. I spoke to Dom a month ago, knowing this court appearance was looming. I wanted to know the whole story – the real one," Bernard began.

"I told him if he wasn't upfront with me, I'd fire him," Bernard chuckled. "I love my son, Ann, but I'm not stupid. A feckin' idiot for doing what he did to you and a feckin' idiot for not supporting you. I'm sorry about that. But you know as well as I do, we can only guide them . . ." He paused, reaching over and resting his hand on hers.

"When he told me about how you went back to Knockmore, what you'd discovered about your mam, how she was trying to protect you, how you'd arrived here in Dublin all those years ago, only a child . . ." He shook his head. "Well, I can't begin to understand what you've been through. And then to meet my son, and to be treated how you were by him. Actually, I'm ashamed to say how you were treated by *all* of my family. You didn't deserve that, Ann. We never asked the right questions of you and for that, I'm sorry."

Ann didn't know what to say. It wasn't what she'd expected.

"Thank you, Bernard. Thank you for that. I felt like I'd let you down. You were so kind to me. I would have stayed with Dom, but the cheating was too much."

Bernard nodded. "I was never once unfaithful to my wife. Not once. Oh, I had plenty of opportunities over the years, on business trips and the likes, but it wasn't how I was reared. I'm sorry Dom did that to you," he told her honestly.

"It's okay," Ann admitted. "In a way, it's all gone the way it was supposed to. It hasn't been easy, but I went home. Dublin wasn't for me, in the end. I'm not like them here. I'm not exactly sure I'm for Knockmore, either, to be honest, but it's starting to feel like home."

"Well, then perhaps what I'm going to tell you won't exactly float your boat, but you can do with it what you feel best. It's not about money, it's about—"

"Choices," Ann finished, remembering what he always used to say.

Bernard laughed. "That's right, girl. *Someone* was listening to me. Your parents would be proud of you, Ann." He stopped, looked down. "*I'm* proud of you."

"Thank you for this chat. I feel so much better. And I mean it, I want nothing. This was enough for me. I can leave with my head high now."

"Would you stop, girl. Now, I know, because you won't stop saying it, that you want nothing, but I want to do this for you. In fact, I've already done it. Dom agrees. Well, it took a while to convince him, but anyway, it's done."

Ann looked at him quizzically.

"The house. The Pembroke house. Your house." He handed her a set of keys. "There's some paperwork, but it's yours. There's no mortgage. I took care of that. I don't suppose you'll want to live in it, but you earned it. Sell it, rent it. Choose, Ann. It's up to you now."

Ann stared at the keys in her hand and back at him. "But, I . . . I . . ."

Bernard laughed. "No arguments. If you're happy to accept, today is just a formality. You walk away with the house and you never have to see Dom again. Don't say no, Ann. You're a clever girl. Accept it. Make a life for yourself. Go find a decent fella, have babies – or don't . . ." He paused again when he saw the tears streaming down her face. He stood and put his hand on her shoulder. "I would have been proud to call you my daughter. Drop me the odd email, won't you? Let me know you're okay. I'd better go in."

The hearing had been quick. Everyone agreed. Dom barely had the decency to look at her and even Sabrina sat outside waiting, staring at her phone.

Ann had no idea what she was going to do with the

Pembroke house, but she couldn't stop smiling as she drove along the motorway back to Knockmore. Choices – she had plenty of them now. But all she could think of was Jason – his smile, his touch. She imagined him picking her up, wrapping his strong arms around her, kissing her. Ann's mind flitted to Mark. She still had to speak to him. No time like the present, she thought as she pulled the car in at the side of the road a few miles from the town.

Mark answered straightaway.

"Ann. Are you okay? Where have you been?"

"Hi. I'm sorry. I couldn't find my phone," Ann lied. "And then I had the hearing. Sorry. How's Jessica? I didn't hear anything. Is there any change?"

"Yes."

He sounded lighter.

"Jessica's okay. She's awake, since the weekend, doing much better. God, I was so worried. I wanted to say sorry for how I spoke to you. It's so good to hear your voice."

"That's great." The guilt surged through her body. "Really great, Mark."

"I thought Mum would have told you, but she said you weren't at the house. Then I remembered you had your meeting today and you're obviously in Dublin. How did it go? I wish I could have been there with you, but it'll be another few weeks before I get back. Are you okay?"

"It was good," she started and then paused. "What do you mean, your mum says I wasn't at the house?"

"Mum flew back on Saturday evening. At first, I was shocked she was leaving, but then it made sense. I think the penny's finally dropped that Jessica needs help – more than we can offer. She flew back to get everything sorted.

Jessica's going to be going into rehab, at last. It's the right decision. I'm just so—"

"Saturday evening?" Ann could hardly breathe.

"Yep. Mum must have got to the house late. I suppose you wouldn't have been there at the weekend, anyway. I haven't spoken to her much, to be honest. When Mum's on a mission, she's on a mission."

"Are you sure she was at the house, Mark?" Ann asked suddenly, trying to think back to Saturday night.

She and Jason had sat outside for hours together. Ann caught a glimpse of her face in the rear-view mirror now, every ounce of colour fading from her recently tanned skin.

"Pretty sure. Then again, she may have stayed in Dublin. I don't know. Why?"

Ann couldn't think.

"Ann, are you there?"

"Yes. Sorry. No reason. The line's bad. Mark, I have to go. I'm in the car. I'm so pleased about Jessica. Really. I'll call you later."

Ann leaned her head back against the headrest and covered her face with her hands.

"You're a rollercoaster, Ann Maguire. Up and down, twists and turns, never a dull moment. One thing happens and then some big bomb goes off." Ann could hear Sophie's words.

Olive Dempsey was the last person she expected to have to think about. Had Olive been there? Surely Ann would have noticed. Maybe she came by the house and left straightaway. Ann felt sick. There was every chance that Olive saw nothing. Then again . . .

Ann put the car into gear and pulled back out onto the road, heading for Knockmore House, dread edging its way up through her limbs. She turned the car off Main Street and drove up the hill, through the granite gateposts. Stopping the car in front of the steps, she jumped out and unlocked the front door.

"Hello," she called, to no reply.

Ann threw open the kitchen door, her brow furrowed as she looked at the empty kitchen. She glanced out at the back. The concrete floor of the conservatory had been poured, as planned, the day before, but the place was deserted – the scaffolding cleared, the tools, cement mixers, wheelbarrows, all gone. Ann walked outside and looked to the left, hoping to see both the caravan and Jason waiting for her.

"Ann, dear. I was wondering when you'd show up." Her little blonde bob jerked up immediately. "My, my, haven't you been the busy bee? Come sit, dear." Olive patted the chair beside her, where the caravan had once been. "I want to talk to you."

Ann took in Olive's red dress, which was the colour of blood, the matching shoes, her large dark glasses, and walked woodenly towards her, feeling as if she were inching her way towards her own funeral.

CHAPTER FORTY-EIGHT

Olive

Olive had left almost immediately. Well, as soon as she'd convinced Mark he was absolutely right and they mustn't wait another second before investigating the right facility for Jessica, back in Ireland.

"I can do nothing here," Olive had explained through forced tears. "I'll go home for a few days, speak to the doctor myself – go and see the various centres personally." Olive still couldn't bring herself to use the word rehab. "We can't wait, Mark. You're right. It was wrong of me to try to manage Jessica alone. It's taken its toll on us all. Such severe depression needs to be dealt with. Sometimes there's no reason for it. Depression can just hit. And I haven't helped by trying to mollycoddle Jessica. I thought I was doing the right thing, but I see now that I was wrong."

Olive thought Mark or even Eugene might have put up more of a fight, attempted to stop her from leaving. They hadn't. Instead, they'd appeared relieved to be rid of her, practically shoving her out of the door.

"I'll go with you in the taxi," Mark offered. "Can I give you a hand to pack?"

After all she'd done for them – the sacrifices, the sleepless nights, the planning, the executing – and they didn't seem bothered if she left or not. Under normal circumstances, it might have hurt, but instead, Olive felt numb. She'd surprised herself, even, that she'd been able to muster tears when Mark had dropped her outside the terminal, still feeling nothing at all. But the closer she got to home, the empty feeling began to gather, propelled by determination. Olive had got this far – she wasn't going to let it all fall apart now.

As soon as Mark had zoomed in on that picture, Olive had recognised him, the scraggly beard not enough to hide his features or those eyes. The last time she'd looked into them, she'd been sitting across from him in that disgusting prison, only a little square table with its thin metal legs separating them.

"You will never cross our door again," she'd told him in no uncertain terms.

"You won't get away with this. The truth will out. It always does."

"I have no idea what you're talking about, Nathan." Olive feigned ignorance.

By then, she'd almost persuaded herself that her twisted version of the story was the truth.

"I rue the day Jessica ever met you. *You* did this. This is on you, and now you want to take her down with you! You're delusional."

"No!" he'd shouted, lowering his voice when the guard looked up suddenly. "*You're* delusional. You spiteful, disgusting excuse for a person. I believed you!" He looked down and then said, "I loved her . . ."

Olive almost felt sorry for him.

"You lied to me," he continued through gritted teeth. "And so did Jessica. How could you? I did nothing. I *am* innocent."

"Hah. I wonder how many others in here have said

that before you. But you did do it, Nathan. It's all there in your statement. What?" Olive threw her hands up. "You think the judge is going to believe you that you made it up? You think at the eleventh hour you can turn round and say it was Jessica?" She grinned.

"You know the truth. So does Jessica. She *has* to tell the truth!" He leaned closer. "It was an accident. They'll understand. This is going to destroy me, my career. Everything. My own family won't talk to me. I've been in here since that night – eight months awaiting trial. For what? To save your reputation!"

"You agreed. You said you love her. Jessica's fragile. She'd never have made it through this. If you're lucky, they'll go easy on you and we can all put this sorry affair behind us. But I will protect her, Nathan. You'll understand one day if you ever have your own kids. You'll do anything to protect them, *anything*."

"You're insane, you crazy bitch. The only person you're protecting is yourself. I swear to God, I'll make your life a misery. Just wait. One day, I'll make you pay."

Olive stood. She'd heard enough. Putting her hands on the table to steady herself, she'd looked down at him.

"If you *ever* come near us *ever* again, you'll be sorry. I'll say you threatened to murder me. I'll throw myself down the stairs if I have to. This is nothing to do with us any more. You're on your own. Do you hear me?"

He'd watched her mouth moving, twisting bitterly as she spoke, his shoulders slumped forwards, his spirit broken.

Olive had picked up her purse and walked away, head in the air. He'd called something after her and she'd heard him, but she'd kept going.

"Was there ever a baby? Did you make that up, too?"

Olive had gone to the trial, sitting down at the very back, hidden under a trench coat, a scarf knotted under her chin. It took two days. All the while, she'd tried to remove herself from it, imagining she was watching a soap opera, hardly able to breathe for fear he'd mention Jessica, or her. There was a possibility Jessica would be called as a witness, but Olive's solicitor confirmed she was unfit to attend, the doctor having recorded a nervous breakdown. The entire time, Olive had expected the barrister to turn and point his finger down the court, at her, but he hadn't. No one had noticed her.

Listening to the other family speaking was harrowing. Olive wasn't a monster, after all. Everyone sitting there could feel the weight in the room. The father was a garda, a superintendent. Olive supposed that's why Nathan had been charged and not released on bail, pending his court hearing. Even Olive felt the tears well as she'd listened to him tell the jury how their lives would never be the same again.

She had to hand it to Nathan's barrister, though. He'd played a blinder. That bit was almost exciting to watch. She wondered afterwards if he knew all along that Nathan would get off: on a technicality, or two. Olive had never heard anyone stammer as much as that poor garda on the witness stand. They'd messed up that night. Failed to caution Nathan, and a few other silly mistakes – quite the disaster.

When it was over and the judge had ruled, giving Nathan a suspended sentence for time already served, Olive had expected Nathan to be pleased. Wasn't that the part in the movies where there was cheering and embracing? Instead, Nathan had sat motionless, staring ahead.

What was done was done. Isn't that what Olive's own father used to say? Forwards, not backwards.

All Olive had needed to focus on then was getting Jessica better. Nathan was free, no real harm was done.

Then Eugene had had the stroke.

Olive took a taxi from the airport all the way back to Knockmore, not caring how much it cost, grateful that the driver left her in peace for the duration. She wouldn't have been able to bear a conversation about taxes, or how the Irish government were a shower of money-grabbers. Instead, Olive focused quietly on what lay ahead. In a way, she'd always known this day would come.

Olive had used Eugene's illness and his extramarital embarrassment as a way to convince him they needed to leave Wicklow. Mark had thrown a spanner in the works by offering to buy the house from them. That part had filled her with constant anxiety, fearful that Nathan would turn up there someday. And of course, Jessica had refused to leave Wicklow at first. But Olive knew it was only a matter of time before Jessica became too much for Mark to handle. It hadn't taken Mark long to telephone Olive, plead with her to remove Jessica from the house. Of course, she'd obliged.

Olive had imagined Mark would meet some nice girl in Dublin – one who wouldn't be seen dead living in the bungalow in Wicklow – and then the house would be sold and Nathan never would find them. Then again, in this day and age, there was always a trail. Olive had been naïve about that. Times were different now – it was harder to vanish.

It took Mark longer than expected to meet someone, but as soon as Olive met Ann, she was sure she could push them together. Look how well that had gone, the young lovers ready to move in with each other! Mark would sell the house in Wicklow for sure, but what did it matter now? It was too late. Nathan had found them.

It had taken all of her restraint not to question Mark about "Jason Brady". She wondered how Nathan had pulled it off, managed to pose as someone else the entire time. But why had he taken the job? That part still puzzled Olive. He was an architect, not a builder. Mark should have been more careful. Of course, Mark had never met Nathan before, supposedly – none of them had. Olive wished she never had, either.

Olive could still remember Jessica telling her all about Nathan's fancy architecture firm in Dublin with his brother.

"Winning awards left, right and centre," Jessica gushed down the phone.

After it all came out about Eugene's affair, Jessica had rarely come home, choosing instead to stay with Nathan in Dublin – *Nathan this, Nathan that.*

"Bring him home. Let us meet him," Olive was always asking.

Jessica never got the chance.

The look of Knockmore House in pitch-blackness made Olive shiver. It looked dark, ominously looming over her as she paid the taxi and walked towards the house. At least there was no one here. She could have a good night's sleep, prepare for Monday, when she'd face Nathan – find out what he was doing here and get rid of him just as fast.

Olive let herself in through the front door and stood for a moment. It was after midnight. Olive dropped her bag on the floor, not bothering to turn on the lights, and made her way upstairs.

It felt good to be back here, on familiar soil, in the house that had offered her a second chance. She sat on the bed, removing her shoes, and lay back, staring up at the ceiling, trying to order her thoughts. There were times Olive wasn't sure what the truth was any more. It was so muddled in her mind that she'd struggle to write it all down chronologically. Sometimes, it woke her from her sleep and she'd try to replay it. But parts were missing – enormous vacant gaps in the story. Looking back, it was as if it were someone else it had all happened to. As if she were a spectator, or had dreamed it.

The emotions hit her suddenly and she gasped, putting her head in her hands.

"I didn't mean it all to happen this way," she whispered to the darkness. "I wanted to protect them all."

Her words were swallowed into nothingness.

"I wanted to keep my family safe," she tried again, the sound vanishing into thin air.

Olive sat up, brushing her hair from her face and looking towards the door. The slightest glimmer of light could be seen in the open crack. Perhaps someone had left a light on. She hadn't seen it when she'd walked upstairs, but her eyes had adjusted now.

Walking from room to room, Olive pushed each door open, feeling slightly apprehensive as she did so, more from exhaustion than fear. There was very little that truly frightened Olive. When you've already lost so much, there was very little to fear in life, except death.

Olive pushed the door of the second bedroom at the rear of the house. From the window, she could see the new extension jutting out below. To the left, Olive noticed a glow. She craned her neck and then walked automatically towards the bathroom at the end of the hall, where she removed her shoes and clambered on the toilet seat to peer out.

CHAPTER FORTY-NINE

"Where is everyone?" Ann sat opposite Olive, shivering despite the warmth. "Where's Jason?"

"Gone, dear."

"What do you mean, gone?" Ann's voice began to quiver.

"Well, I think it's quite obvious, dear. G-O-N-E." Olive spelled it and smirked.

"I don't understand." Ann shook her head, desperately trying to read Olive's indecipherable features.

"Come now, Ann. I think you do understand. Give it a moment."

Ann looked away and then back at Olive.

"Ah! there we are. The penny is dropping. Three, two, one, and it's dropped."

"You saw."

Olive stared ahead. Yes, she'd seen.

The girl was leaning forwards, her hands resting on his chest as he kneeled in front of her. He stood then and pulled her up, lifting her off the ground. Her arms wrapped themselves around him, her legs circling his body as their mouths locked together. Olive thought she was going to be sick, instantly putting her hand over her mouth to stifle the sound she was making as she watched them laugh and disappear inside the caravan. Olive sank to the floor.

What was going on? Was Ann in on it all?

She couldn't be. Perhaps this was part of Nathan's plan: lure the girlfriend in, destroy them all. Ann had the appearance that butter wouldn't melt in her mouth, had seemed smitten with Mark. People never failed to amaze her.

Mark would be devastated. Olive couldn't let that happen to her son. One indiscretion didn't have to ruin it all, did it? She'd fix it . . .

Olive clambered up, hobbled to her room, collected her handbag and crept back out of the house as quietly as she could, up the driveway and out of the gate.

"Aren't the gardens stunning, Ann? Isn't that tree so beautiful?"

Ann followed Olive's gaze.

"A tree full of secrets. Isn't that what you said? I thought it was so very poetic of you. You do know Mark asked me not to cut it down? Such a sweet boy. Don't you think?" Olive turned to Ann.

Ann clasped her hands together and rested them on her lap, staring down.

"I didn't mean to hurt him. I *don't* want to hurt him," Ann whispered.

"But of course you don't. That's what I wanted to tell you," Olive began. "Did Mark tell you anything about Eugene? What he did to me?"

"I guessed. I presumed that he'd been unfaithful from the way you spoke."

Olive laughed. "Such a nice clean term – unfaithful. I prefer deceitful. Backstabbing. Two-faced. How did you describe it when your husband did the same to you?" Olive raised her eyebrows.

"The same," Ann admitted, growing wary of whatever game Olive was playing. "I was hurt."

"I prefer devastated, aching, crushed, broken." Olive stared ahead again.

"Okay, you've made your point," Ann said impatiently. "It's only just happened. I'm not proud of myself, but what's done is done. I can't change it."

"Hah! A phrase I use myself, but you're right, Ann. What's done is indeed done."

"I didn't think it was the right time to tell him with everything going on with Jessica." Ann glanced at Olive. "I'm glad she's okay."

"Yes, Jessica." Olive closed her eyes and exhaled. "What a terrible business, and now this."

"I will tell him, Olive. I'd never hurt him intentionally."

"And why would you do a stupid thing like that?" Olive asked, looking ahead again in a trance. "Now, if you'll let me speak . . ." She smoothed her skirt. "When I found out about Eugene, all I wanted was to make it go away. You can't go back once you know. It turned my whole life inside out, ruined it. Everything – *everything* – that happened after was because of that indiscretion. It ruined us all." She paused and then laughed. "I've thought a lot about your 'grandmother'," she air quoted. "Margot, wasn't it? I admire her. She did what she had to do for her family. Protected a secret. Took it to the grave."

Ann was shocked. "She stole a baby, Olive! She abused a child! That child was my mother."

"Yes, but she wanted to give her a better life. She took action. Can't you see that? Don't you admire someone who'll do what has to be done for their family?"

"Not really. What are you saying?" Ann watched her.

"Oh, I know I must sound crazy to you young people, always wanting to lay all of your cards on the table. Always wanting everyone to know the truth. The truth doesn't set you free, dear. The truth traps you – slowly kills you." Olive looked at her. "So you made a mistake with this—"

"Jason," Ann finished.

"Did you know him before?" Olive asked.

"Jason? No. I know nothing about him, just that he's kind and honest. I don't expect you to understand. I'm not proud of my actions and I will tell Mark," Ann repeated. She needed to get out of here.

"But you won't." Olive glared at her, her eyes narrowing. "Jason's gone. Never to return. I gave him a choice and he took it, Ann. He didn't even spare you a moment's thought. I asked him to leave and he left. Didn't he call you?"

Ann shook her head, barely able to understand what Olive was saying. Jason would never leave without saying goodbye. Ann grabbed her phone from her bag and tapped in his number, putting the phone to her ear.

Sorry, the number you have dialled is not in service.

"What have you done?" Ann stood up.

"I did what you would do to protect your child from hurt. Mark is a good man, Ann. He loves you. And with Jessica sick, how could you leave him?" Olive stood up too, her tiny frame suddenly enormous. "I'm giving you a second chance. I'm not going to tell Mark. And nor are you.

"Lick your wounds, Ann. Mark will be back in a few weeks and you'll have forgotten this Jason. Take it for what it was, a dalliance. You know as well as I do, you're meant to be here, in this house, with Mark, with us."

Ann started to walk away. She'd had an idea that Olive was crazy, but this was outrageous. She didn't want anything else to do with her, with any of them.

"You know, Ann, perhaps I should have had a little affair myself. You were hurt before, like me. Tit for Tat," she smirked. "But, *don't* hurt my son, Ann. I hate to say this, but you'll regret it. We know so much of your story. All the little awkward parts that you want kept secret. Are we so different?"

"Are you threatening me?" Ann turned and walked back towards her.

"Not at all, dear," Olive said sweetly. "Like I said, it's a second chance. Think about it. We never have to speak of it again. Our little secret. I'll take it to the grave," Olive called after her as Ann ran back into the house.

"Jason? Jason?" Ann called frantically, knowing he wouldn't answer.

She *had* to find him.

Ann went into the office, grabbed her guitar and her diary from the desk. The cheque book was open on the table and before leaving, Ann picked it up and flicked to the last stub. She inhaled sharply at the amount, then quickly took out her phone and took a picture of it.

Who the hell was Nathan O'Keefe?

CHAPTER FIFTY

By the time Denise and Ian arrived at the house, Ann was climbing the walls. Not knowing what else to do, she'd issued an SOS, summoning them. Ann didn't want to call Sophie, not yet, anyway, unsure she had it in her to hear another, "I told you so."

Ann had dialled Jason's number a thousand times, to no avail. She'd then googled Jason Brady, builder, scoured social media and finally googled Nathan O'Keefe, whoever the hell he was. She'd watched the results flash up on her phone, scrolled through them and then threw the phone on the kitchen table, with no idea what she was even looking for – it was pointless.

Ann paced the floor, the note she'd found in her hallway still in her hand. As soon as she'd read it, she'd crumpled it up and screamed with frustration. It didn't make sense.

Ann,
Job didn't work out. Moving on. It was great meeting you. Don't feel bad – we all make mistakes. Good luck in the future.
J

Ann couldn't think. It felt as though the bottom was tumbling out of her world once again, just when she thought everything was finally falling into place. *No more rollercoasters*, Ann begged, feeling nauseous at the thought of another unexpected plummet. She was so exhausted, longing to be back in Jason's arms, pining for his touch, for him to tell her what she needed to hear – that everything was going to be all right, that it was all some stupid misunderstanding.

Ann smoothed out the note again and reread it before throwing open the front door, hopping the metal fence and banging on Tracy's door.

"What the f . . ." Tracy opened the door. "Ann? What's happened?"

"Tracy, did you see anything? Was there anyone at my house yesterday? Did you see a blue truck come down here? Or anyone at all?"

"Jesus, Ann, what is it? Are you all right?"

"Yeah, No. I don't know. Please, Tracy," Ann pleaded.

"No, I saw nothing. Boys!" Tracy screamed behind her. "Did any of you see a blue truck here yesterday? Or anyone at Ann's house?"

Ann listened as they all shouted no in unison.

"What's happened, Ann?"

"It's nothing, Tracy, honest. Just a delivery mess-up," she lied before hopping the fence once more, slamming her door behind her and sitting on the bottom tread of the stairs.

Ann was still sitting there when Ian and Denise found her, her face streaked with tears, still wearing the black dress she'd worn to her court hearing.

"Jesus Christ! Ann. What's happened?" Denise sat down and put her arm around her, looking up at Ian, who looked just as puzzled.

"Come on, let's go into the kitchen. I'll make the tea

and, Denise, you can administer the sympathy," Ian suggested, clapping his hands together.

"Nothing we can't fix, Annie, nothing. Come on."

Denise pulled Ann up and they followed Ian into the kitchen, where he already had the kettle on and the mugs out. Ann sank into a kitchen chair, her shoulders slumped forwards, and Denise handed her a tissue.

"Was it the court hearing? Was Dom an arsehole?"

Ann shook her head, gulping back the tears that had turned to little hiccups. "No," she said finally. "That all went well."

"Well, what is it?" Denise asked again before putting her hand over her mouth. "Is it the sister? Is she brown bread?"

Ann looked up sharply. "How did you know about that?"

Denise looked at Ian, who made a face.

"Now, don't be cross, Ann, but Sophie told me and I may have mentioned it to Denise. She was worried about you. Just asked us to keep an eye on you."

Ann sighed. What did it matter who knew now? Nothing mattered.

"She's fine. She's going to be okay."

"Did you have a fight with Mark?" Denise pushed. "He must be under a lot of pressure."

Ann shook her head again.

"Well, for God's sake, Ann, am I going to have to extract it manually from you?" Denise threw her hands in the air and Ann started to cry again – great big, heaving tears of despair.

Ian opened the fridge, took out a bottle of wine, unscrewed the top and poured it into one of the mugs before thrusting it at Ann.

"Screw tea. Lug that back, Annie. Take a deep breath and start from the very beginning."

When Ann had finished telling them all about Jason, from when she first saw him the night of her birthday in the pub, to everything in between, Ian opened the fridge again, took out the wine and poured it into the other two mugs. He handed one to Denise and took a gulp from the other.

"Well, knock me over with a feather. Your life gets more exciting by the second." Ian fanned his face. "I knew it. I just knew it. Didn't I say you were attracted to him? There was more chemistry between you and that Jason fella than there was in the chemistry set I got for Christmas when I was twelve years old. I nearly burned down the house with that set. You could see it a mile off," he told Denise, making an explosive action with his hands. "All those knowing glances . . ."

"Why didn't you tell me before now?"

"I'm sorry, Denise. I didn't know. It wasn't until last weekend that I realised all along I had feelings for Jason. I was ashamed. Turns out I have more than feelings," Ann explained. "I think I might—"

"Don't say it, Ann." Ian shook his head and then took her hand. "Annie, I'm older than you and I know men. This was a fling. A bit of fun. I could tell a mile off that your builder friend is one of those – love 'em and leave 'em. Wham bam thank you ma'am. Don't come a-knockin' if the caravan is rockin'. If you get laid—"

"Okay. Thank you, Ian." Denise held her hand up to stop him and Ann mustered a slight smile. "So, when you got back, he was gone?" Denise asked.

Ann nodded. "Vanished. I don't know what happened between Jason and Olive, but I think she paid him off to get him away from me. All she kept saying was that I should be with Mark, we all make mistakes. And there was just this note . . ." She handed them the note and they both read it.

"Bit vague," Ian said. "See, Ann. I'm telling you. Look, I know you think Olive's crazy, but maybe some of what she said makes sense. Mark is handsome, rich, kind, funny, and he loves you. There *are* worse ways to live your life. Put it behind you and move on, girl, with Mark. We really thought this was it for you. Didn't we, Denise?" Ian asked.

Denise said nothing.

"Denise?"

Denise shook her head slowly and then groaned. "Mark is perfect, yes. He's a lovely guy, but I could see he wasn't for you, not really."

Ann looked up, surprised, while Ian shook his head in disgust.

"Now, don't get me wrong, as a middle-aged woman, having been married for longer than I care to admit, I'd be picking Mark for myself. He's the safe bet. He's the one who'll give you comfort and security." Denise paused as Ian nodded along enthusiastically once more.

"But I could see the scales were tipping in the wrong direction. Mark was smitten by you, Ann, but you didn't look at him the same way. Falling in love should be a two-sided story. Look at Sammy and me! Never would have worked!" Denise chuckled before turning serious again and looking up at Ian. "See, Ian, I saw the way Sammy Maguire looked at Felicity Montgomery – the one we all thought had a perfect life up in Knockmore House.

"Turns out it wasn't so perfect. But what they had, that was real. It wasn't easy. It never is when it's real. Not everyone experiences that, you know. The rest of us get something that's nice, comfortable. Mark is nice. Mark is comfortable."

Ann and Ian watched her talk.

"Maybe this Jason is the real deal, maybe he isn't. But you wouldn't be looking the way you do right now if you didn't care for him." Denise squeezed Ann's hand. "You can't stop the feelings you have for someone, just as you can't lie to yourself, either. Your heart won't let you.

"I know I'm an old romantic, but the day you sang that song that night in Lennon's, you set eyes on a man who turned your life inside out," Denise said. "Now that, to me, is no coincidence. That, to me, is Sammy and Felicity sending you the biggest sign, in flashing lights, with a brass band attached."

Denise smiled sadly and Ann's eyes once again filled with tears.

"But what about this?" Ian held the note up again. "Surely if this Jason is the love of your life, he wouldn't have sent—"

Ian was interrupted by the doorbell. Ann shot off the chair to go and answer it, half expecting it to be Jason.

"Tracy?" Ann looked confused.

Tracy was out of breath. "I ran all the way back from the shops. I was there with the boys, when one of them produces a twenty-euro note from his pocket. I said, 'Where the hell did you get that?'" Tracy paused, still trying to catch her breath.

"Well, you know I said none of us had seen anything, well, the little sod was lying. He says some tiny old woman with blonde hair and a weird face was here, snooping about. When she saw him looking at her, she rooted about in her bag, pulled out the cash and said, 'Our secret.' She told him she worked for the post office and not to tell that he'd seen her."

Ian and Denise had materialised behind Ann.

"Olive," they all said together.

"Who's that?" Tracy asked.

"Mark's mother," Ann explained.

"Ann, can I do anything? Why would she do that?" Tracy looked concerned.

Ann reached over and hugged her. "Thanks, Tracy. I'll let you know, but for now, you've been amazing."

After that, they went back inside. Ann sat down again, trying to figure it out.

"It was Olive who wrote that note. I'm sure of it."

"Maybe she was delivering it for Jason." Ian still wasn't convinced.

Ann shook her head. "No. I know there's more to this, Denise, Ian. I just know it. Jason would never disappear like that. I get the feeling that there's something I'm missing.

"Olive was so strange earlier and she's hiding something. I don't know what it is, but I'm beginning to think this is more than just keeping me away from Jason. I think he might be involved in something, too. Otherwise, why would he vanish? There was something he wanted to tell me . . ." Ann paused. "Oh, God, I feel like I've walked into something bigger than a crazy mother. I just don't know what it is."

It was Denise's turn to speak.

"Look, love. Maybe I'm wrong and I'm giving you the worst advice ever . . ." Denise glanced at Ian, who was shaking his head in dismay. "But there's no harm in seeing what this is all about. Trust your intuition, Ann. If Jason is the man you say he is, if he's in trouble somehow, maybe he needs help. We all need someone to believe in us sometimes. Let's get to the bottom of this, together. Let's give a little fight."

Denise placed her hand on Ann's and Ian reluctantly put his hand on Denise's.

"All right, then," Ian agreed. "I'm still Team Mark, but let's see what we can find out."

CHAPTER FIFTY-ONE

Mark

Mark had spent the weekend ferrying between the villa and the hospital, making sure his father was all right with Olive away, and then rushing back to Jessica. Bit by bit, Jessica was starting to come round. Mark was imploring her to speak, still imagining all the scenarios that may have brought her to this point. Mark couldn't piece it all together. With his mother gone, his father had begun to relax, as if a terrible burden had been lifted from his shoulders. He'd been to visit Jessica that morning. Mark had left them alone, backing out of the room but still able to hear the exchange.

"I'm so sorry, Jessica. So very sorry for everything," his father whispered. "I never meant for you to get hurt. I made so many mistakes, but Mark's going to help me to set it all right, love. He's going to help you, too. I love you, Jessica. Please don't leave me again. I need you."

Mark had closed his eyes, blinking back the tears. When he'd peered back round the door, his father's head was resting on the bed and Jessica was rubbing his hair, the tears flowing freely down her face. It was what they all needed now: honesty, openness, no more hiding, no more brushing it all under the carpet, no more lies.

Mark watched Jessica sleep. The colour had begun to come back into her face and she looked more peaceful than she had in years. He heard his phone vibrate in his pocket and looking at the screen, he crept towards the door.

"Hey, you."

"How's Jessica?" Ann asked.

"Much better. So much better. She's sleeping."

"That's good. Listen, Mark, I can't explain right now. I will, I swear to you, and I don't want you to worry, and please don't call your mother, but I need to ask you something. Can you do that for me?"

Ann was speaking so fast he could barely understand her.

"Is Mum okay?"

"She's fine. Well, I saw her today. She was strange. Mark, tell me to back off if you want, but there's something not right about everything. I can't explain it. Call it a sixth sense. Is there something I should know?" Ann tried to explain.

"I . . . I don't know, maybe," Mark admitted finally, the hairs on his arms standing on end. There was no point in hiding anything any more. "Ann, what's going on?"

"Mark, the builders have gone. Olive fired them."

"What? What the hell? I need to call her."

"No, Mark. Wait, please. Just give me a day. That's all I'm asking. But I need to ask you something. Does the name Nathan O'Keefe mean anything to you?"

"Nathan O'Keefe," Mark repeated. "I don't think so. Why, Ann? Should it? I've never heard of a Nathan O'Keefe."

Mark heard a noise behind him and turned. Jessica was sitting up, her face white, her entire body shaking, a pained sound coming from her mouth.

"I found a cheque stub in the office. It was for a hundred and fifty thousand euros, made out to Nathan O'Keefe. It was Olive who signed the cheque."

"I don't understand."

"Neither do I. I wondered . . ."

"Mark?" It was from Jessica. "Mark?"

"Ann, I'll call you back." Mark hung up and walked towards the bed, putting his hand on Jessica's arm. "Jess? What is it?"

"There's something I have to tell you."

CHAPTER FIFTY-TWO

Jessica

Afterwards, it would replay incessantly, over and over, never ceasing. Not once did it cease, not for one moment, the images flashing before her eyes in slow motion, again and again. Jessica couldn't stop it. It would never end. Doing what she did was the only way she could think to halt it. If she couldn't feel any more, then she couldn't see it.

Everything changed that night.

For Jessica. For Nathan. For Nicola – that was her name. Her mother told her afterwards and then Jessica wished she hadn't. Her name made it all so real. Jessica often tried to imagine what Nicola had been thinking, in what would be her last thought, her final moment. Was it something mundane? Something profound?

Jessica hoped it was something beautiful, or something terribly philosophical. Then again, if Nicola had no idea that it would be her last thought, it was more than likely banal – like what to eat for dinner the next day, or remembering to put on a wash.

It struck Jessica how in one second, none of those stupid little things we think about daily really matter when suddenly you are gone, obliterated, destroyed. It made Jessica believe that life was no longer worth living. It was pointless, ridiculous, hopeless.

Jessica had spent most of that day thinking meaningless

thoughts, like what to wear – in fact, she'd agonised over it. She'd wanted to look right, give off the right impression. She'd had her hair done, deciding not to tip the hairdresser when her beachy waves turned out to be more swept out to sea. She'd called her father, asking could she use the credit card to buy a new dress. Some incredibly expensive one she'd seen – one that could have fed a family for a month. Jessica had bought shoes, too, and a bag – without an ounce of guilt, knowing Daddy dearest would do anything to eradicate his sin. *Prick*.

All those years, never coming home, leaving Mark and her under the suffocating gaze of their mother, only to discover he had another little family tucked away all along, clawing for his attention. Jessica hated him, would never forgive him – not like her mother had. Jessica hated her, too, only staying in touch with her to keep her at arm's length. But Jessica had had a new life then, in Dublin, with Nathan.

Nathan was everything. Handsome, rich – or at least he soon would be. His architecture firm was going from strength to strength, but more than anything, Nathan was the kindest, most open, honest person, she'd ever met. He wore his heart on his sleeve and everyone who met him adored him, but not half as much as she did. Jessica was in love. It took him months to say it. He told her afterwards he was afraid she might not feel the same.

"How can I convince you?" she'd laughed at him, reaching up and kissing him, feeling his smooth face against her own.

They were always together and after nine months, they'd had the conversation.

"A converted farmhouse, three kids, four dogs, you and me."

They'd never be like her messed-up family. Never.

Until they were.

Jessica had laughed when he'd told her that the party they'd been invited to was in Wicklow.

"That's near my folks' house."

"Should we call in?"

"No, thanks. Be hard to get a taxi back to town, though. I'll drive," she'd offered. "They're your friends. You enjoy yourself."

"You sure?"

Jessica had been. Or at least she was until of course she'd walked in, feeling ridiculously overdressed in her little floral dress, her new shoes pinching her feet, her usual confidence waning. They'd all seemed so much older, talking about their careers, their pastimes, politics, global warming.

"What do you do?"

"I work in Fashion PR." Jessica wanted the ground to swallow her when she noticed two of the other girls nudge each other.

By then, Nathan was in full swing, chatting to people, introducing her, knocking back bottle after bottle of beer.

"Want a drink?" One of the girls thrust a glass of prosecco into her hand.

By the time Jessica finished the first glass, she'd relaxed a little. One drink couldn't hurt and they still had the meal to go. But one drink turned to three.

"Do you want to head off?" Nathan asked around ten. "I can't wait to get you home. They loved you. I knew they would," Nathan told her as he threw her the car keys.

Nathan was asleep almost before they were out of the driveway, snoring away peacefully. They were just passing the last small town before they hit the motorway, a clear stretch ahead, when Jessica reached into the glove box to get some chewing gum, removing her eyes from the road for one second – one instant, one moment.

That moment.

The sound was so deafening – earth-shattering – that at first Jessica thought a bomb had gone off. But her eyes flashed up just in time to see it – a wave of red hair, crashing past the windscreen in slow motion.

Jessica had pressed her foot down hard on the accelerator. For as long as she lived, Jessica would never understand what had made her do it. Instinct, fear. Or the thought that her future was entwined in that red hair – and would shatter when Nicola hit the road behind her.

Speeding away, Jessica heard another noise. It took her a second to realise it was coming from beside her.

"What the hell? What the hell!" Nathan bolted upright in his seat, turning round to look at the shape she could see in the rear-view mirror – a darkened shadow in the centre of the quiet road, an unmoving splodge. "Jessica, stop the car. Stop the car!" he screamed. "Stop."

Nathan grabbed the wheel, swerving the car, but Jessica held tight, adrenaline fuelling her muscles as the blood whirled in her head, and kept going.

"Jessica, please. What are you doing? What have you done?"

Nathan grappled for his phone and then she'd pulled in, stopping the car suddenly. Her breathing was ragged as she turned off the engine and then started banging the steering wheel, then thumping her head with her hands.

"I can't breathe. I can't breathe."

Nathan was with her in seconds, throwing his door open, rushing to her side and pulling her from the car.

They both stared at the front of the vehicle – the bonnet crumpled like paper, the lights shattered.

"I was drinking. I didn't mean to. I only took my eyes off the road for a second. Oh, God. I saw her. I saw her go over. I saw her. What have I done?" Jessica screamed, collapsing to the ground beside the car.

"We have to go back," Nathan pleaded. "We have to get help."

"No. No. No." Jessica repeated it over and over, pulling frantically at her hair.

"Where are we? Where the hell are we?" Nathan looked up suddenly, to see lights coming from a house at the end of a lane.

"My mother . . ." She pointed. "My mother will know what to do."

She was out of the door in seconds. A tiny shape materialising from the darkness – slippers, dressing gown, her grey hair loose, a look of shock on her face. Olive was on her knees beside Jessica in an instant.

"Tell me. Tell me what happened."

There was no hugging or dramatics, just a little woman asking for an explanation, the sight of her alone calming Jessica.

"Give us a moment. Nathan, is it?"

Nathan stepped away. Jessica could see him pacing up and down, running his hands through his hair as her mother whispered to her.

"Look at me, Jessica. Look at me! Do you understand what I'm saying? You're pregnant. Do you hear me? You're pregnant. You told me yesterday. Do you hear me?"

Jessica nodded robotically, not comprehending what her mother was saying.

"Stay there."

Her mother took Nathan aside. Jessica couldn't hear them, but Nathan glanced over at her, shaking his head, and then nodded. Olive was gripping his hands. Nathan pulled away and walked towards Jessica, taking her in his arms.

"I didn't know. Oh, Jessica."

Jessica kept nodding, tears streaming down her face onto her shaking hands.

"It's going to be okay. It's going to be okay," Nathan whispered over and over. "There's a baby to think about. Our baby." He smiled briefly. "Your mother's going to drive us back. Don't worry. I'll do the talking. It's going to be okay."

Olive's mouth was set in a line, her eyes narrow.

For as long as she lived, Jessica would never forget that face.

The drive back was a blur. Then Jessica saw the flashing lights of the ambulance, the earlier deserted road now a hive of activity. She barely remembered pulling up outside the garda station and being taken to a room for questioning.

"I was in the passenger seat. I was in the passenger seat," Jessica repeated over and over as instructed by her mother.

The faces of the gardai stared at her sympathetically – one held her hand, another put a blanket around her shaking form. It was going to be okay . . . And then she saw Nathan.

"Nathan? Mum? Where are they taking him?" Jessica tried to stand, losing her footing and landing back on the chair.

"Shush now, love," her mother reassured. "It's going to be okay. Just a formality."

Jessica stared after Nathan, whose hands were cuffed

behind his back, his face broken, his eyes like glass. But he'd smiled at Jessica sadly, given her a reassuring nod.

It would be the last time she saw him. Jessica cherished that vision of him sacrificing himself for her, walking into the unknown like a lamb to the slaughter. It meant that at one time, there was at least one person who'd loved her enough. And in return, she'd destroyed him.

"It was an accident," Jessica whispered.

"I know, love. A terrible accident," her mother soothed.

Then blackness. Black like her heart. Black like her soul.

Once back in Wicklow, Jessica slept for weeks, or for what seemed like weeks. The doctor was called. Medication administered.

"A bad break-up," she heard her mother explain as she drifted in and out of sleep. Jessica tried to scream, unable to free her trapped voice.

"Please. I need to see Nathan," she begged.

"Nathan's gone, Jessica. Here, take this."

Her mother would feed her another tablet, along with little shards of information, broken up into bite-sized portions, which Jessica could swallow. But she couldn't swallow any of it and Jessica would sink back into hell.

Eventually, her mother told her more. But by then Jessica had gone, just like Nicola. Jessica wished she could be Nicola. Longed to switch places with her, although that would mean trapping Nicola in this hell. Lovely Nicola. Jessica was sure Nicola must have been lovely. A young girl with a baby tucked inside her – six months pregnant.

"Out for a walk because she couldn't sleep. The daughter of the superintendent in the local garda station."

Jessica listened to her mother's words.

"The baby is alive. A Boy. Isn't that great, Jessica?"

But Nicola wasn't.

No. Nicola was brain-dead on arrival at the hospital, vanishing from the scene of the crime straightaway, leaving behind only her body, to incubate the baby for another six weeks. As soon as the baby boy was born, they'd turned off the machines.

Jessica could imagine the sudden quiet in the room – silence, except for the cry from a boy with no mother. Did they lay him on Nicola's chest for a moment, letting him feel for a few seconds what he'd never taste? Had Nicola floated above it all, looking down while they cut him from her stomach?

Jessica wondered a lot about Nicola, about the baby and about Nathan. Why hadn't he come for her? At times, her hand would rest on her own stomach, wondering what had happened to her baby. Jessica was pregnant too, wasn't she? Her mother kept saying it. But where was her baby?

As her mother gradually eased back on the medication, Jessica asked more and more.

"What's happening?"

"Where's Nathan?"

Nathan had been remanded in custody with no bail. He was in prison. For her. Jessica rocked back and forth until her mother slapped her across the face.

Then her father had the stroke.

And Jessica knew she could do nothing. Her mother warned her. "It will kill him."

Jessica had already killed Nicola. Nathan was gone. She had to be quiet now.

"It's over, Jessica," her mother told her after eight months. "Nathan's free."

"You saw him?" Jessica's face lit up.

"I did. It's over. I went to the trial. Quite the mess. Apparently, the garda never cautioned him that night and the breathalyser results were lost. What a stroke of luck for him." Her mother rubbed Jessica's face. "See, I told you it would all work out in the end."

"I need to see him."

"No, Jessica. He wants nothing to do with you. He can't forgive you for lying about the baby."

"I . . . I . . . I didn't . . ."

"Come now, Jessica. You weren't pregnant at all. You knew what you were doing. But it's all right, I understand. It was for the best. Now, pull yourself together. We're moving. Far from here. A fresh start. The past is the past. This is your second chance. Someday you'll thank me. Our secret."

At first, Jessica had attempted to stay in Wicklow with Mark, to be rid of her mother, but she was too weak. Jessica despised herself for it, hated herself for wanting to be close to the one person who knew the truth. There would be no second chance for Jessica. Stupid, silly Jessica. She'd destroyed everything. Jessica had loved Nathan, had never meant to hurt him, but she'd ruined it all. One second in time and more lives lost than she could count.

Jessica had wanted to die that night she'd taken all the pills. After all, she didn't deserve to live. But now she wanted something more.

"It's going to be okay, Jessica. I'll help you. I'm so sorry. I was so blind." Mark's eyes were round with disbelief. "As soon as we're home. We're going to set right whatever we can."

Jessica nodded and took a breath. It felt like the first time in years that the oxygen reached her lungs.

"I want to tell the truth for Nathan. I need to do for him what he did for me. I have to free him."

CHAPTER FIFTY-THREE

Mark

Jessica's eyes flickered shut almost immediately, a gentle sigh escaping her lips, her jaw slackening, the relief visible. Mark left her to sleep, ambling outside to sit at the fountain opposite the hospital, aimlessly watching the water spurting upwards and falling with a splash into the pond below. He could barely believe what Jessica had told him, but he knew it was the truth. He didn't question it for a moment. It all made sense now.

Mark closed his eyes, trying to banish the fury he could feel, which was making his hands shake – the same hands he wanted to wrap around his mother's throat. How could she? All the hurt – and for what? All the lives she'd destroyed, trying to protect her own sad little existence. Escaping to Knockmore, reinventing herself, trapping them all there with her, deep inside her elaborate web. His mother had ruined all of their lives in the process, but especially Jessica's.

Mark couldn't understand how his mother believed she could continue to hide it all. Even Jessica, attempting to end her life, wasn't enough to halt their mother in her tracks. The woman had clearly lost her mind – written a cheque for a hundred and fifty thousand euros to Nathan O'Keefe. It was a wonder that Nathan hadn't arrived at the house and murdered their mother with his bare hands years ago. Had Nathan been threatening his mother? Was that the reason their mother had been behaving so oddly the last few years?

In a way, Mark could hardly blame him, if Nathan had been holding her to ransom. Let him have the money, if that's what he thought would repair his tattered life. Good luck to him. Lord knows, he deserved it. But did his mother think Mark really wouldn't notice that amount missing? Was she really that delusional?

Mark exhaled and shook his head, still struggling to make sense of it. His mother had obviously tangled herself up so much in all the lies that she was starting to trip up – badly. He needed to confront her, but he'd already decided he'd do that in person, back in Knockmore, not wanting to give her time to think up another scheme to worm her way out of it all. He'd take her by surprise.

His father would need to know, too. The thought that she'd used his father's illness to threaten Jessica turned Mark's stomach. Jessica had suffered nothing less than abuse at the hands of their own mother and it was time it all stopped. It was up to Mark now to fix whatever was left to fix. He just needed to figure out the best way to do it.

Well, Mark had said he'd get to the bottom of it, and now he had. Except there was still one part that didn't make sense. Why had his mother let the builders go? Was it because she knew it was all about to come crashing down around her? Perhaps she was hatching another plan. Mark had spoken to her that morning and she'd sounded perfectly normal, as if nothing had happened. She hadn't mentioned the builders, the house or Ann.

Mark rubbed at his temples. His head was starting to pound. What a mess. Ann had somehow managed to work out that something was going on. Well, the cheque had been a huge clue, but had she alluded to something more, or was that Mark's imagination? He couldn't think.

What was he missing?

Mark dialled Ann's number and listened to it ring out, again.

CHAPTER FIFTY-FOUR

It had been Denise's idea.

"Isn't your aunt Florrie's son a garda up in Dublin?" she'd asked earlier.

"Good idea," Ian nodded enthusiastically. "Always great to have a member of the gardai at hand. Maybe he can find out who Nathan O'Keefe is. Save us from rifling through the phone directory all evening!"

"Just tell me you're all right, love," Florrie had begged over the phone before agreeing to ask her son, Dermot, to help.

"I'm fine, Florrie, honest. It appears Knockmore House might have more secrets than we thought." Ann tried to explain the situation as best she could.

"Sounds familiar. Imagine, another Margot! Oh, it gives me the shivers," Florrie replied. "Give me the name again. Do you have any idea what we're looking for? The more information I can give Dermot, the better."

"Anything to do with Nathan O'Keefe, or Olive or Jessica Dempsey. Anything he can find," Ann suggested. "God, I hope I don't get him in trouble."

"Ah, you won't. Just don't go using any of the information. Dermot will help. I'll tell him his father will haunt him if he doesn't. It could take a few days, but he'll try," Florrie assured. "I was quite good at solving a mystery in my day, remember? It was me who figured out that your poor mam was in trouble all those years ago, with the help of your grandma, Tess. Over one drink, we worked out Felicity was pregnant, Sammy was the father and Margot was . . . Well, let's not go there now. Don't worry, we'll get to the bottom of this one, too," Florrie had promised.

They'd sat at the kitchen table for hours, with Ian inventing all sorts of far-fetched scenarios to keep them entertained.

"Right. I have it. Picture it, if you will. Olive had a secret love child in her teens . . . let's call him Nathan. Nathan is reared by a pack of wolves. Finally escapes and tumbles out of the woods, to find his long-lost mother and avenge his youth."

"That's the *Jungle Book*!" Denise rolled her eyes.

"Okay. Picture it, if you will . . . "

Ann sneaked away to try Jason's phone again, not sure why she was expecting it to ring magically. The number was dead – gone, just like him.

"Ann, love, you look done in." Denise watched her walk back into the kitchen, pale and downtrodden. "Why don't you get an early night? There's nothing more we can do today. If inspiration hits in the middle of the night, I can call you."

"Okay," Ann nodded, knowing she wouldn't sleep a wink, anyway.

"Come here, Annie."

Ian was hugging her goodbye, when she heard the text message and took out her phone.

"Oh my God . . ." Ann's hand shot to her mouth. "Poor Jessica."

Found him. Drunk driver. Hit and run. Daughter of a garda killed. I remember it. She was pregnant.

Baby survived. Tragic. The passenger in the car was Jessica Dempsey, Wicklow. He was arrested, served time.

"Wow!" Denise exclaimed. "Well, that explains Jessica's despair. How awful!"

"Do you think this Nathan, whoever he was, was threatening Olive and she wrote him a cheque to get rid of him?" Ian wondered.

"That makes sense. Oh, God. I feel bad. I mean, she's still crazy, but I judged her without knowing the full story. I wonder if Mark knows. But it still doesn't make sense."

Ann had hoped that finding this Nathan might shed some light on Jason's disappearance. She shook her head and handed Denise the phone to reread it.

"Ann?" Denise said, her voice barely more than a whisper. "Look."

Ann took the phone and scrolled down. Staring back at her, under the text message, was a picture of Nathan.

"It's Jason."

Fittingly, the rain started to fall in sheets while Ann lay awake, trying to make sense of everything, her own sobs louder than the rain beating against the window. Denise stayed with her, rocking her like a baby, while Ann repeated the same word over and over: Why? Why? Why?

"I'm so sorry, Ann. The way you spoke of him, I thought he seemed genuine," Denise whispered. "If I ever see him again, so help me God, I'll kill him. Do you think Mark knows?"

Ann shook her head. "No. I don't think so. Why would Olive hide all this from her family? I can't believe it. And *him*. How could he? It was all a game. I was a pawn to Jason, or Nathan, or whatever the hell he's called. I told him how Dad died. I told him he was killed by a drunk driver. He never even flinched. What have I done, Denise? Poor Mark. And Olive? She must have been trying to protect us all. How could I have got it so wrong?"

"Do you want to call Mark?"

"No. No. I can never look at Mark again. I don't want to be involved in any of it any more. I just want to get the hell away from it all."

"Come now. This isn't your fault, Ann. It's that Nathan. What a shit! And looking for money. For what? Revenge? Do you think he was going to destroy the house, too? I keep going over it all. I keep thinking there's something we've missed."

"I don't care any more," Ann sniffed. "I thought it was real. I was so sure. Now, I've ruined everything."

By morning, Ann had packed her bags before Denise even woke. It was surprising how she could wrap her whole life up in less than an hour – surprising and sad.

"What are you doing?"

"I'm leaving. I have the house in Dublin. I need to get away from Knockmore. This isn't my mess and I don't want anything to do with it. Will you tell Mark when he comes back? Just tell him I've gone. Please, Denise, swear to me you won't tell him where. Say I've gone to Australia. I can't face him. Say I've gone to see Lucie. Okay?"

Denise nodded. "I think you're making a mistake. This is where you belong. Feck the Dempseys. Pack of blow-ins. So you got messed up in a messy family with a few skeletons. Mark will understand. You don't have to leave."

"I do, Denise." Ann hugged her. "Say goodbye to Ian for

me. You guys have meant everything to me this past while. I'll stay in touch, but for now, it's the right thing to do."

Denise watched her drive away, trying to swallow the lump in her throat, hoping that somehow, they'd missed something vital – something that someday soon would bring Ann Maguire back to Knockmore, where she belonged.

CHAPTER FIFTY-FIVE

"I'm so glad you called, Ann." Bernard Fitzgerald sat opposite her in the hotel lobby.

"Thanks for meeting me, Bernard. I wanted to thank you again, for the house. For everything."

"Stop now. I won't have you thanking me profusely every time I see you. A drop in the ocean."

"I'm back in Dublin . . . for good."

"Really? I thought Knockmore was your home."

"It is. I mean it was," Ann smiled wistfully. "Things didn't work out."

"That seems sudden. You were so sure and if you don't mind me saying, from what I can see, you have a tendency of running away. Would I be right?"

Ann grinned. "Sophie says that, too."

"I told you I always liked that girl. No shit about her. I thought that was the same for you?"

"It is. I think." Ann shook her head, deciding to get straight to the point. "I wanted to ask you for my job back. I heard on the grapevine Dom's no longer working for you. I thought maybe . . ."

"The job is always there, Ann. Are you sure that's what you want, though?" He regarded her.

"Yes. No. I thought it was. Now, sitting here, I don't know. Truth is, I don't know anything any more, or where

I'm supposed to be."

"What did you love about Knockmore?" Bernard asked abruptly.

Ann looked off into the distance. "My friends. My singing. Knockmore House. I miss it. It's not mine, but when I was there, I felt like I was home." Ann sighed then and tutted. "Sounds stupid."

"No, it doesn't. It sounds like your heart is there. Was there a man?"

"There was. But the wrong man."

Bernard smiled. "You're good at finding them, too, aren't you? Like a shite magnet, you are," he chuckled before turning serious again. "It was the house your mother grew up in, no?"

Ann nodded.

"And you spent time there?"

"Yes, I was doing the accounts for the Dempseys. ED Construction. They own it."

"Ah, I knew Eugene in the day. A fine man. The wife was a nutter," Bernard laughed. "They live there?"

"Yes, she is," Ann answered and then grinned. "And yes, they do."

"Can I ask you, if money was no object, Ann, what would you do with your life?"

Ann smiled but said nothing. She thought she knew, but it seemed so absurd, she didn't want to admit it.

"You're a clever girl, Ann. And it looks to me like you already have the answers. When you know, you know. When—"

Ann laughed. "My aunt Lucie says the same thing."

Bernard stood up. "Goodbye, Ann." He patted her shoulder. "Like I always say. The only thing money gives you is choices. The rest is up to you."

And he was gone.

Ann had cried solidly for two weeks, mourning Jason, who no longer existed. He'd been the sanctuary that was going to heal her. Except Nathan O'Keefe, the monster, had taken his place. It was still so hard to imagine it all and to separate one from the other.

Ann despised both versions. She was angry, again, with everyone: her parents, Dom, Mark, Olive, even Sophie bore the brunt of her fury. Ann wondered had Tats, Foxy, Winker and Sully been in on it all, too? They must have been. She'd been so taken in by it all. What a fool.

Ann lay awake at night, in the house in Pembroke, pondering what Jason's plan had been. Had he been planning to destroy Knockmore House, the same house he'd appeared to adore? Had he wanted to bed her to get back at them all?

Ann hated him. Hated herself more for still missing him, unable to stop imagining their moments together. Was he thinking about her, too? No. She'd never mattered to him. At first, Ann debated it, trying to convince both Sophie and herself that there was more to it, but then she'd stopped, overhearing her own pitiful voice.

"Ann, please, this has to stop. You have to stop talking about them as if they're two different people. Jason is Nathan – Nathan is a bad guy. Nathan was playing a game and using you. Please, forget him. Forget Mark. Start again. Just one more time . . ."

Eventually, Ann had wiped her tears and hauled herself out of bed, to aimlessly wander around Dublin, looking for answers. Could she forget it all? Start a life in Dublin again. Reinvent once more.

It took Ann hours to explain to Lucie what had happened over a few months.

"Can I come and visit, Lu?"

"Of course, Ann, but not right now. Things are . . . well . . . a little complicated at the moment. Busy. Could it wait a few months?"

"Sure." Ann was disappointed. Going to Australia and being with Aunt Lucie was what she craved. "Is everything okay, Lu?"

"It is. I think so. I don't want to burden you with anything else. There are a few issues. Nothing too serious. If I'm honest, I'm not ready to talk about it just yet. Besides," Lucie told her down the phone, "you need to sort your life out there first.

"Come and see me when you're happy again. Let it be your goal. I know you'll figure it out." And then, "Are you going to sell the house in the Estates?" Lucie asked suddenly.

"I'll never sell it," Ann promised.

"Good."

"Are you sure you're okay, Lucie?" Her aunt didn't seem herself.

"Yes, love. Just mundane life, is all. You know, kids, marriage, bills. I wish I could be there with you, Ann. You'll be okay. I know it."

"Are you sure, Lucie? I'm worried about you."

"Of course I'm fine! No need to worry about me. I should be the one to worry about you, love."

It was Sophie who finally suggested calling Bernard Fitzgerald and asking for her job back. It seemed like the obvious thing to do. It was funny, though, as soon as Bernard had asked her what she'd do if money were no object, Ann had known straightaway. There had been no second-guessing. Bernard didn't need to tell her that money was no longer an object. Ann knew that, too. The only thing standing in her way now was herself. Perhaps it was time to follow her own heart, instead of being led by someone else's.

"Mark's back," Denise told her over the phone. "I told him you were away, just like you said. Jesus, I couldn't look him in the eye, the poor fecker. He didn't hang around. He looks terrible. He just wanted to know if you were all right . . ."

Later, Mark sent Ann a message asking her to meet him at Knockmore House, saying it was important. More than anything, Ann wanted to ignore it, but she knew this was her chance. So far, Ann had been able to avoid talking to Mark. At first, he'd tried her phone incessantly. Eventually, she'd sent him a message, saying a lot had happened and she wasn't sure she could continue the relationship. It was the cowardly thing to do, she knew that, but it was all she could manage. Mark hadn't answered.

Ann still wasn't sure what Mark knew, or how much Olive had told him. The truth was, she didn't really care, but there was something she needed to do in Knockmore House.

"Are you going to go?" Denise asked her that evening.

"I am."

"Good. Time to stop running, Ann. Face the music and then come home. Please. Everyone misses you. We need you here. This is where you belong."

"I know, Denise. Knockmore is the one answer I do have."

CHAPTER FIFTY-SIX

Ann tucked her hands in the pockets of her jeans to stop them from trembling. She'd almost turned back so many times on the way here, afraid she wouldn't have the courage to say what she needed to, terrified that she'd once again be making yet another mistake. Her thoughts had been drenched for days with what-ifs, fear, exhilaration, resolution and other relentless uncertainties. It wasn't until she stood at the gate, looking up at the house, that Ann understood she was, for once, exactly where she was supposed to be.

Its presence instantly calmed her thoughts. Ann stood there, remembering everything that had happened inside the gates of this house before running her fingers over the name on the gatepost: Knockmore House. Then, she took a breath and walked towards where Mark was sitting, waiting on the steps.

"You came back. It's good to see you."

He was smiling and despite her trepidation, Ann smiled back.

"You, too." Ann stood in front of him.

"You look skinny," he frowned. "Was nobody feeding you?"

He didn't stand up. He looked weary, drawn, his eyes framed with dark shadows, his skin paler than it should be for someone who'd spent the last few weeks in Spain. Ann didn't answer. She sat down beside him, her insides wrenching even more than they already were.

"Mark, I need to talk to you. I need to tell you what happened . . ." she started, but he stopped her.

"Please, Ann."

His eyes were full of sorrow, coupled with a quick flash of hope, and she dissolved. Mark really was one of the good guys: kind, warm, honest. Of course, she'd always known it, wished she could make herself feel for him what she knew he still wanted her to.

"You don't need to explain anything to me. I'm the one who should be doing the explaining." Ann rested her head on his shoulder, closed her eyes, breathing in his familiar scent.

"If . . . if it had just been you and me, could you . . .?" Mark reflected and then exhaled sharply. "In another lifetime, huh?" he said eventually.

"So much happened." Ann lifted her head for a moment, peering up at him, and then rested it down again on his shoulder.

"I keep thinking if we could just go back to that night. The one where I asked you to move in with me and just press pause," he whispered, resting his head on hers. "You think we could ever do that?"

Ann's heart was thumping. Part of her wanted to say yes, if only to heal his pain, but the words wouldn't come.

"No. I suppose not," he said when Ann didn't answer. "You disappeared. Did you figure it all out, in the end?" he asked.

Ann nodded. "Most of it. I found out who Nathan O'Keefe is and what he was doing here. Jessica was in the car while he was driving, wasn't she? Is she okay?"

"She will be." Mark took Ann's hand. So, she hadn't figured it all out. "There's more you need to know, Ann. That's why I asked you here. Jessica wants to see you, too."

"She's here?"

Mark nodded.

"No rehab?"

"Not for the moment. Although Mum thinks she's going tomorrow."

The mention of his mother unnerved her.

"Mark, I'm not sure what this has to do with me. I should go. I don't really want to see Olive, if I'm honest. Sorry." Ann sat up straighter and looked over her shoulder at the front door.

"I know, but you need to hear this." He stood and pulled her up. "Oh, and apologies in advance," he whispered. "Might get a bit messy before the storm clears."

Ann hesitated.

"Please, Ann. I promise you. You'll want to hear this."

Jessica looked drained, but her face was different – more assured. She stood when she saw Ann walk into the room and hugged Ann gently. Eugene also looked up, but he didn't attempt to stand.

"Sit down, Ann, and sorry about the smell . . . not sure what's causing it. Something rotten. Although, I think I have a fair idea," Eugene muttered.

Ann sniffed the air. Eugene was right. It was as if they'd all been plunged into a septic tank. It was foul.

"Mark, what's all this about? I've been trying to get someone to come and fix the . . . oh," Olive said, storming in and stopping abruptly when she saw Ann. "Well, look what the cat dragged in."

"Zip it, Mother," Jessica spat at her mother suddenly. "And sit down."

"Jessica! What on earth?"

Ann was surprised to see an expression flash over Olive's frozen face – terror.

"I wanted to see you all here today because I need to tell the truth. It's something I should have done a long time ago, but I was ill-advised," Jessica began.

"Jessica, dear, what are you doing?" Their mother went to stand up, but Mark gently pushed her back into the chair.

"This is preposterous. What *are* you talking about? Some form of admittance therapy, is it? Jessica, your father . . ." Olive glanced at Eugene.

"It's all right, Olive. The truth surfaced in Spain . . . well, most of it. Let Jessica continue." Eugene nodded in the direction of his daughter.

Olive's face turned puce.

"I need to tell you all about . . . *that* night," Jessica started again, directing the conversation at Ann, who interrupted.

"Jessica, you don't need to do this. I already know. It appears we all know now. You see, I found the cheque." Ann looked at Olive. "Made out to Nathan O'Keefe. You were in the car with him." Ann turned towards Olive then. "Olive, I'm sorry about that part. He came looking for money from you. I had no idea. He lied to us all, posed as Jason. I'm so sorry, Jessica, I really had no idea."

"That's right, Ann. Terrible business. Now, if you'll excuse me—"

"Mother! Enough!"

"Mark? *You* don't speak to me like that."

Jessica stood. "No, but I do. Enough. Enough with the

lies, enough with the games, enough with you controlling us all."

Mark was watching Ann.

"So, you figured out Nathan was acting as Jason. You were quicker than me. I only discovered that part very recently. I still didn't connect it until . . ." Mark drifted off.

Ann looked confused.

"Nathan's an architect. Or at least he was until I ruined his life," Jessica explained, sitting back down and clasping her hands together. "It was me, Ann. I was the one driving. It was me . . ." Jessica exhaled loudly, her face crumpling.

"What?" Ann's entire body was alert. "It wasn't Jason? I mean, Nathan."

Jessica shook her head and grasped Ann's hand.

"Jessica, don't do this, please. It's all contained here, Jessica. Ann won't tell."

Olive had been sitting so silently that they'd almost forgotten she was there.

Ann stared at Jessica. "But wasn't he arrested? I don't understand." Ann was sure the message from Florrie's son, Dermot, had said he'd served time.

Jessica lifted her hand slowly and pointed at her mother. "*She* made him lie. Mother told him I was pregnant. You see, we were together, a couple. Nathan did it for me, but by the time I realised what had happened, it was too late. Nicola was dead. Nathan was locked up and I was so far into the lies, I almost believed them myself," Jessica explained. She was looking directly at her mother now. "You know, I actually believed I was pregnant. You had me so messed up, feeding me a cocktail of God knows what to keep me pliable."

"It would have ruined you. I was trying to protect you. All of you," Olive pleaded, glancing at the door as if she might try to escape.

"You were protecting yourself. Trying to keep us all with you," Jessica said.

"It's his fault!" Olive screamed frantically like a cornered rat, pointing at Eugene. "This is on you. If you hadn't done what you did . . ."

Eugene threw his head back and laughed. "Lord knows I've made my mistakes, Olive, but this one is all yours, my dear, all yours. Thank God for Mark." He smiled at his son before turning to Ann. "And thank God for Ann. I believe that you, young lady, somehow came into our lives to set us all free." Then he looked at Jessica, his face beaming with pride. "And thank God for my beautiful, brave daughter, now willing to face her mistakes."

"Her!" Olive pointed at Ann. "I haven't had a chance to tell you that part, Mark. Oh, she's no angel. Believe me. I saw it with my own eyes. She was overseeing far more than the building work. She took a very special interest in the fictitious builder, Jason." Olive glared at Ann.

Ann looked at the ground, hoping it would swallow her, before bravely lifting her eyes to Mark, ready to admit her mistake. "Mark, I—"

"It's okay, Ann. I already know. You don't need to explain." He walked towards her, removing something from his pocket. "I found this . . ." Mark handed her a piece of paper.

He'd found it the day he'd returned from Spain with his father and Jessica. As soon as Mark was back in Knockmore, he'd called round at Ann's house and then immediately gone to Denise to try to find her. Mark saw the look in Denise's eyes straightaway – pity – and then heard an awkward rehearsed exchange as if Denise had been waiting for him to turn up and had been told what to say.

"She's not here," she'd issued robotically.

Denise had a heart of gold, Mark knew that, but she was no actress. When he'd left the shop, he'd turned to look back through the window. Denise was already on the phone. He didn't need to hazard a guess as to whom she was speaking.

Mark, Jessica and their father had all discussed how things were going to play out with their mother on their return. They were going to have everything arranged and then spring it on her, not giving her time to worm her way out again. Mark was going to contact the gardai on Jessica's behalf and commence the procedure of clearing Nathan's name.

Mark never for a moment planned to involve Ann – at least not until he'd gone outside for some air. He'd found himself wandering towards the end of the garden, resting his hand against the oak tree, perhaps in an attempt to feel close to her. Or maybe he'd been searching for answers against the rough bark, when he saw the letter.

The similarity of the letter's hiding place instantly struck Mark, but there was one glaring difference. One of the letters had been carefully concealed in the earth many years before as if the sender never really wanted it to be discovered and was perhaps writing it as a way of relinquishing heavy guilt. But this letter was taped to the inside of the tree with bright blue insulation tape, as visible as possible, the sender not caring who found it or read the contents, but hopeful that whoever did would ensure it was delivered to the right person.

For a split second, after he'd read it, Mark wanted to ball it up and throw it over the wall, but then he'd remembered the pain that secrets had inflicted upon him and his family, and the hurt they'd already caused Ann. He'd reread it then, the realisation that there'd never be another chance for Ann and him written clearly on the page.

Then again, Mark had already known it without reading the letter. That Nathan had known where to put the letter meant that Ann must have confided in him, which surprised Mark. That *he'd* fallen in love with her, as Mark had, didn't.

"Ann Maguire." Mark had whispered her name. The woman who'd entered his life fleetingly and altered it – for the better, he realised that now.

Now, it was time to do the same for her.

Mark had felt more numb rather than hurt. It *all* made sense now. That was the reason his mother had fired the builders – and not because of the disagreement she'd invented over the god-forsaken orangery. Then he'd remembered the photos on the iPad and he'd gone to see Jessica immediately.

Jessica had confirmed straightaway that Jason was in fact Nathan. So that was why their mother flew back to Ireland after Mark had shown her the photos of the building work. It had been nothing to do with finding a suitable facility for Jessica to recover in – it had been, still, to hide her lies.

The secrets would never stop. He knew now he'd done the right thing, calling Ann here to give her the letter and allow Jessica to tell her the truth. He owed it to her. His father was right – Ann had somehow set them all free.

Ann looked at the piece of paper in her hand.

"Read it alone," he told her. "Now, I think you've heard all you need to hear." Mark turned back to his mother. "The police will be here soon. Jessica wants to come clean about it all. He, Nathan, did nothing. He was a victim, too. A victim of my mother."

Olive sank so far into her chair, she almost vanished.

"We'll be leaving here, Ann," Eugene told her. "I'm going to Dublin," he said proudly. "I have a son and I need to ask him to forgive me. Jessica's coming with me, and Mark, too. Besides, I can't stick this place a moment longer. It's baltic in this house and it smells like shite – nothing more than a damned building site. Mill it down, that's my vote."

"What about me?" Olive looked up meekly. "All I did for you all, all I . . ." She stopped suddenly, like an exhausted wind-up doll.

"Damned if I know. You've plenty of money. Go and get a body transplant, for all I care. Mind you, I'd say the police will want to speak to you first. So maybe stay put for that bit. And then I suggest you let your unrecognisable face disintegrate," Eugene spat.

"I'm so sorry, Mark. I never meant to hurt you. Thank you for everything," Ann said, trying to blink back the tears. Then she turned to Jessica. "I think it's courageous what you're doing."

Jessica's tears prevented her from saying more.

"Perhaps this isn't the time . . ." Ann stood and walked towards Eugene, knowing it was now or never. "But can I discuss something with you quickly? In private."

CHAPTER FIFTY-SEVEN

The entire time Ann spoke with Eugene, she could feel the presence of the letter in her pocket, the heat of her hand around it. All she really wanted was to get away as fast as possible, so she could rip it open, but she'd come this far and it was time to finish this, once and for all. It didn't take long and before she knew it, Ann was rushing out of the gate, hoping that the letter would contain the final piece of the story.

Sitting on the wall opposite Knockmore House, she opened it. Her hand shook as she tried to steady the paper, the words blurred behind her tears.

Dear Ann,

I listened to every word you said. That's why I put this letter here. If you're reading it, then I know you were meant to find it. I asked you to spend the weekend with me. I wanted you to trust me because, from the first moment I saw you, I haven't been able to think of anything else.

I came here to this place for revenge. I wanted to take from them what they took from me: my life. Instead, I found you. I tried to stop it. I stupidly tried to drive you away until I saw you here that night and I knew I was home. Those days . . . those nights – you made me realise there is a life worth living. You gave me hope, where I thought hope had forsaken me.

I was broken. I took the fall for something I didn't do because I thought I was in love. I was – with Jessica. That woman, her mother, told me Jessica was pregnant. She wasn't. It was a lie invented to trap me.

I was in the car that night, but I was the passenger. It was Jessica who was driving. She knocked over and killed a pregnant woman then fled the scene. I tried to stop her. Then Olive convinced me to take the rap for it to protect Jessica. Everything after happened so fast. That poor girl – she was the daughter of a local guard. I didn't stand a chance. I was locked up straightaway, stood trial eight months later, and I got off on some stupid technicalities. I lost everything. I should have been happy. I was free. But the girl was still dead and my life ruined. My family disowned me and no one would have believed me, so I left.

I found the lads and we went from job to job, getting by. Most of what I earned I sent to her family, anonymously. The baby survived. His name is Charlie. I never went near them in person, but I thought I could make a difference in his life. I wanted to make it better for them. I thought the money could help.

Then I came across the Dempseys, living in Knockmore House. I called there that day to confront them and Mark mistook me for Jason. I don't know why I played along. Maybe it was because I saw you in the garden that day – the same girl I heard singing in that pub, the same one who was haunting my dreams. You, Ann. It was all real. That part, anyway. I love you. Is it possible? I've loved you from the first moment I saw you, but you deserve more than a broken man. You deserve the world.

When Olive came back from Spain to confront me, I knew I had to leave. She offered money – enough that will make little Charlie's life easier. It's with him now and in some way, I'm free.

I wanted to tell you in person, but I couldn't face you. When you told me what happened to your dad, I knew it was over. I couldn't risk that you wouldn't believe me, either.

I should never have let Jessica drive that night. That's on me. Olive told me she tried to kill herself. She's been punished enough, it seems.

Mark loves you, Ann. I can see it and he's a good man. Steer clear of the mother, but you're strong and no one can knock you down.

That day in the sea with you, I felt so alive, Ann. That feeling will be with me always.

I'm sorry I lied to you. You have my heart, forever. I don't deserve yours – please give it to someone who does.

Nathan

CHAPTER FIFTY-EIGHT

Ann didn't try to find him straightaway, not sure if he even wanted to be discovered. Instead, she'd read Nathan's letter a thousand times, holding it close to her chest, allowing the words to embrace her through the page – his real words, not the ones that had been scribbled on that note and shoved through her letterbox the day Nathan vanished. Even Olive had the grace to admit it was her who'd forged the emotionless letter from "Jason" that day, still trying to protect her secret, against all the odds.

It was the second time Ann's life had almost been destroyed by someone else's mistruths and the curse of the women of Knockmore House – that beautiful old house on the hill, looking out over the town. The one Ann would always call home. Ann would never doubt it again. It was where she was meant to be. Knockmore – it had her heart, her past, her future.

Ann worked tirelessly for a month, making arrangements, going backwards and forwards to Dublin, making sure everything went as she planned now. It was all sorted quicker than she anticipated, all parties ready for a fresh start, a new phase. Wherever she went, Ann was always looking, keeping an eye out, hoping to see the battered old blue truck, wondering where Nathan was.

The house on Pembroke sold straightaway, for far

more than Ann could ever have imagined. Apparently, it was hugely sought-after. It had been Dom all along preventing any offer from going through. But it was hers to do with as she pleased, that's what Bernard Fitzgerald had said, and Ann didn't want it. All it represented was the emptiness she'd felt there, married to Dom.

Sophie once again attempted to make her change her mind about her plans, but nothing would sway Ann now.

"It was you who gave me the idea, Sophie. Let me do this for you."

In the end, Sophie agreed. Even Ian and Denise were supportive, knowing they had no other choice. Something had changed in Ann, for the better. They all saw it – the sudden shift from continuously uncertain, ever-questioning, to determined and assured.

"That's the girl I always knew you were, Ann. Strong. With the power to turn it all around and take charge of your life," Denise assured.

Ann supposed she'd always known it, too. That eventually, she'd uncover what she really wanted and with whom. It had just taken her a long time to get here.

"Better late than never, Annie." Ian hugged her when she informed them what she was planning.

Florrie had been right. For Ann to work out how it all ended, she needed to go directly back to the start, working her way through all the obstacles, to discover that it was herself, all along, who was the hero in her own story. When it was all done, there was only one matter left to settle – the thing she was most nervous about. Nathan O'Keefe had been right about a lot of things, but wrong about one, and she needed to tell him. Even if he didn't want to see her, she had to try.

Ann had listened to him, too – heard and absorbed every word he'd said. She knew she could always contact his brother, but she hoped that he'd be there. That she'd find him right where he was supposed to be, in the same way his letter had found its way to her. Ann had Mark to thank for that – Marvellous Mark.

They'd promised to stay in contact, but Ann knew deep down they wouldn't. It was a sweet promise, though, made from the heart. The last time they spoke, Mark had assured her that Nathan's name had been cleared. He didn't tell her too much about the others, only to say, "It'll be a long process, but Dad, Jessica and I are all helping each other."

"And Olive?"

"In Wicklow."

"Back to the start. As good a place as any."

Ann slowed the car, carefully reversing it into the small space, grateful that she still hadn't got round to changing her little blue car. Not everything needed to change – some things were a reminder of the journey she'd been on. As she switched off the engine, she could still hear his voice.

"Have you ever been to The Forty Foot in Dublin? Best swimming spot in Ireland, maybe even the world. Sunrise and a sea swim. Set you up for the whole day."

Ann shivered against the early morning breeze, praying Nathan would be here, hoping she was right and he'd sent her a subliminal message of how to find him when she needed to. The sun was barely up, the path silent as she crossed it and made her way up the hill to the stone wall. Ann stood there watching the early morning swimmers bravely entering the icy sea. Many were in and out in minutes, walking back up the slippery steps again, looking invigorated, their skin pink, their faces happy, the sound of chatter coming from the concrete changing cubicle.

Ann moved to the gap in the wall, peering down, wondering if she'd missed him and berating herself for her silly romantic notions. Of course he wasn't there. Ann tugged her jacket around her and lifted the collar to her face to hide her embarrassment.

"Nathan. Get a move on, brother. We have a meeting at nine in town."

Ann whipped round upon hearing the name and looked back at the sea. Still unable to see, she moved through the gap in the wall, looking right, towards the stone archway. His back was to her, his head bobbing there alone, staring up at the sky.

"Not dressed for a swim, are you?"

Ann heard a voice behind her and turned to see a face so familiar, she started laughing. They had the same eyes. He was a little smaller, but she knew who he must be.

"No. I'm here to see him . . ." She pointed towards Nathan.

He looked at her for a moment, recognition slowly registering.

"Ann?"

She nodded and he placed his hand on her arm.

"I've got a lot to thank you for. You brought my brother home."

Ann turned to follow his gaze in Nathan's direction, who was now standing on the top step, framed in the arch, his feet still immersed in water, his eyes unsure, his features even.

"So you found me."

"I knew I would." She walked towards him and stood there, hands by her sides. "I was listening, too."

He didn't move. "And?" he said gruffly.

"Don't you take that tone with me." She wagged her finger and his face softened. "I came to tell you that you were wrong."

"Oh yeah?"

"Yeah." She stepped forwards and rested her hands on his bare shoulders. "About a lot of things. You do deserve my heart, Nathan, if you want it."

He closed his eyes and exhaled.

"Jason, now he was a different kettle of fish, but you, Nathan O'Keefe, you deserve it. Well, with one condition," Ann smirked.

"I will never lie to you again, Ann. I'm so sorry."

"Nope, not that. I'm the one who's sorry. For everything that happened to you." She moved closer still.

"What, then?"

"Well," she grinned. "I've been having a little trouble with my plumbing."

"Oh yeah? How's that?" He was laughing.

"They've gone, Nathan, and I did something. Something I hope you'll be happy about. I bought Knockmore House. It's my home now." Ann watched his face change to one of shock.

"Aren't you impulsive when you want to be!"

"Actually, I was thinking of getting the lads back together. Tats, Sully, Foxy, Winker and me . . . to finish that job they started. There's a few problems that have come to light with the build. Know anything about that?"

Nathan grimaced, shook his head. "Nope."

"Are you sure?"

"Well, I'm not admitting to anything." He pretended to pat down her clothes. "Am I being recorded? Off the record, I've heard that misdirecting a sewer pipe is a great way to piss off tricky clients."

"Is that right? That would explain the smell."

"And there may be a few measurements that are a little off. Not by much. It may have been that Jason. Sloppy work."

Ann laughed.

"I'd like to fire *De Boss*. Jason's work *was* sloppy. This time, the lads should answer to me. Are you in?"

Nathan grinned. "I'll have to think about it. Those old houses can be minefields, loads of problems. I couldn't be sure what we'd uncover there."

"I think everything that could possibly be uncovered there already has been. Don't you? No more secrets, no more lies and no more problems," she promised. "Can you fix it?"

"I can. I never would have done anything too serious to the house," he said soberly. "I know how much you love it. It was so stupid of me. I'm sorry. I was angry. I was hurt."

"I know."

"But you taught me that everything can be fixed, Ann. There's always a way. Always a second chance. A chance to live again. We'll fix it together."

He reached over and picked her up. She wrapped herself around him, never wanting to let him go again.

"I missed you," he said, kissing her.

She kissed him back with every inch of her soul.

"Don't you dare!" Ann screeched as he started to reverse back into the sea. "Nathan! Wait. Please."

He paused.

"Can I say it now?" She looked into his eyes and

whispered the words that had been on the tip of her tongue for so long, resting there patiently until it was time. "I love you."

"I love you too, Ann."

He kissed her again and she inhaled the saltiness, the pain, the joy, all at once. Then he stepped backwards, taking her with him, plunging them right into the frostiness of the Irish Sea.

"Nathan!" she squealed again, gasping for breath as she came up for air. "Jesus Christ. It's freezing."

Ann gripped tight around his neck, feeling the cold water soaking her clothes, penetrating through to her skin, the water rushing around them. Nathan laughed loudly, throwing his head back as a cheer erupted from the small group of bathers behind them.

"Yes, it is, but don't you feel alive, Ann? Because I've never felt more alive in my entire life."

AFTER

Olive had been right about one thing only: the orangery looked stunning at the back of the house. It was the ideal addition to the perfect home: a home now permeated with Felicity's warmth, Sammy's music, Ann's tenderness and Nathan's expertise. Olive Dempsey hadn't managed to break the curse of Knockmore House. It was Ann Maguire who did that in the end, filling the house with music, life, love, truth and new beginnings.

"You look stunning," Ann hugged Sophie tightly. "Are you ready?"

Sophie nodded excitedly.

"Okay. I'll let them know. I'm right in front of you every step of the way."

Ann turned to give a little nod towards the end of the garden, where a pergola had been erected next to the oak tree, built with Nathan's hands and laced with white roses and ivy looping around it. Jack stood under it, anxiously awaiting his bride. A plaque had been erected there, bearing the perfect words to describe its significance:

Love is a tree with deep roots, whose branches extend to heaven.
Sammy & Felicity Maguire
1987 – Forever

"Ann, wait." Sophie beckoned her back. "Thank you for this. For everything. For being the best friend in the world, for this day."

Ann could see the tears welling beneath Sophie's vintage lace veil.

"You'll ruin your make-up, Soph." Ann took her hand and squeezed it.

"Do *not* start crying." Tracy appeared out of nowhere. "And do *not* get your hair caught in that big old trellis thing down the end, Sophie, I swear. It took me all morning to get you looking this way. I call the look Knockmore Knockout and you *are* a total knockout." Tracy leaned over and kissed Sophie. "Welcome to my world. I see boys in your future, loads and loads of little boys."

"Don't you dare, Tracy Doyle. Don't you dare curse me on my wedding day."

Ann started to giggle. One was as bad as the other. Ann should have known that Sophie and Tracy would end up getting on like a house on fire.

"Plot twist," Sophie had whispered to Ann at the opening of Knockmore House. "I think I might adore Tracy."

Tracy turned to Ann now and took her hands.

"Feck it, I'm going to cry now. Thank you for this opportunity, Ann. Resident senior hair and make-up officer of Knockmore House. It's a dream. And I promise I'll never bring the kids to work. Those new ones renting next door to me are super babysitters."

"Make-up officer?"

"We'll talk about the title . . ." Tracy scuttled away to tidy up.

"Okay, pal. Let's get you married."

Ann looked over at where Ian and Denise were seated,

waving frantically at her. Ian was trying to spit out one of the oversized feathers from Denise's fascinator that kept getting in his mouth. Jack glanced over his shoulder as they approached. Ann nodded to him and then focused her attention on Nathan, who was seated up front, a massive smile on his clean-shaven face.

He looked so different from how he had when she'd first met him almost a year ago, when she sang to the stranger who'd change her life and give her the ending she'd hoped for. Nathan O'Keefe. Ann knew someday she'd bear his name proudly when it was their turn, but she'd already given him her heart, as he had given her his, wholly and without condition.

Ann smiled back as she glided confidently up the aisle, towards a new era, a new beginning.

"Are you mad?" Nathan had asked when Ann had revealed her plans.

"Yes. I am. Mad about you. Mad about this house. It's what I want to do. It's what I'm meant to do."

"Well then, I'm in. Here, with you, for as long as you'll have me. I'll get the lads back and let's make this house the best wedding destination in the land."

"But I need to change the plans a little. Know anyone who might oblige? Fewer glass walls, more intimate rooms, more how it always was but better . . ."

"I might just know someone who'd be delighted to assist."

Having "her boys" back at Knockmore House, working for Ann, them calling her boss this time, making sure the house was perfect for Nathan and her to live in together and host weddings, had been a joy. They'd worked hard to turn it around on time – well, with plenty of music therapy thrown in – ready to give Sophie and Jack the wedding of their dreams. Not only them, but also all the other couples who'd someday start their journey at Knockmore House.

Jack took Sophie's hand and lifted her veil. At that moment, Ann knew that today would be one of *those days* – the perfect ones. Her heart was glowing as she watched them exchange vows and when Ann took her place at the microphone and picked up her guitar, she looked out at the crowd of people, feeling only love as she began to sing. Her body tingled as she sang to her friends, those who'd been with her through thick and thin. Today, there was only happiness – and life.

Life is precious, Ann knew that now. With its peaks and troughs, filled with cherished moments and times so painful that you sometimes wonder what it's all about. But if you can look beyond the tough times, if you can uncover the parts in between that are so precious, so unique, so constant, they make every trough worth it. If you can remind yourself that every time the rollercoaster goes down, it will come back up again. If you can push beyond when you feel you can't go on. When life is far too cruel, if you can dig deep and keep climbing, you *will* make your way back up the mountain.

Ann had known more pain than some people experience in an entire lifetime, but she wasn't ready to give up. She would never give up, because she'd also known love. She had Nathan now. They'd found each other, damaged and broken, in the pit of a trough and clung on, gripping tight to the small spark that had the power to light their lives and heal them.

Ann understood that the rest of her life wouldn't be all plain sailing – it never is, it isn't meant to be. There's always something waiting around the corner to surprise you, to pounce on you when you least expect it. That's what life is – an enormous rollercoaster. Sometimes exhilarating, at times terrifying. But while the downs are frightening, ultimately, the highs are worth it.

Life is ever-changing, ever-evolving. People pass through your life fleetingly, put there to guide you. And some are meant to be there forever. Ann knew who her constants were and she was going to cherish them – cherish herself and embrace life.

Most of all, Ann had realised through everything that the first person you have to love is yourself and it was that eventual realisation that allowed everything else to fall into place slowly. Now, when Ann closed her eyes, she could feel Sammy and Felicity here with her. And when she opened them, she could see Nathan. The man who'd helped to sing her home – here in this house, where two love stories had begun. Her parents and hers – and all the other couples who'd swear their unending love to each other here.

Not any kind of love, but the kind worth fighting for. The sort that can overcome anything. Love that will be there until . . .

The End . . .

ACKNOWLEDGEMENTS

Are we here again? I don't think you're ever really ready to bid your book farewell – the thing that's consumed your thoughts for months, the characters who've become like family – but here we are.

I'm forever indebted to all at Poolbeg Press Limited for allowing me to share my dysfunctional family with you. To the proofreaders, typesetters and designers, thank you. To the unflappable Paula Campbell, thank you for all of your support. Two books in and one to go!

To my wonderful, patient editor, Claire Dean, whose eagle eye catches all the silly things I miss, often so caught up in the story that I've forgotten to tell you something. Thank you for your encouragement, your belief and making my book far better than I could manage alone. We did it again and I promise I'll try harder with the commas next time!

To everyone who showed their support for the first book in the Evolve trilogy, *When Destiny Sings*, thank you. To those who bought it, reviewed it, shared it – you're all amazing.

To my husband, Malcolm, who believes in me. Thank you for allowing me the time and supporting us while I invest in my life-long dream. At times, it hasn't been easy, but then again, nothing worth doing ever is.

To my children, Martha, Bruce and Gertie – throughout this entire process, you've grown in inches and met many incredible milestones. Know that I see it all, even with my head stuck in my laptop. You three are the ones who sing me home.

I dedicate this book to Martha, my eldest, at this lovely time in your life and all that lies ahead for you. I couldn't be prouder of who you're becoming, or the fact that you know the words to all those awful eighties songs. (Fear not – I won't rest until Bruce and Gertie each have a book in their name also. It's what will keep me writing!)

To my friends, for allowing me to step away, knowing I was trying to make this writing business a reality, and for continuing to call me, even when I was unresponsive. Everyday Y.C. Everyday!

To Lucie, Nicole and Susan, my early readers. Thank you for helping me to plot the story for this book and for keeping me going. I appreciate it so very much.

To Wilbur, the boxer – at my side through every single draft, he's the best work colleague I've ever had.

My folks – John and Amy Small. Thank you for giving me all the opportunities you did. For those who think it's unrealistic for Ann to have met the love of her life in the same manner that Felicity meets Sammy, I beg to differ! I met mine at a Bective rugby club disco when I was sixteen. So did my mum: same place, same age.

To Jenn Drew, my legal advisor and the best darn sister-in-law in the world.

To Lisa Earlie, one of the most inspiring people I've never met! Thank you for all of your incredible encouragement and online support. For helping to name both books, being strong, positive and wonderful. I know, one day, you'll write your story. I believe!

To Becky Martin, for all of your initial help and for

proving that there are still people who will stick their neck out for you, for no other reason than being lovely.

To Eoin Yoda Dempsey, for all of your advice.

To the Sunday Swim Service friends. I still haven't figured out the benefits of forcing myself into the icy sea each week, but like Nathan shouts in the book: it makes you feel *alive*! I hope we're still doing it until our skin is saggy, our knees buckled and our swimsuits *ginormous*.

And lastly, to me. The final thoughts in this book are my own. I embarked on this journey knowing it would be difficult and that I'd set myself hard targets to reach. I'm still here! If you want to do something, do it. Don't wait. It only takes one person to believe in you – sometimes that person is you!

Book Three coming right up! Hold your horses . . .
Judith
x

Now that you're hooked why not try

Lying With Truth

Until You're Asked, You May Never Tell . . .

coming soon

Here's a sneak preview of the
Prologue and Chapter 1 & 2

"The truth is rarely pure and never simple."
Oscar Wilde

PROLOGUE

Truth

The truth is, no one wants the truth, not entirely, in its sometimes raw and gruesome form. No one wants to hear that they've made mistakes, chosen the wrong path, wronged a loved one, become someone other than the honest person they set out to be. We don't want to hear that we're overweight, underweight, work too hard, not hard enough. We don't want to be told that we don't spend enough time with our children, neglect our partners, have a dependency, have wasted our lives, that we've become stale or bitter, that we've changed. Let alone that we've focused on the wrong thing all of our lives, that we've left it too late, that we've failed . . .

The truth hurts, no matter if it comes from someone else's mouth, or by your own admission. And yet we're told from an early age that the truth will prevail. The truth and only the truth will eventually set us free. The truth will out. Seek the truth. Tell the truth or someone will tell it for you. The truth is the truth.

The truth is, the truth isn't always some huge life-altering revelation, nor some sordid uncovered secret – it can be as simple as an honest declaration. The truth is, life is a series of choices and it's often far more comfortable to cling to what you believe you are, what others see, even if deep down you know it's a lie. The truth is, very few of us tell the whole truth, nor abide by the integrity on which we often pride ourselves. The truth is, we're *all* liars, in some shape or form.

We are *all* liars.

We mislead, deceive, exaggerate, distort, contort, trick, manufacture, twist, bend, inflate, stretch. We all do it – learn what we can and can't say, what will make us stand out, what will make us fit in, what will make us appear *normal*. After all, to reveal all those secret inner criticisms and prejudices, all the little thoughts that pass through our minds when someone is speaking (or lying), would be risking social ostracisation. And so we compromise. We listen to other people's myths while we tell our own, but deep down we *all* know our inner truth – the real story.

"Lies are the one thing I won't stand for," Lucie's mother had told her once. "Always tell the truth unless it's to save someone's feelings. And even then . . ."

"Sorry, Mam, but that dress is pure terrible on you. Gross," she'd giggled from where she was sitting on the end of her mother's bed.

"The cheek of you! I'll tell you, that mouth of yours will get you into trouble someday."

"But you said . . ."

Tess Maguire had sat down beside her and put her hand on her daughter's. "I'm serious, love. I'm trying to tell you everything I know before you head off into the sunset, leaving me here." Mam paused to wipe the sudden tears from her eyes. "The truth can hurt, but I suppose it's better to take the pain quickly and then move on. Lies cause more trouble in the long run. Sure, haven't we seen that with our own eyes with Felicity?" Tess had always had a soft spot for her son's now wife and Lucie's best friend, who'd suffered a miserable childhood by the hand of a dishonest mother. She stood again to look in the mirror, smoothing her hands over her stomach. "It *is* terrible, isn't it?"

"Dreadful," Lucie grinned.

"Right. I'll change it. See – a lesson learned. And another thing. Don't ever lie to yourself, love. That's the worst person you can lie to. Do you hear me? Always be honest with yourself. No matter if you're here or in Australia. Be true to yourself . . . I still can't believe you're going."

Lucie had ignored the last part, knowing it would cause another fit of heaving sobs. "Sure, aren't I the most honest person in the entire world? You said so yourself."

"Don't I know it!" Tess ruffled her daughter's hair. "Too honest. Too bloody honest."

Even then, when she'd yet to embark on her own life, Lucie *had* witnessed first-hand how shattering an illusion can come with a level of discomfort far more damaging than an unflattering dress. Way back then, she'd seen it with her best friend, Felicity, whose so-called perfect life had crumbled when she'd got pregnant as a teen with Lucie's older brother, Sammy.

In more recent years, Lucie's niece's life had unravelled before Ann had found the strength to pick up the pieces and start again. Lucie had observed from a distance, cheering Ann on, marvelling at her courage and wondering when her own turn would arrive – when the make-believe existence she'd created for herself would come undone. In a way, Lucie had become all the things she'd consistently tried to avoid: settled, serious, no longer striving for extraordinary, getting through life, existing.

It wasn't how she'd ever expected to be. It certainly wasn't how it all started when she first arrived in Australia all those years ago as the freckly Irish girl with red hair as fiery as her ambitions. She'd immediately embraced her new life with open arms, finding instant comfort among a nation of people known for their laid-back honesty, their "say it as it is" attitude, their zest for life. As much as Lucie had felt as though she'd found an entire continent of like-minded individuals, she'd always planned to return home to Ireland someday. She had family there. She couldn't stay away forever – eventually, she'd go back. When each year became a new one, she promised herself once more – *next year, I'll go home.* Until next year became the year after and the year after that.

Back then, Lucie told herself her first official lie – that she'd left it too late.

After that, the lies came easier. It wasn't compulsive lying, nor ridiculous fabrications – it was more the silence. The silence had become the lie.

The truth is, it's only ever the good things we want to hear as we travel through life hungrily craving recognition, praise, good news, positivity.

Tell me I'm amazing.

Tell me I'm honest.

Tell me everything will be fine.

Tell me it always works out.

Tell me if it's for me, it won't pass me by.

Tell me I did my best with the choices I had.

But what if it *is* true what they say? That no matter how silent you remain about the rest, the truth will eventually force its way out? And what if there is absolutely nothing you can do to stop it?

People had always liked Lucie. Lucie was honest. Lucie was real. But just as Lucie's mother had warned her never to do, as she'd sworn she never would, she'd been lying to herself for a very long time. It turns out it's quite easy to lie to yourself. The truth is, for a lot of her life, no one had wanted *her* truth – not from Lucie Woods, with the perfect husband, the two adorable children, the enviable figure, the enormous smile, the perfect house, the lovely job – until, that is, someone had. Until out of the blue, a total stranger began to poke at everything she'd kept carefully hidden. Once it was out, as soon as she'd heard herself say it aloud, she'd realised there was no other choice but to confront it.

And here it was – the moment of truth.

Sitting here now, staring at the faces before her, it was as if she were staring straight at the truth of her entire life – past truth, present truth, future truth. For a moment she felt giddy, wondering how she'd kept it in for so long, pondering how on earth she'd found herself in this absurd reality. She'd been gifted a long period of isolated reflection, a time to think back over her life, face what she'd always refused to face. It hadn't been easy. At first, she'd had to force herself to stare at it all, but so far, through some of her earlier admissions, she'd found a piece of the old Lucie again. Perhaps by releasing these final burdens, she would find all of herself, regardless of the hardship that lay ahead, and it would be hard. The truth *was* going to hurt, and not just her, it was going to destroy everyone she held dear.

Maybe in time, she could revert to being the girl sitting on the end of her mother's bed, giggling over the horrible dress, frankness as her secret weapon. But first, she finally needed to relinquish the burden, and it *had* been a burden. Even in happier times, she'd felt it pressing down, weighing heavily on her soul. But in the same way she'd known that it's the truth that has the power to set you free, she'd also known that this day would come.

And here it was, her opportunity for freedom.

Taking a breath, she closed her eyes and exhaled before opening them and finally saying the words.

"My name is Lucie Woods. I swear to tell the truth, the whole truth and nothing but the truth, so help me God."

PART ONE – Present Truth

Chapter One

Seeing Bella sitting there motionless with her back to her instantly infuriated Lucie. Clenching her fists, she had to use all of her reserve to stop herself from reaching out and plunging her fingers into her daughter's freshly ironed sheet of red hair and tossing it about. The outward calm of Bella's hair felt like a taunt, exaggerating the unruly mass that hung around Lucie's own face that morning.

She must have been up for hours already taming it, erasing any resemblance it bore to Lucie's hair – the same hair for which Bella so often criticised her mother for passing down to her. Lucie wondered if the technology had been available in her day, would she have spent as much time flattening her thick wiry hair, smoothing it into something totally different to how it was supposed to be.

Then again, when Lucie had been teen a thousand years ago, it had always been about the bigger, the better. Back then, she'd felt edgier than the pine desk jammed into the corner of her childhood bedroom, despite her voluminous peroxide blonde and red bouffant. She could still remember sitting in front of her red plastic mirror, using a thin comb to backcomb her hair to make it even fuller.

How different everything was nowadays to those innocent times when you had to make the best of what you were given. In Lucie's case: freckles, fuzzy hair and translucent skin. Bella was the same. Of course, you wouldn't know it any more, with her daughter's permanent layer of fake tan, carefully applied concealer and glossy poker-straight hair. It felt like a slight – as if the genetic hand her daughter had been gifted was below standard, not quite good enough. Then again, everything Lucie did lately wasn't to the standard her daughter expected.

"I'll pay for it myself," Bella had been pleading for months. "Let me get highlights, please. I want to be blonde."

"But your hair is beautiful. It's what make you unique. Why would you want to be like everyone else?"

Even saying it, Lucie had known that it wasn't about Bella being like everyone else, it was about not being anything like Lucie.

"Why didn't Declan get this horrible bushy red leprechaun hair and see-through skin? *I'm* not Irish. It's not fair." Bella had pulled at her own hair and then pointed at her mother's accusingly.

Lucie hadn't bothered to answer.

"Did the revolutionary idea of waking me not enter your head?"

Lucie stomped past Bella now, grabbed a cup and stuck it under the coffee maker. Then she grabbed two slices of bread, frantically buttered them and threw a slice of cheese between them.

"Declan, grab the rest of your lunch, quick," she gestured as her ten-year-old son entered the kitchen. "Bella, well?"

"I've never had to wake you before. It's not like you're . . . like busy or anything."

"Don't start, Bella. Not today."

"Whatever."

Bella didn't look up. Instead, she sat staring at her phone, tilting her chin ever so slightly in different directions and snapping photos of her unmoving duck face. Satisfied, she used her thin, elegant finger to swipe the screen shut and then tucked it in the crested breast pocket of her black school blazer before glancing up at her mother.

"Are you seriously wearing *that*? Shouldn't you . . . like, change?"

"Are you wearing *that*?" Lucie mimicked, turning her back and making a face.

Getting into an argument now with her thirteen-year-old daughter would do nothing to improve the type of morning she was already having. Besides, lately, she was sort of afraid of Bella. It was a strange thing when your child was suddenly taller than you. It took away some of your authority, especially now that Bella was able to look down on Lucie with contempt. Or was it disdain? Aversion? Defiance? Hatred? It was hard to tell any more. Perhaps she should try standing on a chair when talking to Bella, look down on her for a change.

Declan poured some cereal, then held the milk carton above his head and poured the liquid from a height. Lucie watched it splash out of the bowl, hit the counter and edge its way towards Bella's check uniform skirt.

"You little shit!" Bella screamed with the intensity one might reserve for having a bucket of water tipped over them and not a few droplets of milk. "I'm a mess." She jumped off the stool, swiped at her brother's head and stormed out of the room.

"Hardly. Just give it a quick wipe and hurry up," Lucie called after her.

She picked up a sodden dishcloth, which had been left to stew in last night's dishwater. Declan's nose turned up as Lucie squeezed the cloth to rid it of the now brown water to wipe up the milk. Then she threw it back in the sink, looked around the kitchen in frustration and groaned. Now, that *was* a mess.

For someone who wasn't *like* "busy", as Bella kept telling her, the house had never been untidier and by the look of her drawn face in the mirror that morning, Lucie had never looked worse.

Initially, Lucie had had all sorts of plans. She'd even written them down somewhere, she couldn't remember where, but she definitely had, she was sure of it. First, she was going to conquer the mountain of washing in the utility room. Like a modern-day Edmund Hillary, she would place a flag on top of the Everest-like washing basket when she did it. She was finally going to uncover the location of the soul mates of all the lonely socks residing inside what had started off as a net bag within which to wash delicate items. *Delicates?!* The delicate items bag was now a dedicated "odd sock bag", which hung on the back of the laundry room door as a reminder that no one may ever know where those socks were. But Lucie would. She'd crack the case of the missing socks, eventually.

Obviously, she was going to take up yoga. She had huge aspirations to be one of those bendy yokes who casually sit with their leg flung around the back of their neck, filing their toenails. Toenails – yes, those, too. She was going to paint them at least once a week, maybe more. Skincare, tick. There would be moisturiser applied *everywhere*, after every shower. Cuticles would be cared for. Legs shaved. Eyebrows plucked. Hair in check.

She was going to get rid of those extra few pounds that had started to hang around like an unwanted stalker. Hell, she may even join a cycling group, cladding herself in unflattering Lycra and those shoes that turned up at the toes. And meditate. She'd meditate three times a day, allowing all of her muscles to sink into the floor and spread out. She'd be so calm that you'd have to use a shovel to scoop her up off the floor and pour her back into her activewear. Activewear! Yes, yes, yes! Every morning, Lucie was going to saunter into the kitchen, having been up since six stretching, hair ironed, wearing activewear, even if she had no plans to be active that day.

She was going to get all of their diets under control, and ensure they were getting all of their daily requirements of vitamins and minerals through food, and not by cheating and taking all those out-of-date bullet-like multivitamins. And best of all, she was finally going to cook. One by one, she'd make her way through all those recipes she'd ripped out of magazines over the years and shoved in the spare drawer beside the cutlery one – the one that contained everything from light bulbs to old batteries, chalk, hair bobbles and keys with no lock that you'd better keep, just in case. As a matter of fact, Lucie was going to clean out that drawer, once and for all. Come to think of it, that was probably where her list was.

It took Lucie a few months to realise that having more time on her hands hadn't prompted her to become utterly fabulous and organised. Waking with Declan's nose pressed against hers, shouting that they were late, had become a regular occurrence. So, too, was the discovery that someone (*Bella*) kept taking her phone charger, despite covering it in bright blue tape to indicate ownership. As a result, her phone was constantly dying. Meaning Lucie rarely got to hear the morning alert of the mystical sounds of the whales and dolphins as they swam peacefully towards her, to wake her from another disturbed slumber.

Mind you, that morning, even from the confines of the dead phone, those mammals had appeared to spray her with half the ocean. Another regular occurrence – waking up drenched in salty sweat. Lucie had stood up too quickly, the ground shifting beneath her. She'd steadied herself on the chest of drawers and peeled off her soaked nightdress before glancing back at the bedclothes, to see the all-too-familiar sign that she would spend another day doubled over in agony.

"Do you have the money for the school trip?"

Bella appeared once more, eyeing her mother with . . . yes, that was contempt. Lucie shivered – Bella really was terrifying.

"I told you to ask your father."

Lucie stared back, trying not to picture the girl from *The Exorcist*. No, Bella's hair was far too neat, but the eyes were similar at times.

"He's not here."

"Well, I can see that. Where the hell is he?"

"He's playing golf."

Of course Hamish was playing bloody golf.

"I'll get it for you later. Come on. We'll be late."

It wasn't until they were halfway down the road with no time to return that Bella dropped another bombshell.

"I need you to come in and sign the permission form for the swim meet."

"What?"

"I told you."

Had she? Oh, Jesus.

Lucie looked down at what she was wearing, wishing she'd taken more heed of Bella's earlier words. In a rush, she'd pulled on a pair of black "inactive" leggings and the same T-shirt she'd been wearing the night before. Lucie licked her finger and rubbed frantically at the sticky red stain on the front. It was either bolognese sauce or ketchup. It could have been either. She had in fact been wearing the T-shirt for two days in a row before putting it on a third time that morning. The splodge, which she'd now made worse, may have been from the actual dinner she'd made two days prior, or from last night's desperation dinner: frankfurters wrapped in slices of bread, since they'd run out of hotdog buns. At least it wasn't red wine. There was always a positive. *Not always. There isn't always a positive.*

She felt her stomach flip and her mind go suddenly hot as the thought of that blasted day suddenly hit her. No matter where she was, or what she was doing, the feeling of that day was always there in some form. It hadn't gone away over time, as she'd kept telling herself it would. *If only. If only. If only . . .*

There were far too many to go through each one every single time. Lately, Lucie had come to settle on what she believed was the most relevant "*if only*" – the reason she was driving towards her destination filled with dread to accompany the dragging in her abdomen. The quick lug from the bottle of children's paracetamol had done nothing to abate what the day had gifted her.

If only that day she'd employed the same mantra she'd tried to drill into her children, the one that so often she'd ignored over the years: stop, breathe, count to ten, and then to twenty for good measure. It will prevent you from doing something you may regret for the rest of your life.

If only.

Chapter Two

It really was beautiful: serene, leafy, safe, sort of lego-ish. "The perfect place to raise a family." The estate agent had taken one look at Lucie's rounded belly and gone in for the kill. Of course, Lucie already knew the area, had driven through years before, giggling at the enormous houses and the type of person she believed would choose to live in a place like Double Bay, Sydney.

"Never," she'd said, looking around her at the groups of yummy mummies, the Stepford-style wives, the bronzed retired men in their seventies strutting about in far less than they should have been. "Not for me."

It was Hamish who'd pushed it, well aware that they weren't only purchasing a home, but also buying into a "way of life". It was the type of plasticky life he adored, but she'd come to appreciate its fabricated prettiness over the years. People changed, priorities changed. Lucie still remembered the day they'd taken a drive to look at the house they could ill-afford at the time, glancing at the brochure:

Capturing ocean views from the master balcony, this first-class entertainer embraces outdoor living with a custom-designed kitchen, a stone-paved terrace that can be used as an outdoor room. Within striking distance of the village shopping hub, with close proximity to the harbour and surf beaches, plenty of top-notch schools, this location couldn't be better – a commuter's paradise.

"It's all a bit much, no?" She'd turned to Hamish in the car on the way there, her hand caressing her stomach as she spoke. She'd only gone along to placate him. There was no way they could afford a house like it.

"It's perfect. What does it say? First-class entertainer? Can you imagine the lads' faces if I invited them over for a few cold ones and they turned up here." He'd looked far too excited, his eyes round with theoretical possibility. "Surfing before work. Hey, and wouldn't you like the shopping hub?"

"There wouldn't be any money left for shopping – the price! Come on, can't we go and look at the other one? The starter one, with room to develop."

"I'm sure those schools will come in handy sooner rather than later," he'd smiled, ignoring her, reaching over and resting his hand protectively on her stomach. "Top-notch schools for a top-notch baby."

"It's totally out of our price range and still a big enough commute to the city, despite what the brochure says, especially in my condition."

"Let's just look." He'd patted her hand before doing some form of cringeworthy American accent. "Stick with me, schweetheart. Anything is possible."

Hamish *had* made it possible, somehow, and even Lucie had to admit there were parts of Double Bay that she adored. But this morning, driving past the buzzing coffee shops and the picturesque jetty already filled with people taking in the outstanding views of the harbour did nothing to lift Lucie's mood. No, this morning, Lucie felt sick.

It hadn't always been this way. Up until *that day*, three months before, leaving the house dressed and ready for the day ahead had always filled Lucie with a sense of fulfilment. Driving past the early morning swimmers on the beach, people out walking their dogs – even the retired men in their too-tight swimming trunks – had given her a form of satisfaction. She, too, was going about her day as they made their way from their home on George Street, watching the road twist towards the gates of the school.

Back then, she'd pull into the staff car park, quickly kiss Bella and Declan goodbye, then watch them run round to the front of the enormous building to join all the other privileged children. Then Lucie would hurry to the staff room for a blast of caffeine with the other socially inferior staff members, as they called themselves, before the day started.

Lucie had known when she took the job as school nurse for the "Illustrious Australian Education System" that was Woodfield Grammar that she'd landed a cushy number. Despite the advantages, she'd had her reservations. It had seemed like a step down from her stressful but adored position at Sydney General Hospital. There, she'd forged a successful nursing career, ending up at the top of her game as Clinical Theatre Manager.

"You Irish love a bit of drama, that's why you like theatre," her oldest friend and hospital work colleague, Nina, had teased Lucie when she first took the managerial role at the hospital. "So, let me get this straight, you have a baby and then you take on more responsibility!"

Nina and Lucie had been pregnant at roughly the same time, both returning to work within weeks of each other.

"Crazy Irish! I'm heading to an easier life in out-patients, edging my way out of the door after them!"

It was Lucie, though, and not Nina, who three years later waved the understaffed hospital and irregular hours goodbye. Working full-time, with Bella as a toddler and pregnant with Declan, commuting in and out to the city, it was too much.

"Stop having babies!" Nina had told her. "I'm happy with one. I'll miss you, Lu. Never thought I'd see the day you'd wave this place goodbye. All those years . . ."

All those years was right. All those memories . . . but even Lucie had to admit that eventually, despite what she adored, she needed to adjust to a life more conducive to raising a family. Didn't she? So, *she'd* taken the step down. The "step down" had come with a step up in salary, no need for childcare, school holidays off and the added bonus of her children receiving a superior education at a fraction of the extortionate fees. Lucie had almost choked when she heard how much the other parents were paying to have their children flourish, with "smaller class sizes, allowing them to reach academic excellence". Apparently, "a Woodfield education results in responsible and well-rounded citizens who are confident in their ability to succeed in their chosen path in life."

Well, you couldn't argue with that. Of course, Lucie was wise enough to know that such well-rounded citizens would come with an air of superiority, backed by their sometimes less-rounded parents. But she'd handled worse. Surely, it would be a breeze.

"It's a no-brainer, Lu. Do it for a few years," Hamish had encouraged. "This new business I'm working on is about to take flight and sooner rather than later, you won't be working if you don't want to. Then you can be just like the other mothers . . . Also, don't forget the contacts I can make here. Woodfield is *the* school for anyone who's anyone around here."

* * *

"Mum, we're going to be late," Bella droned from the passenger seat as she took yet another selfie, pouting her little mouth and pulling free a strand of red hair either side of her face.

"Well, if it wasn't for you forgetting the bloody permission slip, I wouldn't have to go in this morning. Clearly, I hadn't planned to."

"Don't bother, then. I don't want to go on the stupid swim-team meet anyway. I'm still on my . . . period." Bella turned towards Lucie and mouthed the word with a dollop of attitude, then sucked in her cheeks and rolled her eyes.

"You have to go. And you can't still be on your . . . period," Lucie mouthed back. "It's been a week. I'm not stupid, Bella."

Over her years working as the school nurse, Lucie had heard almost every implausible excuse in the book.

"And I'm going as fast as I can," Lucie added.

She looked out of the window as two students sauntered past the car.

"There's people walking faster than you're driving, Mum," Bella exhaled impatiently.

"I'm looking for somewhere to park, okay?"

Lucie glanced over at the group of activewear-clad women gathered in their usual position near the entrance of the car park, probably in full-fledged discussion over whatever piece of idle gossip they'd managed to glean over the weekend. Hamish had been right. The job was a no-brainer, but it hadn't taken Lucie long to figure out that she wasn't like the other mothers, nor would she ever be, and therein lay the reason she was driving into Woodfield Grammar, trying to avoid them.

"How would you know, anyway?" Bella seemed intent on finishing their earlier conversation about her period. "Like, it's not like you even get yours any more."

Lucie jammed on the brakes and swivelled towards her teenage daughter. It wasn't as dramatic a move as she'd hoped for, since the car was barely moving to begin with.

"Bella. I'm warning you. One more word of cheek and so help me God, I'll turn this car round and you'll bloody walk to school." She was speaking with her teeth together, her lips moving in an exaggerated way as if doing a foreign language voice-over. "And for your information, I do still have mine. In fact, I have it right now. I just don't feel the need to tell everyone every five minutes and to use it as an excuse to get out of normal life. It is *not* an illness, Bella. It's life – and the sooner you get used to it, the better," Lucie finished with a crazed shake of her head.

"Sorry, Mum," Bella said, her eyes round from her mother's outburst.

Lucie's shoulders slumped and she exhaled. "It's okay. It gets easier, I promise. I know it's hard." She reached over and patted Bella's shoulder.

It wasn't Bella's fault that her transition to womanhood was coinciding with Lucie's own perimenopausal explosion. Bella had mood swings, and Lucie had lost all patience and clearly her sense of humour. Her daughter getting her period should have been a milestone, but one Lucie couldn't bear to think of, especially with what she was currently experiencing. No one had warned Lucie that going through this phase in her life would take years, coupled with still having to endure what had now become a twice-, and sometimes more, monthly cycle. It was cruel, like having newborn twins and being pregnant with triplets. She'd never had any problems before with her cycles: Why was it bloody starting now?

Lucie glanced over to see the group of women staring at her from where she'd "abruptly" stopped the vehicle.

"Shit."

"Language, Mother." Declan lifted his head from his book.

She'd almost forgotten he was there.

"Declan, I'm an adult, I can fucking well swear if I want."

Lucie could see his shocked little face peering at her from the rear-view mirror. Now she'd gone and upset both of her children. What the hell was wrong with her?

"Shit," she muttered again. "Sorry, sweetie. You're right. Let's try the prayer."

"Hail Mary, full of grace, please find us a parking space," Lucie and Declan whispered together.

"It's worked. Look." Declan pointed out of the window. "Score. Now you don't need to be angry with us."

Lucie felt her heart tug. Poor Declan was far too sensitive for his own good, but then again, that's what she loved about him – so different from Bella, who attracted people like a magnet. For the past few years, Declan had seemed to repel friends until, of course, Lucie had unearthed the reason. But all that was sorted now. Finally seeing him gain a little confidence was what she'd been hoping for for years, even if his blossoming spirit had come at a cost to herself. Still, she supposed, if she was to look at "the incident", as it was politely referred to, from a glass half-full perspective, it had had the desired effect, if not the best outcome. If only . . .

The thought was interrupted by Declan's excited voice.

"Don't forget, Mum. I'm going to Bruce's after school today."

"Copy that, Dec. I'll pick you up later."

"And I'm going for smoothies after school in Cali Press. Sandy's mum is dropping us," Bella added.

"Okay. Well, be safe and call me when you need to be collected. Not too late, okay?"

Lucie waited for the car in front to move off before pulling into the space she'd prayed for. Perhaps it wasn't going to be such a bad day.

She looked over to see Amanda Garth, one of the other mothers, standing with her arms crossed, a brazen look of defiance on her face. Lucie could see Amanda's side-kick, Roberta Williams, too, hanging back looking everywhere but in Lucie's direction, the shame visible across her features. Lucie ignored them, got out of the car and kissed Declan before he fled inside.

"Are you okay, Mum?" Bella stopped briefly on the steps of the school, put her hands on her hips and scowled at the group of women.

"I'm fine, love, honest."

Lucie could see the look of angry rebellion on her daughter's face, so familiar to how she'd once faced the world herself. They were so alike. Sometimes it frightened Lucie.

"Fiery hair, fiery soul," Lucie's father used to tell her.

"Spirited," she'd reply. "Passionate."

"Just make sure you manage that fire well. Hotheads never solved anything."

Didn't she know that only too well . . .

Lucie swallowed the lump that had formed in her throat at her daughter's attempt at support. No matter how terrifying Bella was at times, Lucie adored her. They all said it, didn't they? – that the teenage years are a challenge. Of course, you don't believe it until you're there.

Had she been the same with her mother? she wondered. There was no one to ask. She didn't think she had, but maybe she'd forgotten. She wished she could call her mother now, apologise for how she may have acted during those years. Perhaps her mother could have talked to Bella, or assured Lucie it would pass.

But it wasn't just that. It was watching her daughter grow up and begin to question the world. That was what scared Lucie the most – the thought that Bella was clever enough to figure out someday that Lucie didn't know it all, was just as confused by life as she'd always been and, worst of all, that her fire had gone out.

"Screw them," Bella whispered and then ran up the steps to school.

"Screw them," Lucie repeated and then, "I love you, Bells." Her voice caught.

Bella bounded back down the steps to her.

"I'm sorry I said what I said before. You know . . ." She looked at the ground. "About you ruining my life here. You didn't. I . . . I would have done the same. All of my friends think you're cool." She bent to kiss Lucie on the cheek.

"It wasn't cool, but thanks. Now go – you'll be late." Lucie brushed her away, knowing that the moment of solidarity, the glimpse of the softer side of Bella, had the power to make her crumble.

Glancing back over her shoulder, Lucie could still see them standing there, watching her – Amanda scowling in a way that made her look constipated, her sweet smile anything but.

"Not today, Amanda, not today," Lucie muttered.

She could ignore the stares, the whispers, the glances, knowing what she was witnessing from them was an enormous display of false courage. What she couldn't ignore was the thought of letting her kids down, the repercussions that just kept coming from "the incident". Perhaps she should take a leaf out of Amanda's book – false courage was undoubtedly what she'd need when she was finally forced to admit what she'd been avoiding.

Lucie pulled the door of the school open, staring up at the familiarity, wondering how she was going to break the news to Bella and Declan that this would be their last term at Woodfield Grammar.

Printed in Great Britain
by Amazon

46510853R00271